Praise for *Key Strateg*

C000100198

I wish I had thought of the idea for this book selection of topics is excellent, the commentary astute, and the explanations simple and engaging.

RICHARD KOCH, ENTREPRENEUR, CO-FOUNDER L.E.K. CONSULTING, AUTHOR OF
THE 80/20 PRINCIPLE

This is a new, very practical and delightfully pithy approach to strategy making. It offers a fabulous compendium of the major strategy tools, woven into a no-nonsense, step-by-step strategy process. An enormously refreshing and helpful book, invaluable to novices and strategy experts alike.

MARCUS ALEXANDER, PROFESSOR OF STRATEGY AND ENTERPRISE, LONDON BUSINESS
SCHOOL

A really practical guide to strategy development. All the relevant tools are explained in detail, but highlighting the essential ones is a master stroke that will save endless hours!

ADRIAN BEECROFT, CHAIRMAN, DAWN CAPITAL AND FORMER SENIOR MANAGING
PARTNER, APAX PARTNERS

A comprehensive inventory of the tools and analytical frameworks of strategy. The key value of this book is the guidance it offers on how to apply these tools – and this is rooted in Vaughan Evans' deep experience of working with them.

ROBERT M. GRANT, ENI PROFESSOR OF STRATEGIC MANAGEMENT, BOCCONI
UNIVERSITY, MILAN, VISITING FELLOW AT GEORGETOWN UNIVERSITY, WASHINGTON,
AUTHOR OF THE MARKET LEADING STRATEGY TEXTBOOK FOR BUSINESS SCHOOL
STUDENTS, *CONTEMPORARY STRATEGIC ANALYSIS*

This is an interesting and usable *book. Evans helps you navigate through the myriad of theories and toolkits on business strategy with a highly practical approach. Whether your business is a start-up, an SME or a multi-national, use it to help you devise a coherent strategy.*

ANTHONY KARIBIAN, CEO, BONLINE LTD AND CO-FOUNDER, EUROFFICE LTD AND XLN
TELECOM LTD (BOTH EXITED)

Everything you need from a tool kit, comprehensive, practical and high added value.

MIKE GARLAND, PARTNER AND HEAD OF PORTFOLIO GROUP, PERMIRA ADVISERS LLP

This book really works. I hope it becomes a standard for every management team seeking private equity; it would certainly make my life much easier.

DAVID WILLIAMSON, MANAGING DIRECTOR, NOVA CAPITAL MANAGEMENT

A broad yet accessible explanation of the range of strategy tools actually used by businesses. Whether you are an experienced strategy specialist or newer to the field, you will find this an invaluable guide.

ROBERT SAMUELSON, EXECUTIVE DIRECTOR GROUP STRATEGY, VIRGIN MEDIA

Strategy is at the heart of a successful business – with this excellent book, Vaughan Evans has provided an extremely clear roadmap to achieving that success.

JAMES COURTENAY, GLOBAL HEAD, ADVISORY & INFRASTRUCTURE FINANCE, STANDARD CHARTERED BANK

A very satisfying read. This is a guide to strategy which covers all the necessary ground in a very straightforward and no nonsense way, employing a number of good real life examples of strategy in practice. It is written by a true expert and will prove an invaluable tool for anybody involved in the running of a business.

VINCE O'BRIEN, DIRECTOR, MONTAGU PRIVATE EQUITY AND PAST CHAIRMAN OF THE BRITISH VENTURE CAPITAL ASSOCIATION

It can be difficult to keep up to date with all the latest developments in the world of strategy, let alone how one guru's work blends with those of his predecessors. Vaughan Evans has done it for us. He gives us a thorough refresher course, with each leading strategy theory, model or matrix presented as a tool in the manager's toolkit – and carefully placed in each step of the strategy process. Each tool is described in a lucid and vivid style seldom found in a business manual. Refreshing and invaluable for a DIY strategist.

CHRISTINE HARVEY, FORMER DIRECTOR OF BUSINESS ANALYSIS AND PLANNING, GLAXOSMITHKLINE R&D

A practical approach, easy to read and understand, on how to build your business strategy, the steering direction that any business, large or small, needs to succeed.

JOSE-MARIA MALDONADO, PARTNER, BRIDGEPOINT CAPITAL, MADRID

Every company needs to know where it is headed. It needs a strategy. That doesn't have to be complicated, especially for an SME. Much of it is common sense. Be guided by Vaughan Evans's sensible but sparkling book and you will get the strategy you need.

PETER WRIGHT, INVESTMENT DIRECTOR, FINANCE WALES

I had never come across a strategy manual that was as useful as the Powerpoint slides we used to follow at my former consulting group. Until now. Evans's book is exceptional. It is effectively two books in one: a DIY strategy manual and a toolkit. The manual is arranged around his Strategy Pyramid, with its nine no-nonsense building blocks. Then in each block he lays out a bunch of tools, guiding us as to which are the most essential, for developing a strategy. This is an easy-to-follow strategy process that any manager can run with. A winning book for a winning strategy.

STEPHEN LAWRENCE, CHIEF EXECUTIVE, PROTOCOL EDUCATION LTD AND FORMER MANAGING DIRECTOR, ARTHUR D. LITTLE

Often one of our portfolio companies needs to firm up or redefine its strategy. Sometimes we have to call in strategy consultants to help the management team. With this tiptop strategy manual to hand, we may not need to make those calls.

KEN LAWRENCE, PARTNER, GRESHAM PRIVATE EQUITY

Another excellent book from Vaughan Evans. This time he's achieved the near impossible task of writing a book on strategy formulation that is actually differentiated from the plethora of other offerings out there. By setting out each of 88 strategy models and techniques within a transparent process, this book will be genuinely useful to managers and entrepreneurs.

JAMES PITT, PARTNER, LEXINGTON PARTNERS

Many businesses fail to deliver their potential or fail altogether because they neglect to develop a clear, concise, appropriate and well-communicated strategy. Business books on the subject often don't help – they tend to adopt a theoretical approach, appearing to the manager to lack practical relevance. As a result, they can be unhelpful and uninspiring. This is far from the case in Vaughan Evans's excellent Key Strategy Tools. *He has put together a well constructed compendium of techniques and tools, from Porter to Rumelt, Hamel to Hammer, plus some gems from his own solid experience, and provides clear guidance on their relevance and application. Evans has a 'no nonsense' conversational style of writing and has delivered a book for all managers, regardless of experience. As with his recent guide to writing a business plan, this is not for your business library. It is for action on your desk!*

GRAHAME HUGHES, FOUNDING DIRECTOR, HAVEN POWER LTD.

I am not aware of any other book that brings together so many different business analysis tools into a single volume, cleverly grouped to shape a manual. You can't have a Haynes manual for strategy, but this is as close as you will get to one. It has the potential to become the standard reference text for busy executives.

RICHARD HEPPER, DEPUTY CHIEF EXECUTIVE, CAPITAL FOR ENTERPRISE

This is a most impressive book. I particularly like the approach it takes structurally, with each of the 88 tools assigned its rightful place in the strategy formulation process. It is a comprehensive, practical and highly effective guide to strategy and will prove an invaluable aide to both entrepreneurs and managers of larger businesses. I genuinely like this book.

CHARLES IND, MANAGING PARTNER, BOWMARK CAPITAL LLP

In writing Key Strategy Tools, *Vaughan Evans has provided us with a handy reference book of strategy models and techniques, with the added benefit of a sound process manual. Using his characteristic brand of humour, Evans reminds us of most of the tried and tested tools and introduces some stimulating new ones too.*

MIKE PRICE, CHIEF EXECUTIVE, BETTER STRATEGY LTD

Where else can you find instant access and a user-friendly guide to over 80 important strategy tools? A must for every manager's desktop.

PAUL GOUGH, PARTNER, STAR CAPITAL PARTNERS

Vaughan Evans has done it again. His book on business planning last year showed entrepreneurs how to build a plan that meets investor concerns. But a winning plan hinges on a winning strategy. Now Evans sets out how to build such a strategy, clearly and progressively. Follow this book and you'll build a strategy to win over investors."

JONATHAN DERRY-EVANS, PARTNER, MANFIELD PARTNERS

A successful strategy requires an intellectual framework, clear analysis and the tools to construct it. Vaughan Evans' new book brings all these together and explains, in jargon-free language, how to choose and use the tools most relevant to your needs to create a compelling strategy. Comprehensive, but clear and concise, and evidently honed from practical experience, this is the go-to strategy guide for entrepreneurs and managers alike.

RICHARD KEMP, MANAGING PARTNER, SEPHTON CAPITAL

Key strategy tools

PEARSON

At Pearson, we believe in learning – all kinds of learning for all kinds of people. Whether it's at home, in the classroom or in the workplace, learning is the key to improving our life chances.

That's why we're working with leading authors to bring you the latest thinking and the best practices, so you can get better at the things that are important to you. You can learn on the page or on the move, and with content that's always crafted to help you understand quickly and apply what you've learned.

If you want to upgrade your personal skills or accelerate your career, become a more effective leader or more powerful communicator, discover new opportunities or simply find more inspiration, we can help you make progress in your work and life.

Pearson is the world's leading learning company. Our portfolio includes the Financial Times, Penguin, Dorling Kindersley, and our educational business, Pearson International.

Every day our work helps learning flourish, and wherever learning flourishes, so do people.

To learn more please visit us at: www.pearson.com/uk

[VAUGHAN EVANS]

Key strategy tools

The 80+ tools for every manager to
build a winning strategy

PEARSON

Harlow, England • London • New York • Boston • San Francisco • Toronto • Sydney • Auckland • Singapore • Hong Kong
Tokyo • Seoul • Taipei • New Delhi • Cape Town • São Paulo • Mexico City • Madrid • Amsterdam • Munich • Paris • Milan

Pearson Education Limited
Edinburgh Gate
Harlow CM20 2JE
Tel: +44 (0)1279 623623
Website: www.pearson.com/uk

First published 2013 (print and electronic)

ISBN: 978-0-273-77796-0 (print)
        978-0-273-77911-7 (PDF)
        978-0-273-77912-4 (ePub)
        978-0-273-77910-0 (eText)

British Library Cataloguing-in-Publication Data
A catalogue record for the print edition is available from the British Library

Library of Congress Cataloging-in-Publication Data
A catalog record for the print edition is available from the Library of Congress

The Financial Times. With a worldwide network of highly respected journalists, The Financial Times provides global business news, insightful opinion and expert analysis of business, finance and politics. With over 500 journalists reporting from 50 countries worldwide, our in-depth coverage of international news is objectively reported and analysed from an independent, global perspective. To find out more, visit www.ft.com/pearsonoffer.

10 9 8 7 6 5 4 3 2 1
17 16 15 14 13

Cover design by Heat Design
Print edition typeset in 9.25 Helvetica Neue Pro by 3
Print edition printed and bound in Great Britain by Henry Ling Ltd, at the Dorset Press, Dorchester, Dorset

NOTE THAT ANY PAGE CROSS REFERENCES REFER TO THE PRINT EDITION

To Carys, Natasha and Stefan
and their nascent strategy pyramids

Contents

About the author xvi
Publisher's acknowledgements xvii

INTRODUCTION 1

The Strategy Pyramid 2
How to use this book 2
Business vs corporate strategy 9

SECTION 1 Knowing your business 11

Overview 12
Essential tools
1 | Identifying key segments 13
2 | Issue analysis (Minto) 19
Example: British Aerospace's super segment 23
Useful tools
3 | The 80/20 principle (Pareto) 24
4 | The segmentation mincer (Koch) 27
5 | 5C situation analysis 29
6 | SWOT analysis (Andrews) 31

SECTION 2 Setting goals and objectives 35

Overview 36
Essential tools
7 | Setting long-term goals 38
8 | Setting SMART objectives 41
9 | Maximising shareholder value 43
10 | Balancing stakeholder interests 45
Example: Which goals count for RBS? 49
Useful tools
11 | Creating shared value (Porter and Kramer) 50
12 | Economic value added (Stern Stewart) 53
13 | Balanced scorecard and strategy map (Kaplan and Norton) 55

14 Core ideology (Collins and Porras) 58
15 Business as a community (Handy) 60

SECTION 3 Forecasting market demand 63

Overview 64
Essential tools
16 Sizing the market and marketcrafting (Evans) 66
17 The HOOF approach to demand forecasting (Evans) 70
    Example: Galileo's hiccup in market demand 76
Useful tools
18 Smoothing with moving averages 78
19 Income elasticity of demand 80
20 Survey methods of demand forecasting 82
    • Survey of customers' intentions 82
    • Salesforce estimation method 83
    • The Delphi method 83
    • Pilot test marketing 84
21 Statistical methods of demand forecasting 85
    • Trend projection 85
    • Regression analysis 86
    • Barometric method (NBER) 87

SECTION 4 Gauging industry competition 89

Overview 90
Essential tools
22 The five forces (Porter) 92
23 Assessing customer purchasing criteria 97
24 Deriving key success factors 101
    Example: Woolworths succumbs to the five forces 105
Useful tools
25 Weighing economies of scale 107
26 Corporate environment as a sixth force 110
27 Complements as a sixth force (Brandenburger and Nalebuff) 112
28 PESTEL analysis 114

SECTION 5 Tracking competitive advantage 117

Overview 118
Essential tools
29 | Rating competitive position 119
30 | The resource and capability strengths/importance matrix (Grant) 124
Example: Cobra Beer's clever competitive advantage 127
Useful tools
31 | The value chain (Porter) 128
32 | The product/market matrix (Ansoff) 131
33 | Cross, spider and comb charts 133
34 | Benchmarking 136
35 | Structured interviewing 139

SECTION 6 Targeting the strategic gap 143

Overview 144
Essential tools
36 | The attractiveness/advantage matrix (GE/McKinsey) 146
37 | The growth/share matrix (BCG) 151
38 | Profiling the ideal player 155
39 | Identifying the capability gap 158
Example: Komatsu targets the cat 163
Useful tools
40 | The strategic condition matrix (Arthur D. Little) 164
41 | The 7S framework (McKinsey) 167
42 | The opportunity/vulnerability matrix (Bain/L.E.K.) 170
43 | Brainstorming 173
44 | Scenario planning 175

SECTION 7 Bridging the gap: business strategy 177

Overview 179
Essential tools
45 | Three generic strategies (Porter) 180
46 | The experience curve (BCG) 183
47 | Strategic repositioning and shaping profit growth options 186
48 | Making the strategic investment decision 191
49 | Blue ocean strategy (Kim and Mauborgne) 197
Example: Could Facebook be undone the way it undid
MySpace? 201

Useful tools

50	The tipping point (Gladwell)	204
51	Price elasticity of demand (Marshall)	207
52	PIMS (GE/SPI)	211
53	The 4Ps marketing mix (McCarthy)	214
54	Product quality and satisfaction (Kano)	218
55	The hierarchy of needs (Maslow)	221
56	The bottom of the pyramid (Prahalad and Leiberthal)	223
57	Business process redesign (Hammer and Champy)	226
58	Outsourcing	229

SECTION 8 Bridging the gap: corporate strategy 233

Overview 235
Essential tools

59	Optimising the corporate portfolio	237
60	Creating value from mergers, acquisitions and alliances	240
61	The corporate restructuring hexagon (McKinsey)	249
62	Creating parenting value (Goold, Campbell and Alexander)	252
63	Core competences (Hamel and Prahalad)	256
64	Strategically valuable resources (Collis and Montgomery)	260
	Example: Virgin's brand as resource-based strategy 263	
	Useful tools	
65	Strategically distinctive resources (Barney)	265
66	Distinctive capabilities (Kay)	268
67	Distinctive competences (Snow and Hrebiniak)	271
68	Dynamic capabilities (Teece, Pisano and Shuen)	274
69	Deliberate and emergent strategy (Mintzberg)	277
70	Stick to the knitting (Peters and Waterman)	280
71	Profit from the core (Zook)	283
72	The market-driven organisation (Day)	286
73	Value disciplines (Treacy and Wiersema)	289
74	Disruptive technologies (Christensen)	293
75	Co-opetition (Brandenburger and Nalebuff)	296
76	Growth and crisis (Greiner)	299
77	Good strategy, bad strategy (Rumelt)	302
78	Innovation hot spots (Gratton)	305
79	Strategy as orientation or animation (Cummings and Wilson)	307
80	The knowledge spiral (Nonaka and Takeuchi)	309
81	The eight phases of change (Kotter)	311

SECTION 9 Addressing risk and opportunity 313

Overview 314
Essential tools
82 Strategic due diligence and market contextual plan review
    (Evans) 316
83 The suns & clouds chart (Evans) 321
    Example: Were the Beatles worth the risk? 325
    Useful tools
84 The composite risk index and the 5×5 risk matrix 327
85 The risk management matrix 330
86 Expected value and sensitivity analysis 332
87 Black swans (Taleb) 335
88 Strategic bets (Burgleman and Grove) 337

Conclusion 339
References and further reading 340
Glossary 347
Index 351

About the author

Vaughan Evans is an independent strategy consultant (www.managingstrate gicrisk.com), with a background in industry economics – the analysis of market demand and industry competition which lies at the bedrock of business strategy. He has also specialised since the mid-1980s in strategic due diligence, a discipline which focuses on the risk and return of a company's strategy and lends valuable insights to the strategy process itself.

He worked for many years at management and technology consultants Arthur D. Little and at investment bank Bankers Trust. An economics graduate from Downing College, Cambridge University and a Sloan Fellow with distinction from London Business School, he is the author of four previous books, including the best-selling *Financial Times Essential Guide to Writing a Business Plan: How to Win Backing to Start Up or Grow Your Business*.

Publisher's acknowledgements

We are grateful to the following for permission to reproduce copyright material:

Figures

Figure 3.1 Pearson Education Ltd (left) Sozaijiten, (right) Photolink.Photodisc; Figure 11.1 adapted from *Strategy Maps: Converting Intangible Assets into Tangible Outcomes*, Harvard Business School Press (Kaplan, Robert S. and Norton, David P. 2004) Figure 3.1; Figure 14.1 from *Built to Last*, Copyright © 1994 by Jim Collins and Jerry I. Porras. Reprinted with permission from Jim Collins; Figure on page 106 and Figures 22.1, 26.1, 27.1 adapted with the permission of Free Press, a Division of Simon & Schuster, Inc., from COMPETITIVE STRATEGY: Techniques for Analyzing Industries and Competitors by Michael E. Porter. Copyright © 1980, 1988 by The Free Press. All rights reserved; Figure 30.1 adapted from *Contemporary Strategy Analysis*, 7th, Blackwell (Grant, Robert M. 2011) Figure 5.4, p.141; Figure 31.1 adapted with the permission of Free Press, a Division of Simon & Schuster, Inc., from COMPETITIVE STRATEGY: Techniques for Analyzing Industries and Competitors by Michael E. Porter. Copyright © 1980, 1988 by The Free Press. All rights reserved; Figure 32.1 adapted from Strategies for Diversification, *Harvard Business Review*, Sept–Oct, pp.113–25 (Ansoff, Igor 1957); Graphic used in Figure 36.1 from shutterstock.com/Z-art; Figure 37.1 adapted from *THE BCG PORTFOLIO MATRIX FROM THE PRODUCT PORTFOLIO MATRIX*, THE BOSTON CONSULTING GROUP (1970), adapted from The BCG Portfolio Matrix from the Product Portfolio Matrix, © 1970, The Boston Consulting Group; Figure 42.1 adapted from *Financial Times Guide to Strategy*, FT Publishing (Koch, Richard 2011) p.59, Figure 1.9; Figures 49.1 and 49.2 adapted from *Blue Ocean Strategy: How to Create Uncontested Market Space and Make the Competition Irrelevant*, Harvard Business School Press (Chan Kim, W. and Mauborgne, Renee 2005) Figure 4–6 and http://www.blueoceanstrategy.com/abo/4_action.html; Figure 56.1 adapted from The End of Corporate Imperialism, *Harvard Business Review*, Jul–Aug, p.113 (Prahalad, C.K. and Lieberthal, Keith 1998); Figure 61.1 adapted from *Valuation: Measuring and Managing the Value of Companies*, 5th edn, John Wiley & Sons (Koller, Tim, Goedhart, Marc and Wessels, David 2010) Exhibit 2.2, Copyright © 2010 McKinsey and Company Inc. All rights reserved. Reproduced with permission of John Wiley & Sons; Figure 62.1 from *Corporate-Level Strategy: Creating Value in Multi-Business Companies*, John Wiley & Sons (Goold, Michael, Campbell, Andrew and Alexander, Marcus 1994) Figure 2.3, Copyright © 1997 Michael Goold, Andrew Campbell and Marcus Alexander. Reproduced with permission John Wiley & Sons, Inc.; Figures 63.1 and 63.2 adapted from *Competing for the Future*, Harvard Business School Press (Hamel, Gary and Prahalad, C.K. 1994); Figure 69.1 adapted from *The Rise and Fall of Strategic Planning*, Pearson Education (Mintzberg, Henry 2000) Figure 1–1, and adapted with the permission of Free Press, a Division of Simon & Schuster, Inc., from THE RISE AND FALL OF STRATEGIC PLANNING by Henry Mintzberg.

Introduction

Do you, as a manager, find the idea of drawing up a strategy daunting? Does it conjure up images of impenetrable business school textbooks, with esoteric, quasi-academic theories? Or of global companies engaging gold-plated consulting groups to produce bamboozling bubble charts?

Let's settle these concerns upfront. Strategy need not be complex. And you do not need to spend a fortune on a platoon of consultants.

Strategy should be readily doable by every manager.

But you do need a process. And a toolkit – and know which tools to use and why in which part of the process.

Or you are an entrepreneur. You know your company and its markets inside out, and yet over lunch with your bank manager the other day you hesitated. You didn't sound that convincing when she asked you where the firm was headed. There were a number of exciting options, you had said, and proceeded to elaborate. 'But surely you can't pursue them all', she had commented, hitting the nail on the head.

You need a robust strategy to take your creation to the next level.

Whether you're a manager or entrepreneur, you don't require an academic treatise or an encyclopaedia of strategic theories, randomly or alphabetically arranged.

What you need is a practical manual on how to build a winning strategy for your business.

And the manual needs to deploy carefully selected, critiqued and grouped strategy tools.

This book delivers just that. And more.

It will guide you into building a strategy which is tight enough to withstand the scrutiny of your board of directors.

And beyond. You will build a strategy that is so robust that, should you so choose, it can stand up to the cross-examination of an outside backer, such as a private equity house, along with their forensic advisers on strategic due diligence.

This book will deliver you a strategy that is, in short, backable.

The Strategy Pyramid

Key Strategy Tools introduces you to a straightforward, practical, proven strategy development process, the Strategy Pyramid. The pyramid is made up of nine building blocks, ranging from Section 1, Knowing your business, to Section 9, Addressing risk and opportunity.

Each of the 88 strategy tools will be slotted into place in one of the nine building blocks.

You will have a framework, a manual and a toolkit for building a winning strategy.

But, first things first, what is 'strategy'? What do we mean by it?

There is a myriad of definitions, ranging from General Sun Tzu's 'know your opponent' in the sixth century BC to Kenichi Ohmae's rather more recent 'in a word, competitive advantage' (that's actually two words, but we'll let that pass!).

I am an economist by training, so feel the need to bring the word 'resources' into the broader definition. Just as economics can be defined as the optimal allocation of a nation's scarce resources, so can a company's strategy be defined thus:

> Strategy is how a company achieves its goals by deploying its scarce resources to gain a sustainable competitive advantage.

Your strategy will set out how you plan to allocate your firm's scarce resources to meet your goals and objectives. These resources are essentially your assets – your people, physical assets (for example, buildings, equipment and inventory) and cash (and borrowing capacity). How will you allocate – or invest – these resources to optimal effect?

How to use this book

Key Strategy Tools is two books in one, a tool book and a how-to manual. It presents 88 tools, grouped within one coherent strategy development framework, the Strategy Pyramid.

The pyramid consists of nine building blocks, into which is slotted the appropriate set of tools – each of which is categorised as either essential or useful.

You are given a choice. You can apply just the *essential* tools, using them as a manual to build a potentially winning strategy.

Or you can go further. Skim through the other, *useful* tools, pluck out those which are particularly appropriate to *your* firm in *your* situation and apply them too – thereby improving *your* odds of building a winning strategy.

Let this book be your guide in building the strategy you need for your firm to succeed.

Where to start, then, in drawing up a strategy and where best to invest your resources? First you need to know your business. Where exactly do the sources of profit lie in the business? In other words, which are the product/market segments you serve and which make the greatest contribution towards operating profit? Business segmentation is the foundation for strategy analysis (see Figure 0.1).

Figure 0.1 Lay the foundation: know your business

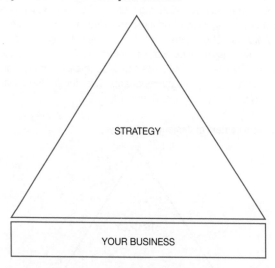

Once you've laid the foundation, the single most important factor in strategy development is to root it firmly within the context of the micro-economy in which your firm operates. Whatever key assumptions you make down the line on, for example, product development, pricing, service enhancement or cost reduction

Figure 0.2 Set strategy in a micro-economic context ...

must reflect the reality of market demand and industry supply, today and tomorrow, in *your* micro-economy.

I have seen scores of strategies over the years built on inadequate research on the micro-economic environment. They are built on sand. Some succeeded, though deserved not to. They succeeded through rare intuition or luck. Many faltered.

Micro-economic analysis must underpin the Strategy Pyramid (see Figure 0.2).

There are two distinct components of the micro-economy, market demand and industry supply, and they must be analysed separately. Failure to separate them can lead to muddled thinking. The tools used to analyse each component are entirely different. And both sets are equally important. Thus, the micro-economy building block can be split in two (see Figure 0.3).

Figure 0.3 ... or a context of demand and suply

Within the context of the micro-economy, the crux of the strategy development process now rests on the analysis of your firm's competitiveness – how your firm measures against a whole range of factors critical to success. As many strategic insights will flow from this analysis of *internal* competitiveness as from the *external* micro-economic analysis (see Figure 0.4).

Figure 0.4 View strategy as the output of competitive analysis …

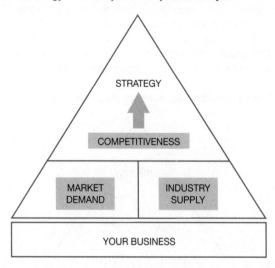

Competitive analysis is best undertaken in two steps. The first is the current reality of how your firm stacks up to its peers in today's marketplace. And the second is how you envisage your firm rating against its competitors in the future – your target competitiveness. The competitive situation 'as is' and 'to be' form two building blocks in the Strategy Pyramid (see Figure 0.5).

Figure 0.5 … both as is and to be

But there is something we have missed. How you see the future competitiveness of your firm depends partly, even largely, on what your aims for the firm are. What are your goals and objectives? To make a reasonable existence, to maximise profit growth, to keep your employees in their jobs, to satisfy a range of stakeholders? These overarching aims are fundamental to the strategy development process and belong to the foundation of the Strategy Pyramid (see Figure 0.6).

Figure 0.6 Target competitiveness also depends on your aims

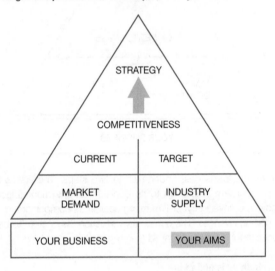

Now it is time to make an important distinction. There are two components to strategy: business and corporate. Business strategy is concerned with maximising the competitiveness of a single strategic business unit (see Section 6 for a full definition). Corporate strategy is how you optimise your portfolio of businesses, whether through investment, acquisition or disposal, and how you add value to each through exploitation of your firm's overall resources and capabilities. The tools used for analysing business and corporate strategy are largely different, though there is overlap and some essential tools can be used for both. Unless yours is a single business firm, you need to address both elements of strategy (see Figure 0.7).

Figure 0.7 Strategy has two components: business and corporate

We're almost there. There is just one final building block needed to complete the pyramid. The analysis of market demand, industry supply and your firm's competitiveness will encounter risk at every turn, likewise opportunity. Uncertainty is unavoidable and will be ever-present. It must be addressed systematically in the strategy development process. It is core to success and should be wrapped around every part of the micro-economic and competitiveness analyses of the Strategy Pyramid (see Figure 0.8).

Figure 0.8 Strategy development is wrapped in uncertainty

The building blocks of the Strategy Pyramid now emerge, numbers 1 to 9 (see Figure 0.9).

Figure 0.9 The nine building blocks of the Strategy Pyramid

All that remains is to convert the building block headings into task-oriented clauses and we have the nine section headings for this book:

1 Knowing your business

2 Setting your firm's goals and objectives

3 Forecasting market demand

4 Gauging industry competition

5 Rating your firm's competitive position

6 Targeting your firm's strategic gap

7 Bridging the gap: business strategy

8 Bridging the gap: corporate strategy

9 Addressing risk and opportunity.

Each section will set out the tools and techniques you need to build the block. Some are essential. If you want to take a short-cut route to building your strategy, just follow them. They will surely suffice. If you want to see what else might be pertinent to your firm's situation, take a look at the other tools, designated 'useful'. They could well improve the odds of your firm developing a truly winning strategy.

Finally, may I welcome you to the strategy development process. I hope you find the Strategy Pyramid and its 88 tools both useful and stimulating. My purpose is not to write an academic tome, but a practical and lively guide to help you build the strategy you need for your firm to succeed.

Business vs corporate strategy

One thing we need to address upfront is how this book approaches the two distinct but related fields of strategy, business strategy and corporate strategy. A business, or, more technically, a strategic business unit ('SBU'), is defined as an entity with a closely interrelated product (or service) offering and a cost structure largely independent of other business units. Thus, in a large corporation, an SBU may well have not only its own CEO, CFO, COO, CSMO and CIO, but its own CTO, head of all R&D in that SBU.

An SBU is a substantive enough entity to warrant drawing up its own strategy, independent of strategies its fellow SBUs may be drawing up.

SBU strategy is known more simply as *business strategy*.

Corporate strategy is in the first instance how you allocate resources between your SBUs. Which will you invest in, which will you hold for cash generation, which will you sell, which may you be forced to close down? This is corporate strategy as portfolio planning – see tools such as Optimising the Corporate Portfolio (Section 8).

But corporate strategy is more than that. It is about how you strive to attain synergies between your SBUs, how you create value in the centre, how you initiate a winning culture or capability that permeates the entire organisation. This is the resource-based theory of corporate strategy – see, for example, Hamel and Prahalad's Core Competences (Section 8).

Most of this book is about business strategy. The Strategy Pyramid is essentially a business strategy tool (right up to Section 7 and including Section 9). Each step of the process can be followed by a single SBU.

Corporate strategy is addressed (in Section 8), and all the main portfolio-based and resource-based models are set out.

The differentiation between corporate and business strategy can be temporary. Large corporations often spin off an SBU, whether through IPO, MBO or trade sale. That SBU becomes its own entity and may decide to set up its own SBUs, based on the key product/market segments formerly analysed in its business strategy. That entity's business strategy is now corporate strategy. The entity may soon decide to hive off one of its newly created SBUs, which then becomes its own entity, and so on.

Finally, many of the portfolio planning tools of corporate strategy apply no less readily to business strategy. Where corporate strategy can be seen as the optimal allocation of resources between SBUs, so too can business strategy be seen as that between key product/market segments. The same tools, in particular the GE/McKinsey and BCG matrices (Tools 36 and 37), can and should be deployed for both. The difference is that for corporate strategy the bubbles plotted on the matrix will be SBUs and for business strategy they will be key product/market segments.

[SECTION 1]

Knowing your business

Overview

Essential tools

1   Identifying key segments

2   Issue analysis (Minto)

Useful tools

3   The 80/20 principle (Pareto)

4   The segmentation mincer (Koch)

5   5C situation analysis

6   SWOT analysis (Andrews)

Overview

How well do you know your business? In which deep, dark recesses do the profits reside? And what are the issues that could affect those profits?

These are the two essential starting points in strategy formulation: clarifying where your sources of profit reside and taking a first look at the issues that may impact them.

First, you need to know your business. You need to clarify the major business segments you compete in and which contribute most to the bottom line. Only when you have a clear perspective on which business segments are material to your firm's strategy should you proceed.

Then think about what are the main questions you will need answers to during the process to arrive at a winning strategy. And to answer those main questions, what other questions need answering? And so on. Setting out a structured waterfall of questions will help guide you through the research and analysis needed to draw up your strategy – and hopefully leave no major stones unturned.

These two starting points are set out as the two essential tools in this chapter: namely, key segment identification and issue analysis. Then we address some other tools which may be useful in knowing your business.

First things first, then. What are the key product/market segments in your business? Identifying them is the first essential tool in knowing your business.

Identifying key segments

1

The tool

Does your firm serve some segments where you generate good sales but frustratingly little profit? And what of those merrier segments where sales are modest but margins meaty?

Step one in building block one of the Strategy Pyramid is to know your business – where the profit resides.

There are two components to this:

- Which business segments does your firm compete in – which products do you sell to which sets of customers? (Products or services, henceforth to be referred to in this section as just 'products'.)
- Which of these segments delivers the most profit?

Only once this segmentation process is complete should you embark on developing your strategy. There is no point devoting hours of research, whether in analysing competitor data or gathering customer feedback, in a segment which contributes to just 1 per cent of your operating profit – and which offers little prospect of growing that contribution over the next five years.

How you could strengthen your capabilities in that segment may be fascinating, but is not material to your business strategy and of little interest to your board or backer.

You need to devote your time and effort to strengthening your firm's presence in those segments that contribute, or will contribute, to 80 per cent or more of your business.

How to use it

In an established business

What is your business mix? What products or services does your business offer and to which customer groups?

Which count for most in your business?

Businesses seldom offer just the one product to one customer group. Most businesses offer a number of distinct products to a number of distinct customer groups.

A product tends to be distinctive if the competition differs from one product to another. Some competitors may offer all your services; others may specialise in one or two of them. Others still may offer just the one as a spin-off to a largely unrelated business.

A customer group is distinctive if the customers have distinct characteristics and are typically reachable through distinct marketing routes.

Thus, a customer group can be defined by who they are (e.g. leisure or business visitor, young or old, well or less educated), what sector they are in (especially for business-to-business ventures), where they are located (e.g. town or suburbs, region, country) or in other ways where different marketing approaches will be needed to reach them.

Each distinct product offered to a distinct customer group is a segment, termed, in rather ungainly business-speak, a 'product/market segment' or, more simply, a 'business segment'.

If your business offers two products to one customer group, you have two business segments. If you stick with the same two products but develop a new customer group, you'll have four segments. Introduce a third product and sell it to both customer groups and you have six segments.

How many products does your business offer? To how many customer groups? Multiply the two numbers together and that's how many business segments you serve.

Now, which two, three or four segments are the most important? Which contribute most to sales (let's assume to start with that each segment has a similar cost profile, so proportionate contribution to operating profit is the same as for sales)?

And will these same segments be the main contributors to sales over the next few years?

Set this out precisely and succinctly here. In too many strategic plans this basic information is absent. Often one sees a pie chart or two of sales by main product line, or sales by region or country, but what is left out is:

● Sales by product/market segment – that is, sales of a specific product line *to a specific customer group*

● That same information over time, say over the last three years.

Let's take a simple example. Your company makes widgets, small, medium and large, which you sell to three sectors, manufacturing, engineering and construction, in each of two countries, UK and France. You operate in 3 * 3 * 2 = 18 product/market segments.

By far your biggest segment is large widgets to UK engineering, which account for 40 per cent of sales. This is followed by medium widgets to UK engineering at 25 per cent of sales and large widgets to French manufacturing at 15 per cent of sales. Together these three segments account for 80 per cent of sales. The remaining 15 segments account for just 20 per cent of sales – see Figure 1.1.

Figure 1.1 Key segmentation: an example

Sales by product/market segment

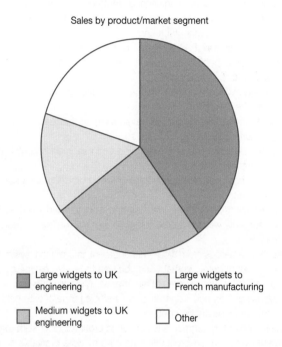

■ Large widgets to UK engineering

□ Large widgets to French manufacturing

▦ Medium widgets to UK engineering

□ Other

Very often, what would be set out here would be a pie chart showing a break-down of sales by widget size – large, medium and small. Alongside might be another pie chart showing sales by country, UK and France. Better, it might combine both country and end-user data, breaking down sales into four customer groups, UK engineering, UK manufacturing, French engineering and French manufacturing.

This is useful information, but what would be very much more useful would be a pie chart showing the real product/market segmentation as set out above. It would show one segment alone – large widgets to UK engineering – accounting for 40 per cent of sales and another for 25 per cent.

That would show that the key issues impacting on your firm's strategy development, whether relating to market demand, competition or your firm's competitiveness, are those pertaining to *one* particular segment – large widgets to UK engineering. Not large widgets in general, not small widgets, not UK as a whole, not all of France, not French engineering, not UK construction, but specifically one product/market segment – large widgets to UK engineering.

Engineering customers will have different demand influences to those in construction. The UK may be at a different stage in the economic cycle to France. French engineering companies may have different solutions favouring medium over large widgets. Small widget producers may be more numerous and have more flexible, short-run production facilities than those making large widgets.

For any or all of these reasons, you need to know that one product/market segment, large widgets to UK engineering, matters most in your business. And what matters next is the segment of medium widgets to UK engineering, followed by large widgets to French manufacturing.

And what of the future? Perhaps you are set to launch an extra-large widget tailored to the UK aerospace sector, which, if all goes to plan, could account for 20 per cent of sales in three years' time.

So let's have a second pie chart alongside the first, showing forecast sales by main product/market segment in three years' time.

And what of profitability? So far we have assumed that each segment has the same cost structure. This is unlikely to be so.

We need to repeat the exercise examining each segment's contribution not to sales, but to operating profit.

That data may not exist. You surely have sales by product/market segment and probably gross profit too.

But it is operating profit or at least contribution to fixed overheads that we need. Some segments will be heavier consumers of the marketing budget or travel expenses than others.

The data that emerges from your management information system probably won't give this level of detail. In that case you need to make estimates. Reasoned estimates are far better than no data at all. After all, in drawing up your strategy you will soon be making reasoned judgements on a whole range of external factors, like market demand and industry competition.

The contribution of key segments to operating profit will differ from that for sales. Some segments will be more profitable than others. More profitable segments will have a higher share of operating profit than of sales.

But that doesn't mean that the breakdown by operating profit is necessarily more useful than that by sales. The latter can be most useful in highlighting where profitability in certain segments is lagging behind others and potentially how that gap can be narrowed.

Returning to the example of the engineering company, where the segment of large widgets to UK engineering contributes to 40 per cent of sales. Suppose the contribution to operating profit was only 30 per cent, the same as that of the second largest segment (in terms of sales), medium widgets to UK engineering – despite the latter only contributing to 25 per cent of sales.

Both sets of data are important. There may be structural factors influencing the disparity in profitability – the large widget business may face competition from Far Eastern imports, with medium widgets less affected. This will limit the firm's choice of strategic options.

But it may be that the firm's manufacturing efficiency has fallen behind that of its domestic competitors, which have invested in capital equipment ideally suited for the larger widgets. This will lie within the firm's scope to act upon.

In a start-up venture

If you are planning a business start-up, you may still need to segment. If you are to launch just the one product (or service) to one group of customers, fine, you won't need to segment any further. But are you sure you'll only have one product? One customer group?

Try categorising your products. And your customers. Is further segmentation meaningful? If so, use it. If not, don't waste time just for the sake of seeming serious. Stick to the one product for the one customer group, i.e. one business segment.

But there is one big difference. No matter how you segment, no matter how many customer groups you identify, they are all, at present, gleams in the eye.

You have no customers. Yet.

Your product must be couched in terms of its benefits to the customer. That is the business proposition.

Not the way in which your product can do this, do that, at this price. But in the way in which your product or service can *benefit* the target customer.

Who is the target customer? In which way will he or she benefit from your offering?

And that is just in the one segment. Are there others?

Segmentation may lie at the very heart of your business proposition. It may have been in the very act of segmentation that you unearthed a niche where only your offering can yield the customer benefit. And you have since tailored your offering to address that very niche, that customer benefit.

For further stimulating thoughts on this, see the chapter on 'Will the fish bite?' in John Mullins' indispensable guide to business start-ups, *The New Business Road Test: What Entrepreneurs and Executives Should Do Before Writing a Business Plan*.

Here is a slightly different way of looking at it. Does your offering address some 'unmet need' in the marketplace? Does it fill a gap in a target customer's needs? This is one of the secrets to a new venture's success highlighted by William Bridges in his book, *Creating You & Co*. He suggests that an 'unmet need' could be uncovered by spotting signs such as a missing piece in a pattern, an unrecognised opportunity, an underused resource, a signal event, an unacknowledged change, a supposedly impossible situation, a non-existent but needed service, a new or emerging problem, a bottleneck, an interface, or other similar signs.

However you define the customer benefit, whether in terms of unmet needs or in a way more meaningful to your offering, you need to undertake some basic research to dig up whatever evidence you can glean of customer benefit.

An understanding of customer benefit will help you to clarify segmentation.

In summary, what we need from this essential tool is a breakdown of what matters most in your business mix, now and in the near future. Which product/market segments will make or break your business?

When to use it

Use it always. Segmentation is critical to the strategy development process.

When to be wary

Be careful of paralysis through analysis. Don't end up with dozens of segments. Concentrate on the half-dozen or so product/market segments that truly drive your firm's profit.

Issue analysis (Minto)

2

The tool

What is the key question you are trying to answer in your strategy development process? And to answer that, what other questions need answering, especially those relating to certain rather worrying risks or exciting opportunities?

These risks and opportunities may be external to your firm – like economic recession (or, conversely, economic recovery) or a new Eastern European market entrant (or exit).

Or they may be internal to your firm – like the loss of a key customer (or gain) or a competitor poaching your Sales Director (or vice versa).

These issues all need to be taken into account in drawing up your strategy. The main ones will be assessed for how likely they are to occur and their impact on value if they do occur (see Section 9).

But you need to get the key issues on the table right at the start of the strategy development process, to make sure that the research and analysis needed to answer the most important questions is carried out.

And these issues need to be embraced in a structured framework: an issue analysis.

How to use it

Each strategy consulting group has its own in-house approach to issue analysis. My former group had an excellent methodology, adapted largely from the issue analysis work of Barbara Minto and her *Pyramid Principle*.

Her issue analysis always starts with the S-C-Q framework, adapted below for purposes of strategy development:

- *Situation* – what is the situation of the firm, in a paragraph – which markets is it in, how well is it doing, now and in the recent past?

- *Complication* – what are the major constraints on further profit growth for the firm, again in a paragraph?

Figure 2.1 The pyramid principle: an example

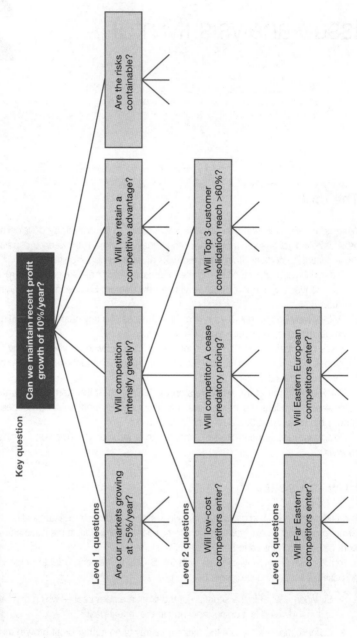

Key question

Can we maintain recent profit growth of 10%/year?

Level 1 questions

Are our markets growing at >5%/year?

Will competition intensify greatly?

Will we retain a competitive advantage?

Are the risks containable?

Level 2 questions

Will low-cost competitors enter?

Will competitor A cease predatory pricing?

Will Top 3 customer consolidation reach >60%?

Level 3 questions

Will Far Eastern competitors enter?

Will Eastern European competitors enter?

Source: Adapted from *The Pyramid Principle*, Barbara Minto, Pearson Education, 2002

- *Key question* – what is the key question this strategy development process should set out to address?

Once you have formulated the single key question, you draw up a set of 3, 4, 5 questions which need answering before you can answer that key question. Then you draw up a set of second-level questions you need to answer before you can answer each of the first-level questions. And so on, down to perhaps a third or fourth level in some cases.

You have built a pyramid of questions, with these characteristics:

- Each question follows a logical order, arranged, for example, by time, structure or rank.

- Each question should be independent and non-overlapping with others, but together exhaustive (that is, they should cover all possibilities).

- Each question can only have a yes or no answer; questions starting with 'why' or 'how' are not permissible, but questions such as 'will market demand growth exceed 5 per cent/year?' would be (as opposed to 'what is the growth rate of market demand?') – this forces you to be conclusive, all the way up the pyramid.

- The number of sub-issues under any issue should not exceed seven and should be more than one – otherwise the pyramid should be reformulated.

Here's a simplified example – see Figure 2.1.

Note that only a selection of boxes has been illustrated, with most branches left dangling due to limitations of space. In this issue analysis, working from the bottom up, the conclusions might be that:

- Far Eastern competitors will enter the market, but the Eastern Europeans will not.

- This will intensify competition greatly.

- We can maintain recent profit growth of 10 per cent/year despite intensified competition due to fast-growing markets, retention of our competitive advantage and containable risks (relevant boxes not shown).

The key question forces you to think of what you want to come out of the strategy development process. It is the only question which does not have a yes or no answer!

Questions at all other levels require you to come to a firm conclusion, yes or no. It is a powerful tool.

When to use it

Upfront in the strategy development process. It serves three main purposes:

- Brainstorming – your team will be stimulated to think about markets, industries, customers, competitors, prices, trends, etc. at an early stage in the process.

- Highlighting data gaps – the tool should make clear where further research and analysis is needed.
- Structuring your thoughts – by building a pyramid of questions, to be answered with a yes or no, but not too many questions, or too few, you will be *converging* on a strategy solution, *not diverging* into an unstructured array of ideas and observations (as with some other tools – see situation analysis and SWOT analysis later in this section).

When to be wary

Don't be too rigid in the issue analysis. This is an upfront, brainstorming exercise. Not all issues will be identified, some will only become more apparent later on. Some issues may turn out to be non-events. Return to the analysis now and again during the strategy development process and add, delete or amend the questions at each level as appropriate. But retain the pyramid structure.

British Aerospace's super segment

In 1988 British Aerospace bought Rover Group – in a flagrant breach of some fundamental rules of corporate strategy, as in focus (Tool 45), sticking to the knitting (Tool 70), profit from the core (Tool 71) *et al*.

BAe was Britain's premier aerospace and defence manufacturer, its largest exporter and supplier of many of the world's fighter planes, radar, missiles and warships, as well as munitions, having purchased Royal Ordnance in 1986. And it was profitable.

The Rover Group, manufacturers of Rover and Land Rover automobiles, was all that was left of the former troubled, state-run British Leyland, manufacturer of Leyland trucks and buses, Austin, Rover and MG cars and Land Rovers. Its finances were precarious.

Segmentation of BAe's businesses, breaking down sales by major product/market segment, would have been difficult enough, given the array of aerospace and defence-related segments, without the complication of the automobile arm. Segmentation by contribution to operating profit would have added yet another layer of complexity, given the highly uncertain future profitability of the car division.

Yet, in 1990 BAe set off in yet another direction. It joined a consortium with Pactel Communications, Millicom and Matra in Microtel Telecommunications to bid for a licence to develop a mobile telecommunications network in the UK. Following award of the licence, the consortium soon sold out to Hutchison Whampoa, with BAe retaining a 31.5 per cent stake in the venture.

In 1990 BAe's stake in Microtel would not have registered in a segmentation exercise. Analysts would have been more concerned with the core defence businesses and the strategically dubious venture into automobiles. By 1992, with investment in the network roll-out, it should have started to register.

Yet, when BAe came to divest its stake in Orange Personal Communications Services, as Microtel was curiously renamed, via an IPO in 1996, a placement in 1998 and a Eurobond issue backed on its remaining 5 per cent stake in 1999, BAe was to realise £1.7 billion gross receipts, of which £1.4 billion was profit.

Compared to BAe's group profit before tax in 1999 of £790 million (1998: £708 million), that initial investment in a telecoms license bid had made an impressive contribution.

The moral of the tale? When you are identifying key segments at the start of the strategy development process, don't segment on the basis of today's sales and today's profits. Think forward. One of your segments, even one breaching the rules of corporate strategy, might prove to be a Microtel.

P.S. BAe went on to divest Rover Group in 1994, selling to BMW for a healthy £800 million and proving that in business, as in life, luck can at times play as large a role as strategic forethought!

3

The 80/20 principle (Pareto)

The tool

Do you enjoy pottering about in the garden? Or are you an avid gardener with a flourishing allotment and bounteous vegetable harvest?

If the latter, you will know that (roughly) 80 per cent of your peas tend to come from 20 per cent of your pods (see Figure 3.1).

Figure 3.1 The Pareto principle

Source: Adapted from Vilfredo Pareto, *Manuale di Economia Politica*, 1906

This observation is widely attributed to that of the Italian economist, Vilfredo Pareto, writing around the turn of the twentieth century. He is said to have contrasted his horticultural findings with those of his economic research, which showed that 80 per cent of Italian land was owned by 20 per cent of the people, and deduced a principle in the making ...

Yet this story seems apocryphal. As set out in Richard Koch's best-selling 1997 reinterpretation, *The 80/20 Principle: the Secret of Achieving More with Less*, there is no record of Pareto mentioning the numbers 80/20, let alone peas and pods.

What is certain is that Pareto studied the hugely lop-sided distribution of land, wealth and income in nineteenth-century England and derived a mathematical relationship between the proportions of people and wealth. He found that the distribution of wealth was *predictably* unbalanced – *and* that the mathematical relationship held firm across other time periods and other countries.

Pareto's work was built on in the 1940s, notably by quality management guru, Joseph M. Juran, who found that 80 per cent of production problems came from 20 per cent of the causes. He called this effect the 'Pareto Principle' or the 'Rule of the Vital Few'.

Other business writers have developed this principle further, with common business applications including:

- 80 per cent of your sales come from 20 per cent of your products
- 80 per cent of your profits come from 20 per cent of your customers
- 80 per cent of your profits come from 20 per cent of the time put in
- 80 per cent of your complaints come from 20 per cent of your customers
- 80 per cent of your sales are made by 20 per cent of your salesforce
- 80 per cent of your business boost comes from 20 per cent of your advertising.

One I like, which applies to relationships both personal and commercial, is that 80 per cent of frustrations come from 20 per cent of causes (one: 'you're always watching football on TV'; the other: 'you're always watching cookery on TV'!).

Koch encourages people to 'think the 80/20 way', recognising that there is an inbuilt imbalance in three broad areas of business and life:

- 20 per cent of inputs lead to 80 per cent of outputs
- 20 per cent of causes lead to 80 per cent of consequences
- 20 per cent of effort leads to 80 per cent of results.

This self-confessed 'lazy entrepreneur' thinks and lives the 80/20 way in London, Cape Town and 'the sunnier parts of Southern Europe'.

How to use it

The 80/20 principle can be especially useful in segmenting your business for purposes of strategy development.

Here are two potentially revealing business applications of the principle:

- 80 per cent of your profits may come from 20 per cent of your product/

market segments – so concentrate your research and analysis on the latter; indeed, concentrate on those segments which together account for 80 per cent of your cumulative profit over the next five years, whether they represent 20 per cent, 15 per cent or 25 per cent of your segments.

- 80 per cent of the value created by your new strategy may come from 20 per cent of the insights – the challenge is to identify those value-enhancing insights!

It is a stimulating tool. On the one hand it is encouraging, since we know that we can gain 80 per cent of the benefit by just putting in 20 per cent of the effort. On the other hand, which 20 per cent?!

When to use it

Bear it in mind when drawing up your business mix. Don't spend too much effort researching and analysing those segments that contribute to just 20 per cent of the value of your firm.

When to be wary

It is a general, surprisingly widespread principle, but not to be taken too literally. It is the lop-sidedness of effect and cause, outputs and inputs that is important, be it 80/20, 65/35 or 99/1. Be cognisant of the innate imbalance more than the numbers.

The segmentation mincer (Koch)

4

The tool

Sticking to Pareto's horticultural theme in the previous tool, a common concern of the hopeless gardener is the dilemma you face as you stand there, trowel in hand, poised over some curious, ominous green shoot: when is a weed not a weed?

Luckily, for the dilemma of when a segment is not a segment, a tool stands ready to answer it – the Segmentation Mincer.

This was developed by Richard Koch with some former consulting colleagues at L.E.K. in the 1980s. It asks a structured series of questions designed to discover if two segments are genuinely distinct or whether they should be treated for strategy development purposes as being one and the same. It can be viewed as a kind of cluster analysis, without all the complex statistical formulae.

How to use it

The questions shown in Figure 4.1 compare one product/market segment with another to investigate whether they are genuinely distinct segments.

After answering all these penetrating questions and totalling the scores, you should treat the two segments as distinct if the total emerges positive. If the score is negative, the two are best treated as one and the same segment.

Figure 4.1 The Segmentation Mincer

	Yes	No
1. Are the competitors the same?	−30	30
2. Is market share relative to the leader roughly the same?	−50	50
3. Are the customers the same?	−20	20
4. Are customer purchasing criteria and their importance roughly the same?	−30	30
5. Are they substitutes for each other?	−10	10
6. Are prices roughly the same?	−20	20
7. Is profitability roughly the same?	−40	40
8. Do they have similar capital needs?	−10	10
9. Do they have similar cost structures?	−10	10
10. Do they share at least half of their costs?	−30	30
11. Are there barriers to competing in both areas?	−20	20
12. Can a cost advantage be gained by competing in just one area?	−30	30
Total		

Source: Adapted from *Financial Times Guide to Strategy*, Richard Koch, FT Publishing, 2011

When to use it

Use it if you are uncertain about your segmentation and might benefit from a more structured approach.

When to be wary

Some of the questions require answers that tend to emerge later in the strategy development process, such as the nature and weighting of customer purchasing criteria (see Section 4). But there is no harm in taking a first shot now – you can always return to the segmentation later on if necessary and consolidate or split up segments as appropriate.

5C situation analysis 5

The tool

'Strange is our situation here upon earth', mused Albert Einstein. How strange is your firm's situation?

Situation analysis is a tool used primarily in marketing strategy, but it overlaps with strategy in general. It is defined by marketers as the process of identifying the environment the firm is working in, and how the firm slots into that environment, to improve its capabilities and better meet customer needs.

A popular form is the 5C analysis (see Figure 5.1), where the firm takes an environmental scan in five areas:

- *Company* – your goals, culture, product line, strengths, weaknesses, unique selling point, price positioning, image in market
- *Collaborators* – suppliers, alliances, distributors

Figure 5.1 5C analysis

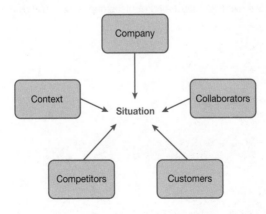

- *Customers* – customer groups, market size, growth, segments, benefits, channels, customer buying decisions, customer behaviour
- *Competitors* – direct/indirect, new entrants, substitutes, market shares, barriers to entry, relative positioning, strengths, weaknesses
- *Context* – the political, economic, social, technological, environmental and legal environment (or PESTEL analysis, see Section 4).

How to use it

Through a series of workshops, marketers study each of these five areas and consider to what extent issues identified impact on key marketing decisions.

When to use it

If you are familiar with this tool, you may choose it instead of issue analysis (Tool 2). Both tools encourage the brainstorming of ideas and issues upfront, something which is essential in strategy development.

When to be wary

The tool is rather unfocused and lacking in structure.

Many of the areas to be scanned require in-depth research or analysis. Take market size and growth – that is the subject of a whole building block (Section 3). Likewise barriers to entry (one of the key forces in Section 4). Your firm's competitive position is another (the subject of Section 5). At best, all that can be accomplished at this stage of the strategy development process is to identify key questions – and that is better done in issue analysis.

The beauty of issue analysis is its pyramid structure. The answer to one question contributes towards the answer to the question in the level above. Situation analysis has no vertical structure: it is just a horizontal grouping of issues by area.

SWOT analysis (Andrews)

6

The tool

Swat away the SWOT?

SWOT analysis is ubiquitous. It pops up all over the place, in market research reports, stockbroker analyst reports, even in financial due diligence reports, drawn up by accountants keen to impress perhaps that they are *au fait* with strategic concepts.

It is popular because it is easy to understand and apply. And it encourages the brainstorming of issues.

But it is a tool of limited merit. It provides no answer and little help to any strategic question. Nor does it suggest in which direction to proceed in order to find an answer.

How to use it

SWOT analysis is a 2 × 2 matrix, with factors internal to the firm (Strengths and Weaknesses) along one row and external factors (Opportunities and Threats) along the other – see Figure 6.1.

In its original formulation in the 1960s it was designed by Kenneth R. Andrews of Harvard Business School to aid strategists in distinguishing between factors they could influence (the internal ones) and those they could not (the external ones). The optimal strategy is seen as one where there is strategic fit between the firm's internal resources or competences and the external market opportunities.

The intended end-result is worthy, but the tool does not help much in getting there.

Figure 6.1 SWOT analysis

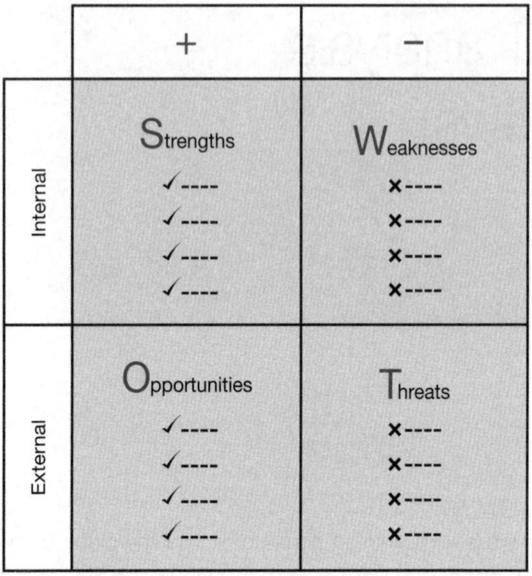

	+	**−**
Internal	**S**trengths ✓---- ✓---- ✓---- ✓----	**W**eaknesses ✗---- ✗---- ✗---- ✗----
External	**O**pportunities ✓---- ✓---- ✓---- ✓----	**T**hreats ✗---- ✗---- ✗---- ✗----

When to use it

As with situation analysis (Tool 5), with which it is sometimes combined, it is an aid to the brainstorming of issues. Use it if you are familiar with it (and understand its limitations). But there are better, more structured aids, such as issue analysis (Tool 2).

When to be wary

There are grave flaws with the SWOT tool itself and yet more in how it has come to be used:

- The juxtaposition on one page of external opportunities and threats, themselves worthy of two whole sections in this book (Sections 3 and 4), and internal observations on strengths and weaknesses (Sections 5 and 6), gives little help to strategy formulation; it is too general, insufficiently specific in terms of the impact on key product/market segments over time of trends in market demand, industry competition, customer purchasing criteria, key success factors, company performance and competitive position.

- There is no assessment of the importance or relevance of the SWOT issues identified – no weighting of the SW issues (as in Section 5 of this book), and no ranking by probability or impact of the OT issues (as in Section 9).

- Users tend to dump their ideas, often the output of offsite brainstorming sessions, into the boxes; I have seen SWOT matrices on PowerPoint presentations where 15–20 observations or issues have been placed *in each box*, so that each is in tiny 6-point text; the matrix can be confusing at the best of times: at other times it is unreadable.

The main problem with SWOT analysis is this: great, but so what? What conclusion can be drawn from the matrix?

At best, it is a considered assessment of issues key to strategy development, grouped by whether these issues are internal or external to the firm and whether they are beneficial or detrimental to the firm. At worst, too often experienced, it is a depository, a jumble of random observations and issues, fluffy and meaningless.

[SECTION 2]

Setting goals and objectives

Overview

Essential tools

7   Setting long-term goals

8   Setting SMART objectives

9   Maximising shareholder value

10 Balancing stakeholder interests

Useful tools

11 Creating shared value (Porter and Kramer)

12 Economic value added (Stern Stewart)

13 Balanced scorecard and strategy map (Kaplan and Norton)

14 Core ideology (Collins and Porras)

15 Business as a community (Handy)

Overview

So, you know your firm as it is today, its segments, its issues. But where do you want it to be tomorrow? What sort of a firm do you want it to be? On which parameters will you measure performance success?

In short, what are the aims of your firm?

There are numerous treatises written on the relative merits of a company articulating its vision, mission, aims, purposes, goals, objectives, values, principles, ideals, beliefs, principles and so on and so forth. The sound of hair splitting can be deafening.

It is simpler and adequate to stick to two of these: goals and objectives.

A goal is something your business aims to be, as described in words. An objective is a target that helps to measure whether that goal is achieved, and is typically set out in numbers.

One of your goals may be for your business to be the most customer-centric supplier of your services in Northern Europe. Objectives to back up that goal could be the achievement of a 'highly satisfied' rating of 30 per cent from your annual customer survey by 2014 and 35 per cent by 2016, along with 80 per cent 'satisfied' or better by that year.

Goals are directional, objectives are specific. The former should look beyond the short term and set out where you see the firm in the long term. The latter should be 'SMART', namely Specific, Measurable, Attainable, Relevant and Time-limited (see Tool 8).

Other aims can readily slot into a simple goals and objectives framework:

- *Mission* – in theory, what sets your business apart from the rest of the competition; in practice, you can treat this as a goal
- *Vision* – in theory, where your business aims to go or become; again, you can treat this as another goal
- *Aims* – they can be taken as roughly synonymous with goals
- *Purposes* – ditto
- *Values* – in theory, a set of beliefs and principles that guide how your business should respond when there are moral, ethical, safety, health, environmental or other value-related demands on the business that may conflict with the goal of shareholder-value maximisation; in practice, this can be identified as a separate goal
- *Beliefs* – as for values
- *Ideals* – ditto
- *Principles* – ditto.

The setting of long-term goals and SMART objectives are essential tools in strategy development. So too are the maximising of shareholder value and the sometimes conflicting but potentially reinforcing tool of balancing stakeholder interests.

We shall look at each of these four essential tools first and then consider other useful tools and techniques in setting goals and objectives, ranging from the ultra-hard Economic Value Added from Stern Stewart to Charles Handy's ultra-soft Business as a Community.

7 Setting long-term goals

The tool

D'où Venons Nous? Que Sommes Nous? Où Allons Nous? (Where do we come from? What are we? Where are we going?) inscribed Paul Gauguin on his hauntingly existential Tahitian painting, in those long-distant, post-Impressionist days when art was artistic. You have dealt with the former two (Section 1), now for the third: where are you going?

Goal setting is the cornerstone of business strategy. Goals should underpin each of your company's main strategic initiatives over the next five years or so.

Goal setting should also prove motivational. Goals can enhance employee performance in four ways, according to Latham and Locke:

- They focus attention towards goal-relevant activities
- They have an energising effect
- They encourage persistence
- They help staff cope with the task to hand.

How to use it

Here are five considerations when setting goals:

- Goals differ from objectives
- Short-term goals have little place in strategy development
- The best goals for motivational purposes may be market related
- Financial goals may need to resolve the shareholder/stakeholder trade-off
- Value-related goals are no less valid.

A goal is something your business aims to be, as described in words. An objective is a target that helps to measure whether that goal is achieved, and is typically set out in numbers. Your goal may be to become a low-cost provider in a key segment. An accompanying objective might be to reduce unit operating costs in that segment within three years by 10 per cent.

Second, think of short-term goals as what lies within and behind this year's budget. These may be important in the short term, whether for keeping the financial markets or your private owners happy or for you landing that performance-related bonus.

But what lies within that budget may have little impact on strategy development. Strategy takes into account market demand trends and industry competition forces that go well beyond the short term. It is no good gearing up your business to compete ferociously in the short term, only to be exposed to a drop-off in demand or intensified competition in the medium to long term.

Third, there are various types of goal. Market- or customer-oriented goals are often the most motivational and easy enough to monitor. Market-share data are readily collected by companies beyond a certain size. A goal could be market leadership in Segment A within three years. Such a goal is motivational for the salesforce, and it is often simple to assess progress.

Customer satisfaction or retention goals (or objectives – see the next tool) can also have the same effect.

Operational goals are also incentivising for the operations team – and even simpler to monitor than market-related goals. A goal of cost leadership in Segment B within five years can dynamise performance-improvement teams. Progress within the company on unit cost reduction can be tracked over time and compared at annual intervals with those of your competitors.

The fourth issue concerns financial goals. If the goals (or objectives) relate to segment prices or margins, whether gross margin or contribution, they can be treated in the same way as market-related goals. Motivational for the salesforce, easy to monitor.

Figure 7.1 An example: Google's goals

Focus on the user and all else will follow

Its best to do one thing really, really well

Fast is better than slow

Democracy on the web works

You don't need to be at your desk to need an answer

You can make money without doing evil

There's always more information out there

The need for information crosses all borders

You can be serious without a suit

Great just isn't good enough

Source: Adapted from www.google.com

But when they relate to the overall financial performance of the company, whether return on sales or capital, the goals may need to resolve the shareholder/stakeholder benefit trade-off – see later tools on maximising shareholder value and balancing stakeholder interests.

Finally, your value-related goals may be just as important – see Google's in Figure 7.1. One such goal could be an ethical sourcing policy – for example, no child labour used by suppliers or no genetically modified cereals bought in. This is your call, though you will be aware that this may be in conflict with a goal of shareholder-value maximisation.

When to use it

Always.

When to be wary

Don't have too many goals. They say people can't remember more than three of any list, but you may choose to stretch that to four or five.

Go for a dozen and you'll be lucky to attain half of them. Go for a handful and you may bag the lot.

Setting SMART objectives

8

The tool

'Institutions mistake good intentions for objectives', cautioned Peter Drucker. Not if they are SMART.

Objectives are intimately linked to goals. Your firm aims towards a goal, a destination typically articulated in words. Objectives are targets, whether along the route or at the final destination, and are typically set out in numbers.

You may aim for the goal of UK market leadership in a key segment by 2017. That is a worthy goal, but a bit too vague for a robust strategy. More precise would be the corresponding objectives of attaining 33 per cent market share by 2015 and 35 per cent by 2017. This objective should help deliver your goal of market leadership in that segment.

How to use it

Where goals are indicative and directional, objectives are precise. You should set objectives that are:

- *Specific* – a precise number against a particular parameter
- *Measurable* – that parameter must be quantifiable – for example, a market-share percentage in a segment rather than a woolly target such as 'best supplier'
- *Attainable* – there is no point in aiming for the improbable – disappointment will be the inevitable outcome
- *Relevant* – the objective should relate to the goal; if the goal is market leadership, an objective of winning 'best marketing campaign of the year' in the trade journal would be inappropriate
- *Time-limited* – you should specify the deadline for the objective to be achieved; an objective with no time limitation would serve no motivational purpose and result in the slippage of difficult decisions.

Objectives should be *S-M-A-R-T* (see Figure 8.1). The best objectives are indeed smart. As in the example above, the objectives are: *Specific* (a market share target in that segment), *Measurable* (market research to which you subscribe will reveal whether the 35 per cent is met), *Attainable* (you are at 29 per cent now and your new product range has been well received), *Relevant* (market share is the ultimate measure of market leadership) and *Time-limited* (2017).

Figure 8.1 SMART objectives

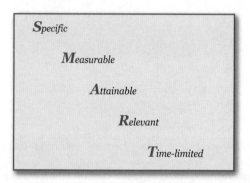

Here is another take on the same theme. Richard Rumelt, in his best-selling book of 2011, *Good Strategy, Bad Strategy*, states that strategy implementation is greatly assisted by the identification of 'proximate objectives'. Each of these is a target that is close enough that the firm 'can reasonably be expected to hit, or even overwhelm it'. He is emphasising the attainable 'A' component of a SMART objective.

He cites the example of President Kennedy pledging to place a man on the moon. The objective sounded fanciful, but it conveyed ambition. And Kennedy had an ace up his sleeve – he knew the technology already existed for such a mission to succeed.

When to use it

In strategy development, always. Objectives are also very important in strategy implementation. Gaining buy-in from key managers and staff can be the key to successful implementation of strategy.

Remember, strategy development should be underpinned by smart goals and *SMART* objectives.

When to be wary

As with goal setting, keep it simple. One or two objectives against each of 4 to 5 goals should be fine.

Maximising shareholder value

9

The tool

Firms exist to create value for their shareholders. The so-called 'Anglo-Saxon' business model is nothing if not straightforward. The interests of other stakeholders, be they employees, suppliers, financiers, government, community or the environment, are not the direct concern of the firm.

Milton Friedman and others have argued that a firm's purpose is to maximise shareholder value and that, since only people can have social responsibilities, firms are responsible solely to their shareholders and not to society as a whole. If directors or managers choose to disburse their personal earnings in a charitable or socially responsible manner, that is their prerogative. It is not in their remit to disburse shareholders' funds in like manner.

The contrary viewpoint is discussed in the next tool.

How to use it

Note the references above to shareholder *value* maximisation. Why not *profit*, you may ask?

The choice of word is fundamental to business strategy. Value and profit are not the same thing. The value of an enterprise is defined strictly as the value of the equity plus the value of the long-term debt. The latter is easy to measure in any company, as is the former in a publicly quoted company – it is simply the market capitalisation of the company at any given moment of time.

That market capitalisation is not a profit, nor is it a sum of profits, nor should it be seen a multiple of today's profits, via a ratio such as P/E. It is the sum of free cash flows likely to be generated over the length of life of the company discounted at the opportunity cost of capital to the value of cash today.

Value is a measure not of profit but of cash. And it is a measure of future cash flow, not a multiple of this year's.

A company can boost short-term profit through a number of ways that may be detrimental to shareholder value, such as:

- Hiking up pricing in the short term, boosting profits from those customers less able to switch to another provider owing to contractual or commercial constraints, but ultimately alienating and potentially losing much of the customer base
- Chopping prices in the short term, boosting market share, but ultimately denting the long-term value of the brand
- Perhaps most commonly, cutting back on capital expenditure so that it falls below provision for depreciation, boosting profitability but damaging long-term competitiveness
- Slashing operating costs, to the extent that product quality and/or service are impaired, but with little detrimental impact on sales in the short term.

The goal of shareholder-value maximisation (see Figure 9.1), as opposed to profit maximisation, forces the strategist to give priority to:

- The medium to long term, rather than the short term
- The building of sustainable competitive position, rather than temporary profit
- Cash flow, rather than profit.

Figure 9.1 Shareholder-value maximisation

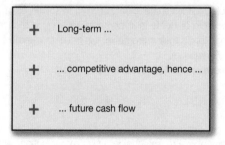

```
+    Long-term ...

+    ... competitive advantage, hence ...

+    ... future cash flow
```

When to use it

Always.

When to be wary

Likewise, always. There is an omnipresent trade-off between this goal and the next, balancing stakeholder interests. Ultimately, it is your call.

Balancing stakeholder interests (corporate social responsibility)

10

The tool

'A company's primary responsibility is to serve its customers … Profit is not the primary goal but rather an essential condition for the company's continued existence. Other responsibilities, e.g., to employees and society, exist to support the company's continued ability to carry out its primary purpose', wrote Peter Drucker in 1954, an original variant on the Anglo-Saxon business model of maximising shareholder value.

There have been many other variants, each with its own take on the divvying of the pie, the optimal balance of shareholder and other stakeholder interests. Some argue that companies should exist to serve not solely the interests of their owners, but also of their employees and managers. They should also act in the interests of other stakeholders with whom they interrelate – their customers, suppliers, landlords, the local community, Government, the environment.

However, the goal of balancing stakeholder interests needs to be treated with care. If you give too much weight to the interests of those other than shareholders, you won't remain in business too long. As Adam Smith wrote in his *Wealth of Nations* in 1776:

'It is not from the benevolence of the butcher, the brewer or the baker, that we expect our dinner, but from their regard to their own self interest. We address ourselves, not to their humanity but to their self-love, and never talk to them of our own necessities but of their advantages.'

The Continental European (and Asian) business model gives greater credence to stakeholders other than shareholders, especially to employees. In the two-tier corporate governance structure in Germany, for example, the management board is composed largely of the executive, but the supervisory board has as many members chosen by employees as by shareholders (excluding the shareholder-appointed Chairman).

How to use it

Debate is ongoing on the efficacy of the European model – on the one hand, proponents claim it encourages companies to plan for the long term and aim to grow the business at least as fast as to maintain levels of employment. On the other hand, opponents argue that it makes the company less flexible and less nimble in response to technological change. Fine, they generalise, for mature engineering and manufacturing firms, less so for hi-tech firms, fine in commercial banking, less so in investment banking.

Under the goal of balancing stakeholder interests, here is your opportunity to clarify the values and principles underpinning your firm. You don't need a comprehensive statement on values and principles, as set out by many large companies – partly for PR reasons, though arguably too for employee motivational purposes. Many of these values can also seem trite and obvious, hardly worth stating – for example, 'we believe in honesty and integrity in business' or 'we comply with all applicable laws and regulations'. It is hard to imagine a firm flaunting contrary goals: 'we believe in dishonesty and duplicity, and strive to evade all laws and regulations that constrain our profitability'! But you may want to pull out one or two values which are crucial, but not self-evident, to the way in which your firm wishes to do business.

The goal of balancing stakeholder interests has become more formalised in the past two decades through the promotion of corporate social responsibility ('CSR'), sometimes referred to as 'corporate conscience', and the advent of 'social accounting'. Large corporations have devoted teams and budgets to CSR and many set out progress against CSR objectives at length in their annual reports. All sorts of CSR indices have been constructed, typically by consultants for specific clients, tailored to the nature of the business.

Business in the Community produces an annual index of CSR performance, published in a *Financial Times* special report on corporate responsibility, which attaches awards ranging from bronze to 'platinum plus' to companies meeting set criteria (Figure 10.1). Fifteen companies achieved platinum plus status in 2011, ranging from BT to the Co-operative Group, and from Heineken to Unilever.

Figure 10.1 The Annual Corporate Responsibility Index

Award	Criteria	No of companies
Platinum plus	CR underpins business strategy	15
Platinum	CR embedded	42
Gold	CR performance reported	25
Silver	CR data collected	18
Bronze	CR goals articulated	7

Source: Adapted from Business in the Community (www.bitc.org.uk) and www.ft.com

Three of the most common qualifiers to a simple goal of maximising shareholder value come in the areas of employment, sourcing and the environment:

- Written into law in countries such as Germany, a corporate goal could be either the maintenance of employment or the guarantee to make every effort, in the event of unavoidable downsizing, to find each redundant employee a similarly attractive alternative source of employment.

- Ethical sourcing policies have become mainstream in the 2000s – pioneered by the likes of The Body Shop – and movements such as the FAIRTRADE mark have greatly increased awareness of ethical sourcing; even low-cost retailers now have to take great care over selection of suppliers in low-cost countries: see, for example, Primark's vigorous response to a programme by BBC TV's *Panorama* on the company's alleged use of child labour in India; footage was subsequently found not to be authentic and an apology was duly issued by the BBC. With today's global and social media, maximising shareholder value and conducting an ethical sourcing policy have become for many firms complementary goals.

- The trade-off between maximising profit and minimising environmental damage used to be straightforward – mining, chemical, energy and manufacturing companies in particular were tightly regulated and forced to incur the full costs of clearing up the mess made in the extraction or conversion processes. The trade-off has since become broader: one of the leading companies in pursuing alternative energy sources, designed to combat global warming and climate change, is the very same leading global extractor of non-renewable hydrocarbons, BP – it has been a pioneer investor in technologies such as solar, wind and geothermal energy; ironically it has also had to face the greatest opprobrium through its failure to do its basic health, safety and environmental protection job properly, with the tragic rig explosion and catastrophic oil spill in the Gulf of Mexico in 2010.

Some argue that the whole doctrine of CSR has been not just a con trick designed to woo customers, but even an abnegation of corporate responsibility. David Henderson's 2001 paper on *Misguided Virtue* lambasted CSR and predicted that managers who over-committed to meeting social and environmental goals risked betraying the interests of shareholders – if only because they might take their eyes off the ball of what they were supposed to be doing.

One such firm he highlighted was BP, and that was well before its *annus horribilis* of 2010. Perhaps greater attention to refinery and oil-rig safety procedures rather than green energy development might have better served the interests not only of shareholders but of the environment. I know what I would think if I were a brown pelican, sea turtle or hermit crab residing on the Louisiana coast.

[David Henderson also believed, and this is especially pertinent in the climate of the 2010s, that CEO compensation should be held to no more than 20 times what the rank and file made. He was enraged by managers receiving massive pay packets while firing thousands of their workers: 'This is morally and socially unforgivable, and we will pay a heavy price for it.']

When to use it

Always …

When to be wary

… but to be approached with care. Your firm's prime goal might be to maximise shareholder value, albeit balanced, as appropriate to your firm's culture and circumstances, by the interests of specified stakeholders. But should the latter interests gain precedence over those of shareholders, your firm may be destined for trouble. And that will be in the interests of no one – not your owners or employees, not your suppliers or customers, not the community or the taxman – other than your competitors.

Which goals count for RBS?

One company that attaches much importance to corporate responsibility is the Royal Bank of Scotland. On its website it sets out proudly its sustainability credentials in the fields of fair banking, enterprise support, employee engagement, safety and security, citizenship and the environment.

Indeed, in July 2008 RBS was being feted on the website Ethical Performance for launching its fifth Corporate Responsibility Report. This showed, inter alia, that RBS was sourcing 100 per cent of its electricity needs from renewable sources.

Highly commendable. Shame about the loan book.

A few months later the bank posted record losses and had to be bailed out by the Government.

CSR is important. But it must not permit directors to take their eyes off the business ball. A bust bank is of little benefit to customers or the environment – and none whatsoever to the 'safety and security' of employees.

11

Creating shared value (Porter and Kramer)

The tool

Many companies pay mere lip service to corporate social responsibility ('CSR'). They treat it as separate from, and a voluntary add-on to, their real goal of shareholder-value creation.

Thus argued Michael Porter and Mark Kramer in two influential articles of 2006 and 2011, in which they introduced the notion of creating shared value, a cross between maximising shareholder value and balancing stakeholder interests.

They believe it is time to move beyond the obvious trade-offs and intertwine CSR with the very core of value creation:

> The concept of shared value ... recognizes that societal needs, not just conventional economic needs, define markets. It also recognizes that social harms or weaknesses frequently create internal costs for firms – such as wasted energy or raw materials, costly accidents, and the need for remedial training to compensate for inadequacies in education. And addressing societal harms and constraints does not necessarily raise costs for firms, because they can innovate through using new technologies, operating methods, and management approaches – and as a result, increase their productivity and expand their markets.

How to use it

Creating shared value is in part simply a repackaging of the tools we have mentioned above on maximising shareholder value and balancing stakeholder interests, but the authors claim to go beyond the blending of conflicting goals. They believe the creation of shared value should be part and parcel of the company's values and culture.

Their model faces much the same criticism discussed above in Tool 10 on balancing stakeholder interests. Critics would argue that the creating shared value model works well when the pursuit of environmental or ethical goals is in harmony with maximising shareholder value but, since the company is pursuing the latter goal anyway, the creating of a shared-value model becomes effectively irrelevant.

Where ethical or environmental goals are in conflict with maximising shareholder value is where the difficulty lies and creating a shared-value model offers little help in resolving this clash. In the interests of long-term survival of the firm, critics argue such conflicts should be resolved in favour of maximising shareholder value.

Nevertheless, even critics would welcome the impetus that this and similar models have given towards reconceiving product/market opportunities benefiting worthy causes, such as poverty relief, sustainability or environmental enhancement. Examples include:

- Nestlé's development of a low-cost milk supply chain in India to benefit the rural poor
- ecomagination, GE's commitment to imagine and build innovative solutions to today's environmental challenges while driving economic growth, has chalked up US$85 billion in revenues, while reducing greenhouse gas emissions by 22 per cent and water use by 30 per cent, and making US$130 million in energy-efficiency savings (see Vice President's letter to investors, customers and other stakeholders of 20 June 2011)
- Marks & Spencer and the Shell Foundation's created a trade aid joint venture in South Africa to invest US$1 million/year in helping 3000 farmers grow, harvest and export exotic flowers.

In each of these cases critics would no doubt counter that the companies involved have been aiming at maximising shareholder value, albeit by cleverly targeting innovative niche opportunities which also happen to improve the public good.

When to use it

Consider using it as an alternative to the tools set out above of maximising shareholder value (Tool 9) and balancing stakeholder interests (Tool 10) – see Figure 11.1.

When to be wary

Conflicts will arise and decisions will need to be taken on sharing the value created. Should the value accrue to the public, in social or environmental benefit, or to shareholders? Trade-offs will be no less difficult to resolve whether the goal is creating shared value or a blend of the goals of maximising shareholder value and balancing stakeholder interests.

Figure 11.1 Creating shared value

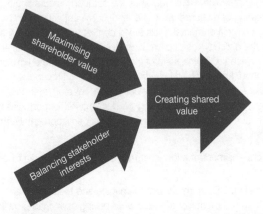

Source: Adapted from Michael E. Porter and Mark R. Kramer, 'Creating Shared Value', *Harvard Business Review*, Jan–Feb 2011

Economic value added (Stern Stewart)

12

The tool

If a company makes a return on capital of 12 per cent, is that good news or bad news?

Well, that depends, primarily on two factors:

- The element of risk in investing in the company
- The extent of long-term debt carried by the company.

Each company has its own cost of capital which reflects both those factors, called the *weighted average cost of capital* ('WACC'). The WACC consists of two parts: the cost of long-term debt times the share of debt in capital employed (fixed assets plus net current assets) plus the cost of equity times the share of equity in capital employed.

The cost of long-term debt is easy enough to assess – it's the rate you need to pay the bank on, say, a three-year secured loan.

The cost of equity is less simple, but, according to the capital asset pricing model, is equal to the risk-free rate (yield on long-term Government bonds) plus the market risk premium (typically 6–7 per cent – the premium investors require to invest in the stock market rather than in government bonds) times a factor representing the risk of the sector your business operates in (called beta, it varies typically in the range 0.5, in steady, low-risk sectors such as utilities, food or insurance, to 1.5, in volatile, high-risk sectors such as construction, capital goods or retail).

When an investor backs your firm, he expects a return equivalent to your WACC. If the return is higher, it is because of *economic profit* or *residual income* or, most popularly and developed by the consulting company Stern Stewart & Co., *economic value added*® ('EVA').

How to use it

EVA is a useful tool in comparing performance in a range of companies – for example those in the FTSE 100. A ranking based on ROCE alone will not necessarily tell you which company is performing best. A company with a high ranking may be in a risky sector and highly leveraged – it could well plummet to the bottom of the ranking in a year or two.

A ranking based on EVA return (EVA/capital employed) is a better indicator. It tells you how companies are performing relative to the sector risk and financial risk each is exposed to. The top-ranking companies will be outperforming investor expectations and 'creating shareholder value'. The lowest, where EVA returns are negative, falling below WACC, are underperforming against investor expectations and are 'destroying shareholder value' (see Figure 12.1).

Figure 12.1 Economic value added

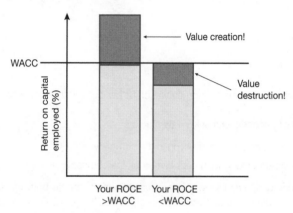

Source: Adapted from www.sternstewart.com

EVA is included in this chapter because you could set an EVA return objective for your firm – say of 5 per cent. That means you aim to achieve a ROCE 5 per cent over and above your firm's WACC – an ambitious target, only achievable if your firm has a sustainable competitive advantage.

EVA is also useful in ranking divisional or business unit performance in your firm. If each business has the same element of risk, there is no advantage to using EVA over ROCE. But this is unlikely, or the businesses would be one and the same. Where businesses are exposed to varying risk, EVA is a better indicator of performance and the ranking can influence strategy development.

When to use it

Use it when you feel comfortable about the theory and calculations and where you want to set a challenging objective for investor returns over and above the usual.

When to be wary

Take care if you find the concept (and the mathematics) difficult. Or unnecessary.

Balanced scorecard and strategy map (Kaplan and Norton)

13

The tool

'Management by objectives works if you first think through your objectives. Ninety percent of the time you haven't', opined Peter Drucker.

The balanced scorecard, a means of translating corporate goals and strategy into a series of defined, measurable objectives, spanning key departmental functions, has become the most commonly used framework of management by objectives.

Derived from earlier metric-driven incentive schemes and work by French process engineers on *tableau de bord* (a dashboard of performance measures), it was developed (from a concept by Art Schneiderman) by Robert Kaplan and David Norton in a 1992 article (and subsequently in a 1996 book). Their objective was to aid strategy implementation and monitoring by defining a set of measurable objectives.

How to use it

The balanced scorecard is typically drawn up for purposes of strategy implementation, but later generations aimed to make it applicable too in strategy development.

The original balanced scorecard method proposed the addition of three non-financial sets of performance measures over and above the standard set of financial objectives of a firm. Thus:

- *Financial perspective*: e.g. revenues, gross and operating margins, return on capital employed, cash flow
- *Customer perspective*: e.g. market share, customer satisfaction, quality performance, delivery performance, customer retention
- *Internal business processes perspective*: e.g. productivity, process measures such as bottlenecks
- *Learning and growth perspective*: e.g. job satisfaction, training as a share of operating costs, employee turnover.

Subsequent generations of the balanced scorecard, by the original developers and a host of others, have streamlined the tool. In their follow-up book of 2000, Kaplan and Norton highlighted the importance of communication in strategy implementation. In their third book of 2003, they introduced the strategy map as the key aid to clarity of strategy creation and communication: they transformed the balanced scorecard from a one-column list to a two-dimensional chart – see Figure 13.1.

Figure 13.1 Strategy map: an example

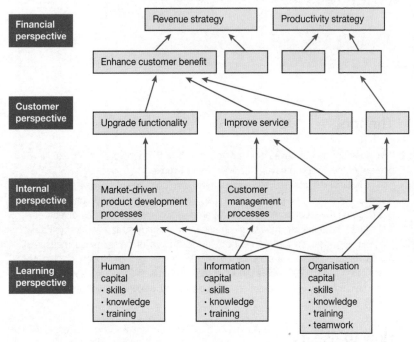

Source: Adapted from Robert S. Kaplan and David P. Norton, *Strategy Maps: Converting Intangible Assets into Tangible Outcomes*, Harvard Business Press, 2004

The strategy map, which can be taken as the second generation of the balanced scorecard, sets out to show how a firm can create value by connecting strategic objectives in cause-and-effect relationships, displayed by arrows in the map. It highlights the route needed to ensure organisational alignment with the strategy.

Many organisations and consultants have tailored the balanced scorecard to fit with their own prioritisation of perspectives. Kaplan and Norton's four perspectives are sometimes extended to five or six, with information management, environmental impact and innovation seen as perspectives of similar validity.

The third generation can be viewed as a derivative of results-driven management. The insertion upfront of a 'destination statement', the outcome of strategic success, with end-results shown against each of the perspectives, purports to galvanise managers in their pursuit of meeting balanced scorecard and/or strategic mapping objectives.

When to use it

The case for using a balanced scorecard in strategy implementation is stronger than for its use in strategy development.

When used effectively in strategy implementation, a balanced scorecard should help in streamlining processes, informing and motivating employees, begetting greater customer satisfaction and demonstrably improving financial results emanating from the strategy.

When to be wary

The danger is self-evident: too many objectives with too little prioritisation in the balanced scorecard, and too much information with too many boxes and arrows on one strategic mapping page, can blur the landscape and hinder coherent strategy development.

The balanced scorecard has an undisputed place in strategy implementation and is used in its various forms by many companies worldwide. This is less so in strategy development.

Critics see strategy mapping as both confusing and over-simplistic, with action items and causal effects unclear and inadequate attention given to uncertainty, risk and sensitivity.

14 Core ideology (Collins and Porras)

The tool

Successful companies set 'big, hairy, audacious goals'.

They also possess a core ideology and create cult-like cultures, claimed Jim Collins and Jerry I. Porras in their influential book *Built to Last: Successful Habits of Visionary Companies* in 1997.

Product lines can change – completely in some cases, such as at Nokia, leaders can change, profit can go up or down – but core ideology should remain for long-term success.

How to use it

You should break core ideology down into core purpose and core values – see Figure 14.1. Core purpose is your firm's 'fundamental reason for being'. Core values are your firm's 'essential and enduring tenets – timeless guiding principles that require no external justification'.

You should set highly challenging big, hairy, audacious goals ('BHAGs') to align ambition and enhance team spirit – for example, Boeing's entry into the commercial aircraft market and President Kennedy's goal to land a man on the moon.

Visionary companies should have cult-like cultures, ones which are demanding of all employees, so much so that some, even many, might feel uncomfortable and quit. Such cultures should exhibit a fervently held ideology, mechanisms for indoctrination, procedures to ensure cultural fit and a feeling of pride, bordering on elitism.

The authors go beyond goals and objectives to identify other sources of success, but that lies outside this chapter. One such merits highlighting, since it is in part contradictory to the purpose of this book. Successful companies never cease to innovate and test their output fast in the marketplace. The authors extol the virtues of continuous opportunistic experimentation, trial and error, giving ideas a quick try, but letting them die quickly if they do not work. And they place this as preferable to strategic planning!

Figure 14.1 Built to last

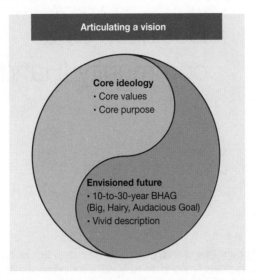

Source: Adapted from James C. Collins and Jerry I. Porras 'Building Your Company's Vision', *Harvard Business Review*, Sep–Oct 1996. *Built to Last*, copyright © 1994 by Jim Collins and Jerry I. Porras. Reprinted with permission from Jim Collins

The authors are as stimulating on what they debunk as on what they promote. In particular, they claim to disprove the notion that a great idea or a charismatic leader is needed to start a company. On the contrary, they see a core ideology and a focused leader as key to long-term success.

When to use it

The concept of the BHAG is memorable, stimulating and as appropriate to the average company as it was to Boeing.

When to be wary

Core ideology as the cornerstone of success may seem a stretch to many firms. They may see purpose and values as less crucial to successful strategy development than goals and objectives.

15

Business as a community (Handy)

The tool

Charles Handy is a sage and national treasure. He was my lecturer on the corporate environment at business school in the early 1980s and talked of concepts that were decades ahead of the time.

He teased, he twinkled, he posed questions and posited trade-offs, typically between efficiency and equity. He seldom supplied answers. They were personal, for us to figure out and to own.

He has long questioned the Anglo-Saxon business model. He believes that it may have worked fine when owner directors and investors were one and the same. Then their interests and those of the company tended to be more aligned. They shared in the pride and responsibility of corporate success.

Now shareholders are largely investors, punters, sometimes gamblers. The law, the rules have become outdated.

Figure 15.1 Business as a community

Source: Adapted from Charles Handy, 'What's a Business For?', *Harvard Business Review*, December 2002

He likes to quote Dave Packard, who, with Bill Hewlett, founded the eponymous computing giant in a one-car garage:

'I think many people assume, wrongly, that a company exists simply to make money. While this is an important result of a company's existence, we have to go deeper and find the real reasons for our being. As we investigate this, we inevitably come to the conclusion that a group of people get together and exist as an institution that we call a company so that they are able to accomplish something collectively that they could not accomplish separately – they make a contribution to society, a phrase which sounds trite but is fundamental.'

Corporate law needs to be updated. In Handy's words:

'The employees of a company are treated, by the law and the accounts, as the property of the owners and are recorded as costs, not assets. This is demeaning, at the very least. Costs are things to be minimized, assets things to be cherished and grown. The language and the measures of business need to be reversed. A good business is a community with a purpose, and a community is not something to be "owned." A community has members, and those members have certain rights, including the right to vote or express their views on major issues.'

He is in favour of the corporate governance found in Germany, where employees take equal responsibility for corporate strategy, but recognises that only aspects can be transferred to the Anglo-Saxon model. Nevertheless, firms should strive to foster a greater sense of community.

How to use it

You should see your business as a community, says Handy. You should strive to take the lead in areas such as social and environmental sustainability, not be reluctant followers.

If business keeps waiting for government to pass more laws and enforce more regulation, 'this minimalist and legalistic approach leaves business looking like the potential despoiler who must be reined in'.

With intangible assets now accounting for over 75 per cent of the market capitalisation of leading companies across the world, it is time too to be more appreciative of the creators of that value:

'Many people have seen their ability to balance work with the rest of their lives deteriorate steadily, as they fall victim to the stresses of the long-hours culture. An executive life, some worry, is becoming unsustainable in social terms. We are in danger of populating companies with the modern equivalent of monks, who forgo all else for the sake of their calling.'

Neglecting the environment may drive away customers, says Handy, but neglecting your workforce may drive away employees. You should see yourself as a community, of people striving for the betterment of that community, including its wealth, welfare and the environment.

Handy's views are echoed by those of former Shell executive, Arie de Geus, who writes in 'The Living Company' that companies become imperilled when managers focus too much on producing goods and services and forget that they are a community, a company of people. He shows that long-living companies possess that sense of community, as well as a distinct identity, a learning culture and an appreciation of the society and environment in which they operate.

At a time of great disillusionment with the capitalist model, as a result both of the corporate excesses of the likes of Enron and Worldcom of the early 2000s and of the sub-prime mortgage-induced credit crunch of the late 2000s, Handy warns that business should take their community responsibilities seriously and soon – before governments step in and shackle them.

When to use it

Handy's works are a joy to read. Sit back with a glass of wine and let his ideas gently waltz with yours.

When to be wary

He seldom gives answers. That's the challenge.

[SECTION 3]

Forecasting market demand

Overview

Essential tools

16 Sizing the market and marketcrafting (Evans)

17 The HOOF approach to demand forecasting (Evans)

Useful tools

18 Smoothing with moving averages

19 Income elasticity of demand

20 Survey methods of demand forecasting

- Survey of customers' intentions

- Salesforce estimation method

- The Delphi method

- Pilot test marketing

21 Statistical methods of demand forecasting

- Trend projection

- Regression analysis

- Barometric method (NBER)

Overview

Henry Kravis is a firm believer in a solid foundation: 'If you build that foundation, both the moral and the ethical foundation, as well as the business foundation, and the experience foundation, then the building won't crumble.'

One foundation he omitted, perhaps because it was implicitly part of the business one, was the micro-economic foundation. It is the bedrock of strategy, the base of the pyramid. Only when you fully appreciate the micro-economic context in which your firm operates and with which it interacts will you have the depth of understanding on which to build a robust strategy.

Micro-economics concerns the economic behaviour of individual units of the economy, whether a person, household, firm or industry – as distinct from macro-economics, which deals with the economy as a whole.

There are two distinct but interrelated aspects of micro-economic behaviour to grasp: market demand and industry supply. The latter deals with the forces driving industry competition and their impact on market share, pricing and profitability in your industry – and will be addressed in the next section.

This section will focus on the former, market demand, and where it is headed. It will introduce two essential tools for forecasting market demand – sizing it, perhaps using the marketcrafting tool, and forecasting it, often via the HOOF approach.

These tools are essential because they will enable you to put numbers to market-growth outlooks. Some argue that such quantification is superfluous in strategy formulation. All that is needed is to understand that demand in one business segment is growing faster than another – or that demand in one segment is growing fast, another is mature and a third is declining. Quantification is needed for preparation of a business plan and financial forecasts, but not for strategy development. Managers can make decisions more effectively from strategy charts than from numbers, they say.

I disagree. Sure, much of strategy development hinges on analysing competitiveness (see Sections 5 and 6), which does not lend itself to meaningful quantification. And strategy charts certainly have their place (and will be duly lauded in Sections 5–8).

However, strategy ultimately does involve the allocation of scarce resources. That is its aim. At the end of the strategy development process, strategic investment decisions will be taken. That decision (see Section 7) will compare with and without scenarios of deploying the strategy. Cash flows will be forecast, which will need revenue forecasts, which in turn need market demand forecasts as a reference.

Ah, they say, but quantification can await the analysis of the strategic investment decision, once the right strategy has been selected. But rough quantification is an invaluable aid to that very strategy-selection process. If a segment is identified as 'fast growing', it helps if we have some concept of what is meant by 'fast'. Is demand growth of 10 per cent/year fast, or 25 per cent/year? Is 2 per cent/year slow, or 5 per cent/year? Is that 5 per cent/year in real terms or nominal (money of the day)? Rough quantification helps in assessing the risk and return trade-off between strategic alternatives.

The counter-argument only has substance if it is difficult or expensive to derive meaningful market-demand forecasts. And that is seldom the case. The essential tools presented in this chapter – market sizing and the HOOF approach – are simple, straightforward and inexpensive.

These basic tools are tried, tested and proven. I have deployed them countless times.

More sophisticated survey and statistical tools also have their place and are included here as useful tools – one or more of which may be pertinent to forecasting demand in your firm's market.

16

Sizing the market and marketcrafting (Evans)

The tool

Size matters.

Without market size you won't know market share. Without market share, you'll find it hard to judge competitive position – and you won't even be able to use that most evergreen of tools, the Growth/Share Matrix (see Section 6). Without competitive position by segment, you'll find it hard to draw up a winning strategy.

The larger your company, the easier it is to find data on market size. Industry associations proliferate and many either compute market share themselves or contract out the job to specialist market research firms. The latter compete fiercely with each other to cover each and every market where they perceive there to be a sufficient number of customers to turn a profit.

SMEs don't enjoy such lavish attention from market research firms. Some do, and I am often pleasantly surprised when a client turning over £10–20 million reveals monthly market data provided to the firm and its half dozen competitors by some enterprising market researcher, often a one-man band.

Most SMEs don't. And they are not alone. A medium-sized firm turning over £100 million may well have the bulk of its business covered by market research reports, but not necessarily that star business segment turning over £10 million, with only two main competitors and growing at 15 per cent/year. That segment may as yet be too small with too few potential customers to entice a market researcher.

Where no data on market size can be found off the shelf, you have to size the market yourself.

How to use it

First you must decide what you are looking for: your addressed market or your addressable market. The difference can be huge:

- Addressed market – those to whom you currently offer your goods or services and who may or may not purchase them

- Addressable (or available) market – all those whom you *could* serve should you extend your offering.

There are six main ways of sizing a market:

- *Top-down market research* – start with a known, researched market size and chop out inapplicable sections, or make appropriate assumptions on relevant proportions, to drill down to the target market.

- *Bottom-up market research* – take disaggregated data from a market research report and assemble the relevant bits that make up your target market.

- *Bottom-up customer sizing* – estimate how much each major customer spends in this target market and make an allowance for other, minor customers.

- *Bottom-up competitor sizing* (or 'marketcrafting', see below) – estimate the scale of your competitors in the target market.

- *Related market triangulation* – use two, three or more known sizes of related markets to gauge a rough estimate of the target market.

- *Final triangulation* – juggle the estimates from the above sources and subject them to sanity checks (why the differences? with which method do you feel most confident? on balance, what *feels* right?); consider giving each estimate a reliability rating, work out relative probabilities and compute a weighted average estimate of target market size.

Marketcrafting is a particularly useful method, since it gives you the base data needed not just for market demand analysis (Section 3) but for industry supply too (Section 4). It is a technique I developed some years ago for clients who knew their customers and competitors well enough but had no firm grasp on market scale. I have used it primarily in niche markets, or in segments of larger markets, but now and again in larger markets too. I recently used it to estimate a market size of around £175 million in an engineering segment left curiously unattended by market research groups.

There are seven main steps in marketcrafting:

1 Select your main competitors – those you pitch regularly against, those you exhibit alongside at trade shows – and don't forget the foreign competitors, especially those from lower-cost countries.

2 Take competitor A: do you think they are selling more or less than you into this market? If less, by how much less, *very roughly*? Are they selling half as much as you? Three-quarters? If they sell more than you, by how much more, very roughly? 10 per cent more? A third more? Is there any publicly available information which can guide you on this? – competitor A's sales to this market are unlikely to be available if it is a private company, but employment data can be indicative. What do customers tell you? And suppliers?

3 Taking your current sales level as an index number of 100, assign the appropriate index number to competitor A; if you think they sell less than you in this market, but not that much less, say 10 per cent less, give them an index number of 90.

4 Repeat steps 2 and 3 for each of the competitors named in step 1.

5 Make an allowance for any other competitors you have not named, those who are small or those who only appear now and again; this should also be an index number; if you think all these others together sell about half what you sell to the market, give this 'Others' category an index number of 50.

6 Add up all the index numbers, divide the total by 100 and multiply by your level of sales – that is your preliminary estimate of market size.

7 Ask your sales director to do the same exercise; get her to talk to the guy in the sales team who used to work at competitor A and the woman in R&D whose former boyfriend now works at competitor B; get their inputs, and those of your operations director and head of R&D; where their views differ from yours, discuss and refine the numbers; you now have built a reasoned estimate of market size.

Marketcrafting is hardly an accurate process, nor can it be guaranteed that the final number will not be some way out. But it is better than nothing, very much better, because you can now use the results to get values of three parameters key to strategy development:

1 Market share – now you 'know' market size, you also know your market share (your sales level divided by estimated market size); you also have an estimate of the market share of each of your competitors.

2 Market growth – repeat the marketcrafting exercise above to estimate the market size of three years ago; for example, did competitor A sell more or less than you to this market three years ago, before that new plant came into operation, and by how much? and so on; you now have two data points – market size of today and that of three years ago; punch them into your calculator and out will come an average compound growth rate over the three years, an estimate of recent market growth.

3 Best of all, market share change – you now have your market share of three years ago, as well as that of today, so you have an estimate of your market share gain (or loss), as well as for each of your competitors; these estimates will be most useful in assessing both competitive intensity (Section 4) and relative competitive position (Section 5).

Figure 16.1 is an example of the findings that can be deduced from the process, adapted from the engineering company I worked with referred to above.

The company's turnover in this segment was about £30 million, so the market size could be estimated at 585/100 × 30, or around £175 million. The company's market share emerged at 17 per cent (100/585), rather lower than the 25 per cent management had quoted prior to the marketcrafting exercise. Likewise, the market share of the Far Eastern competitors, group D, though significant at 21 per cent,

Figure 16.1 Marketcrafting: an example

Competitor	Estimated index number for sales (latest year)	Implied market share (%)
The Company	=100	17%
Competitor A	120	21%
Competitor B	85	15%
Competitor Group C	125	21%
Competitor Group D	65	11%
Competitor E	30	5%
Competitor F	20	3%
Others	40	7%
Total	**585**	**100%**

did not seem to be as high as the one-third quoted rather sensationally in the trade press.

When we repeated the exercise to estimate market size of three years earlier, we found that the market had contracted heavily during the post-credit-crunch recession, falling by one-third, or by roughly 10 per cent/year. Meanwhile, Far Eastern competitors had grown share greatly from 9 to 21 per cent, with corresponding share losses by the domestic players, including that of the company, from 20 to 17 per cent.

These were important findings. The trends were of course known beforehand, but their quantification through the marketcrafting method, though very rough, put some of the wilder assertions into perspective and helped focus attention on the strategic challenge ahead.

When to use it

Use marketcrafting or other market sizing methods whenever you have no third-party data source and need to create a market size from scratch.

When to be wary

Treat the results with caution. If your marketcrafting suggests a competitor's market share of 25 per cent and you hear that their sales director has been boasting of 30–35 per cent share at a recent trade show, don't dismiss it offhand as sales spiel. Take another look at your numbers. Is there any way they may be right? Do they have access to information that you don't? What would that imply for your share, or other competitors' shares?

The numbers are rough, very rough. But they are better than nothing and seldom misleading. (And they will come in handy in Sections 4 and 5.)

17

The HOOF approach to demand forecasting (Evans)

The tool

'It's better to have the wind at your back than in your face', one often hears in the business world.

It's a question of odds. You have a better chance of prospering in a market that's growing than one that's shrinking.

Market size is all very well, but what often matters more in strategy development is what the market is doing, where it is going – the dynamics, as opposed to the statics. Is market demand in your main business segments growing, shrinking, or flat-lining?

This is the big question. It's not the only one, of course. Equally important, as we'll see in the next couple of chapters, is the nature of the competition you face and how you're placed to compete. But it's the first big question.

I developed many years ago a four-step process for translating market demand trends and drivers into forecasts. I call it the HOOF approach, for two reasons. HDDF, the strict representation of the first letters in each of the four steps, would be an unattractive, unmemorable acronym – but, with the appropriate creative licence, the circular O can be borrowed as a lookalike to the semi-circular D!

And also because it reminds me fondly of the junior football team I coach. No matter how many times I screech at some lads to play the simple ball out of defence, head up, along the ground, to a nearby player, they blindly HOOF it down the pitch with all their might, as far as their youthful muscles can propel it!

As the ball leaves the foot, the HOOF starts the perfect trajectory of growth – the kind of market demand forecast we would all love for our business (before the ball reaches its summit and plummets to the ground, the standard path of the product life cycle – Tool 40).

How to use it

There are four distinct stages in the HOOF approach to demand forecasting. Get this process right and all falls logically into place. Get it out of step and you may end up with a misleading answer. You need to apply these steps for each of your main business segments.

The four steps are:

1 *Historic growth* – assess how market demand has grown in the past.

2 *Drivers past* – identify what has been driving that past growth.

3 *Drivers future* – assess whether there will be any change in influence of these and other drivers in the future.

4 *Forecast growth* – forecast market demand growth, based on the influence of future drivers.

Let's look at each of these briefly, then at some examples.

Historic growth

This is where you need to get some facts and figures. If you have access to market research data, whether on a regular basis or with a one-off purchase, all your needs should be in there. If not, you may have to do some marketcrafting – see the previous tool.

Be careful not to fall into the trap of relying on one recent number. Just because demand for a service jumped by, say, 8 per cent last year doesn't mean that trend growth in that market has been 8 per cent/year. The latest year may have been an aberration. The market may have dipped two years ago, remained static last year and recovered by 8 per cent this year. Average annual growth over the three years might only have been 2 per cent/year.

You should try to get an average annual (compound) growth rate over a number of recent years, preferably the last three or four. As long as there haven't been serious annual ups and downs, and there may well have been in the period 2008–11, you can usually get a usable approximation of average annual growth by calculating the overall percentage change in, say, the last four years and then annualising it. If there have been ups and downs, you should smooth them out with three-year moving averages before calculating the percentage change – see Tool 18.

One word of caution: market demand growth is generally measured, analysed and forecast in real terms. You should take care to understand the differences between these growth rates:

- *In nominal terms*: with goods (or services) priced in the money of the day
- *In real terms*: the growth rate in nominal prices deflated by the growth rate in the average prices of goods in that market; as long as the correct deflators are used, this growth rate should be a measure of volume growth.

You should be consistent and restrict all analysis of comparative market growth rates to those in real terms in this chapter and throughout the strategy development process.

But should you need to proceed to business planning and financial forecasting, you must bring average price forecasts back into the mix. Then your revenue forecasts, as well as the whole P&L, will be able to be compared directly with market growth-rate forecasts in nominal prices.

Drivers past

Once you have uncovered some information on recent market demand growth, find out what has been influencing that growth. Typical factors that influence demand in many markets are:

- Per capita income growth
- Population growth in general
- Population growth specific to a market (for example, of pensioners or baby boomers, or general population growth in a particular area)
- Some aspect of government policy or purchasing
- Changing awareness, perhaps from high levels of promotion by competing providers
- Business structural shifts (such as toward outsourcing)
- Price change
- Fashion, even a craze
- Weather – seasonal variations, but maybe even the longer-term effects of climate change.

Or your sector may be heavily influenced by demand in other sectors, typically customer sectors. Thus, the demand for steel is heavily dependent on demand for automobiles, ships, capital goods equipment and construction. Demand for automobiles is also the major driver for demand for Tier 1 car seat suppliers, which in turn drives demand for Tier 2 steel seat reclining mechanism suppliers, who in turn buy from specialist steel producers.

A vertical sector relationship may be so close that you may be able to obtain sound estimates of derived demand. You can obtain excellent automotive market forecasts from specialist market research companies, thereby guiding Tier 2 suppliers like seat mechanism producers in their forecasts.

But be careful of derived demand forecasts – there are always *other* drivers. The average number of seats per car sold may be changing due to the popularity of 4x4s. A major car company may decide to opt for an alternative car seat technology.

The same applies in deriving demand forecasts from those in complementary or related sectors. Thus, demand growth for accommodation in 3-star hotels in the West Country will be influenced by demand growth for coach package tours, but it will not be the same. The latter will not be the only driver of the former. Another driver is the sterling–euro exchange rate, which will be a major influence on whether cost-conscious coach travellers from the North of England opt for destinations in the West Country, France or further afield.

Drivers future

Now you need to assess how each of these drivers is likely to develop over the next few years. Are things going to carry on more or less as before for a driver? Or are things going to change significantly?

Will, for instance, immigration continue to drive local population growth? Is the government likely to hike up a local tax? Could this market become less fashionable?

What are the prospects for growth in vertical or complementary sectors?

The most important driver is, of course, the economic cycle. If it seems the economy is poised for a nosedive, that could have a serious impact on demand in your business over the next year or two – assuming your business is relatively sensitive (or 'elastic', in economics-speak) to the economic cycle (see Tool 19). Or maybe your business is relatively inelastic, as is the case, for example, in much of the food industry? You need to think carefully about the timing of the economic cycle and the elasticity of your business.

Forecast growth

This is the fun bit. You've assembled the information on past trends and drivers. Now you can weave it all together, sprinkle it with a large dose of judgement, and you have a forecast of market demand – not without risk, not without uncertainty, but a systematically derived forecast nevertheless.

Let's take a simple example of the HOOF approach in action. In one of your business segments, your firm offers a relatively new service to the elderly in the US. Step 1 **(H):** You find that the market has been growing at 5–10 per cent per year over the past few years. Step 2 **(O):** You identify the main drivers as (a) per capita income growth, (b) growth in the elderly population, and (c) growing awareness of the service by elderly people. Step 3 **(O):** You believe income growth will continue as before, the elderly population will grow even faster in the future, and that awareness can only become more widespread. Step 4 **(F):** You conclude that growth in your market will accelerate and could reach over 10 per cent per year over the next few years.

The HOOF approach is best used diagrammatically. The example above is simple, but becomes even simpler when displayed on a diagram – see Figure 17.1. The impact of each demand driver on demand growth is represented by varying numbers of plus and minus signs, or a zero. In this case you can see that there will be more pluses in the near future than there were in the past, implying that demand growth will accelerate – from the historic 5–10 per cent/year to the future 10 per cent/year plus.

In real-world strategy development, there will be more such charts, one for each key product/market segment, and each will have more drivers. But the fundamental principles of the HOOF approach will remain. The chart will show the historic growth

Figure 17.1 The HOOF approach to demand forecasting: an example

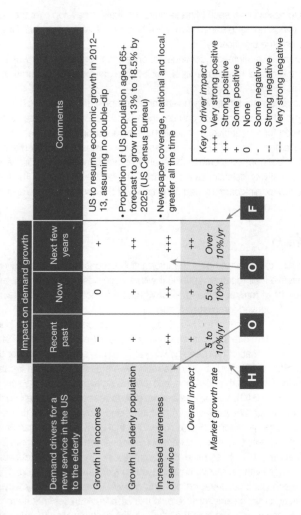

Demand drivers for a new service in the US to the elderly	Impact on demand growth			Comments
	Recent past	Now	Next few years	
Growth in incomes	–	0	+	US to resume economic growth in 2012–13, assuming no double-dip
Growth in elderly population	+	+	++	• Proportion of US population aged 65+ forecast to grow from 13% to 18.5% by 2025 (US Census Bureau)
Increased awareness of service	++	++	+++	• Newspaper coverage, national and local, greater all the time
Overall impact	+	+	++	
Market growth rate	*5 to 10%/yr*	*5 to 10%*	*Over 10%/yr*	

H   O   O   F

Key to driver impact
+++ Very strong positive
++   Strong positive
+   Some positive
0   None
–   Some negative
– – Strong negative
– – – Very strong negative

rate (H), identify the relative impact of drivers past and future (O and O) and conclude with a growth forecast for that segment (F).

And now for an example of how not to do it. Many years ago I was doing some work for a crane manufacturer in the North of England and came across a draft business plan. In the section on market demand, its young author had stated there were no data on UK demand for cranes to be found anywhere. So, for the purposes of the financial forecasts, he assessed real growth in the crane market to be the same as for UK engineering output, forecast then by OECD at 2.4 per cent/year.

Oops! The mistake was one of exclusion. Yes, macro-economic demand was an important driver of demand in the crane market, as for all engineering output. But there were three or four other drivers of as great importance, on which there were, admittedly, no hard-and-fast data, but plenty of anecdotal evidence. They included evidence of crane destocking, a thriving second-hand market and, above all, an imminent downturn in high-rise construction activity.

None of these drivers bore any relation to engineering output as a whole and their combined impact served to translate a 2.4 per cent/year crane market growth forecast into one of steep decline, possibly at 10 per cent/year for two or three years.

The moral of the tale is to make sure *all* drivers are taken into account, *irrespective of whether hard data can be found on them*. The HOOF process encourages you to seek out all relevant drivers and assess their influence in a structured, combined quantitative and qualitative context.

When to use it

Whenever you need to forecast market demand.

When to be wary

Take care to identify all relevant drivers. Use whatever evidence you can muster, dashed by a strong dose of reasoned judgement, in assessing their influence on demand growth, past, present and future. And be wary when computing historic growth rates (see next tool).

Galileo's hiccup in market demand

Back in the 1990s, when you popped into your local high street travel agent to book a trip, your agent would have picked up the telephone and made half-a-dozen calls. But if you had called or walked into one of the larger chains, and certainly one of the business travel agencies, the agent would have punched in your request to a computer terminal.

The agent would have been using a computerised reservation system, or 'CRS'. It would probably have been one of the four worldwide systems, each of which could access the in-house reservation systems of all the major scheduled airlines, hotel chains and car hire firms – Sabre (owned by American Airlines), Worldspan (Delta, Northwest and TWA), Galileo (British Airways, KLM, Alitalia *et al*.) and Amadeus (Air France, Lufthansa, Iberia and, initially, SAS).

Competition between the four of them to sign up the major travel agencies was fierce – and complex. The kinds of deals needed to win an agency account had to be compatible with the deals being offered by the airlines themselves – who were, of course, competing with their co-owners of the CRSs.

There were major economies of scale (see Tool 25) in the CRS business, the most obvious being the investment required for huge data centres and continuous software development. So, there was constant discussion about further consolidation in the industry, with merger and acquisition permutations hot on the agenda, some of which I was party to.

It was a complex but fascinating industry. On the one hand, each airline wanted to maximise its distribution coverage but minimise its (high) distribution costs. On the other hand, each airline owner of a CRS wanted to maximise the value of its stake, whether for purposes of merger or IPO.

And overhanging all these discussions in the mid-1990s was a cloud. Was this an industry that was living on borrowed time? Did the airlines really need to keep stumping up large injections of capital for a business which might be headed for obsolescence?

Five years earlier the main demand drivers of reservation volumes in the CRS industry were simple. The more people travelled, the more they needed to make reservations. So the main drivers were:

- Personal disposable incomes
- The income elasticity of demand for travel (see Tool 19)
- Scheduled air travel for leisure (package tour operators used their in-house reservation systems)
- Business travel by air
- Pre-booking of hotels and car hire
- Proportion of hotel chains linked in to CRSs
- Proportion of car hire firms linked in to CRSs
- Proportion of cruise ship firms linked in to CRSs.

These drivers combined to yield market demand growth rates typically of around 5–7 per cent/year in Western Europe and North America.

But reservations made via CRSs are expensive for the airlines. And this expense led to the cloud hovering above the industry. It was known by the rather ungainly term of *disintermediation*.

In simple terms, it meant the customer booking directly with the airline, bypassing the intermediary – that is, the agent. It meant going back to the old ways, when most bookings were made directly with an airline's in-house reservation system.

In the mid-1990s no one knew how large an effect disintermediation would have. It would certainly be a negative driver to offset the known positive drivers, but by how much?

At the time, we felt that it would depress CRS booking volume growth by around 1–2 per cent/year, due primarily to the airline owners encouraging consumers to book directly via the airline's call centre.

But it was to become a greater dampener than that:

- Consumers increasingly made their bookings online, given the growing household penetration of laptops, the advent of broadband and the benefits of price, quality and timing comparisons available on the Web.
- Low-cost airlines emerged to challenge the CRS airline owners and take market share, most of which was booked online, bypassing a CRS.
- Online travel agencies arose to compete with the bricks-and-mortar firms, not necessarily booking via a CRS.

Booking growth through the CRSs (now called GDSs, or global distribution systems) slowed, but remained positive. They went ahead with their consolidation – Galileo, having floated, merged with Worldspan. So too did their owner airlines – British Airways merged with Iberia, Air France with KLM, United with Continental, etc. And, thoroughly squeezed and disintermediated, so did the travel agents, including Thomas Cook and Co-op Travel in 2011.

That one demand driver, disintermediation, has had a major impact on the travel industry.

18

Smoothing with moving averages

The tool

'Life is a roller-coaster, just gotta ride it', crooned Ronan Keating. As with life, so too perhaps with a market. You have just got to ride it.

Where markets have been up and down, showing no consistent trend, take care with the H step of the HOOF approach to demand forecasting of the previous tool.

The best way to deal with market volatility is to plot a graph on logarithmic paper and draw a line of best fit through the points.

But you may not be comfortable with graphs, especially those of the logarithmic variety. A simple, non-graphical alternative is to translate the data into moving averages. This enables annual fluctuations to be smoothed out, making it easier to decipher and calculate trend growth rates.

How to use it

Take the set of market data and apply these steps:

- Observe the length of the cycle and select an appropriate time period for smoothing, often a three-year period.
- Take the annual average of values during that time period around any given year (if the cycle is three years, take an average of values for the given year, the previous year and the succeeding year).
- Calculate compound growth rates between appropriate start and end points to establish the trend.

The example in Figure 18.1 may help, taken directly from a job I did a few years ago.

If we were to ignore all that happened in the middle years of this period, and just consider growth between the start point of 2000 and the end point of 2007, that would give an overall increase of 5.4 per cent, or growth (compound) of 0.75 per cent/year.

Figure 18.1 Smoothing with moving averages: an example

	2000	2001	2002	2003	2004	2005	2006	2007
Actual demand (£m)	1426	1223	1150	1201	1387	1452	1582	1555
Actual change/year (%)	n/a	–17%	–6%	4%	15%	5%	9%	–2%
Smoothed demand (£m)	**n/a**	**1283**	**1191**	**1246**	**1347**	**1474**	**1530**	**n/a**
Implied change/year (%)	n/a	n/a	–7%	5%	8%	9%	4%	n/a

But 2000 was the peak of the dot-com boom, so using that as the base year would underestimate trend growth in the 2000s. Likewise, if we'd used the trough year 2002 as the base, that would have produced an overestimate. We therefore translate the above data into three-year moving averages – namely, the sum of each year's number plus the previous year's number plus the following year's number, divided by three.

This has the effect of smoothing the annual fluctuations and we begin to see a clearer pattern. Taking 2001 as the start point and 2006 as the end point now gives an overall increase of 19 per cent, or an average of 3.6 per cent/year (over five smoothed years, not seven actual years). The one decimal point suggests spurious accuracy, but a conclusion of 3.5 per cent/year, plus or minus 0.5 per cent/year (or, in other words, 3 to 4 per cent/year), seemed reflective of trend growth in the 2000s in this market.

When to use it

Use it when historic market size data show ups and downs or an irregular pattern.

When to be wary

Don't just compute the numbers blindly. Try to understand what was happening in each of the years to produce such irregular numbers. That will help you avoid the trap of selecting a boom (or bust) year as the starting point and a bust (or boom) year as the end-point. Taking boom to boom, bust to bust, average to average periods should give similar answers, but mixing them up can be severely misleading (and is a much-loved ruse of the politician!).

19

Income elasticity of demand

The tool

'Success is how high you bounce when you hit the bottom', said General George Patton, emphasising the elasticity of life and business as much as warfare.

There is a venerable and much-loved concept in micro-economics of the income elasticity of demand ('IED'). It is a measure of how demand for a good (or service) changes in relation to change in the income of customers. It is defined as the percentage change in demand divided by the percentage change in income.

If your business, or one of your product/market segments, addresses a market which is large and generic, you may be able to use IED in your market demand forecasting.

If income, as measured, say, by GDP, increases by 3 per cent and demand for a good thereby increases by 4.5 per cent, that good has an IED of 1.5. If another good only sees a demand increase of 1 per cent, its IED is 0.33.

Different types of goods have different IEDs (see Figure 19.1):

- Normal goods have a positive IED.

- If an IED is less than 1, the good is a necessity – demand doesn't rise much in good times, nor does it fall back too much in bad times; examples are fresh fruit and vegetables, even tobacco.

- If an IED is greater than 1, the good is a superior good – people buy it aplenty in good times, but cut back in bad times; examples are books, meals out.

- If an IED is greater than 2, the good is a luxury – demand fluctuates widely between good and bad times; examples are sports cars, haute couture, Michelin-starred restaurants, holidays in the Seychelles.

- If an IED is around 0, the good is inelastic or sticky – demand doesn't change much in relation to changes in income; examples are bread, baked beans.

- If an IED is less than 0, the good is an inferior good – demand drops during the good times and returns in bad times: the classic examples are margarine and bus travel.

Figure 19.1 Income elasticity of demand

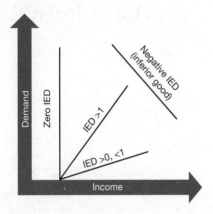

How to use it

If your market is a whole sector or sub-sector, you may well find an estimate of IED for that sector on the Web. To forecast market demand, you:

- extract economic forecasts from a reputable source (for example, the Treasury, London Business School, ITEM)
- multiply by the income elasticity of demand.

Hey presto, you have a preliminary market demand forecast!

When to use it

Use it when your market (or segment) is sufficiently large and homogenous to merit the calculation by some public or academic institution of its income elasticity of demand.

When to be wary

Are you sure your firm addresses that whole sector market? After the process of product/market segmentation in Tool 1, the resultant segments tend to emerge as rather specific, both to a product or product type and to a customer/end-user group, not to a whole sector market. You may need to revisit your segmentation.

20 Survey methods of demand forecasting

The tool

'*USA Today* has come out with a new survey – apparently, three out of every four people make up 75 per cent of the population', quipped David Letterman.

Surveys can be a bit more useful than that, and there are a number of survey-based methods for forecasting demand which you may find pertinent to your strategy development process:

- Survey of customers' intentions
- The salesforce estimation method
- The Delphi method
- Pilot test marketing.

A brief summary of each tool is presented below.

How to use them

Survey of customers' intentions

This is where you choose a representative sample of customers from each major product/market segment and call them up. You ask them what volumes of product they are intending to buy over the next 12, 24 months, not just from you, but from all competitive suppliers.

This can be part of the same survey you will be carrying out to solicit customer views on purchasing criteria and their rating of your firm's performance and those of your rivals against those criteria – more detail in Section 5.

But you should not expect spectacular results. You are likely to be talking to someone in purchasing and s/he may have little knowledge of sales targets for the following year – you may well be referred to someone from sales. Your relationship with the salesperson will not be as developed as with the purchasing person, so you might not get much out of the discussion.

Alternatively, you could carry out an additional survey, targeting salespeople at your customers. Again, though, you would not know these people very well, if at all, and the results might be disappointing – and probably unable to justify the carrying out of a separate survey.

Better to accept limited expectations from the outset and tack these questions on to your survey of purchasing people at your customers – which is a necessary, not an optional, component of your strategy development process.

Figure 20.1 Survey methods

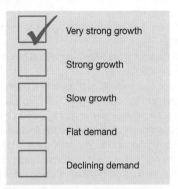

Salesforce estimation method

This is a method that works well for revenue forecasting, not necessarily so well with market demand forecasting. Essentially, you get together, either in a conference room or in an email forum, a group of key salespeople and ask them to debate where they believe market demand is heading. You act as orchestrator and assemble the accumulated opinion of the group.

Salespeople get close to their customers and can often be prescient in forecasting a sales stream from their customers.

But some find it difficult to step back and see the market as a whole – all customers to all suppliers. They spend so much of their lives with each of a handful of trees that the wood can become a blur to some.

You will know the capabilities of your salesforce. It may be worth a go – there is little to be lost in the effort.

The Delphi method

The Delphi method, named curiously after the ravings of an entranced priestess possessed by the spirit of Apollo, is a structured analysis of independent, informed, 'Apollonian' opinion. You email or write to a bunch of reputable, even 'expert' industry observers and ask them a few carefully worded questions on market demand prospects.

You collate the replies, but anonymously, and return a summary of the findings to the observers. They look at what others are saying and have the option of sticking to their initial answers or modifying them, with the appropriate justification.

You amend this summary accordingly and there is your demand forecast, a balanced assessment of the combined wisdom of a handful of Delphic oracles.

You may choose to send your draft final summary to these industry observers, inviting one final round of amendments, or you may decide that further iterations will not be worth the time and effort.

Pilot test marketing

This is most appropriate where you are introducing a new product or venturing into a new product/market segment.

Yours may be a new product or service designed to convey a customer benefit not previously realisable.

How can you convince your boss that there will be buyers of your product, and at that price? You need evidence.

You'll have to do some test marketing. If yours is a business-to-business proposition, get on the phone and set up meetings with prospective corporate buyers. Explain the benefits of your product and why at that price they have a bargain.

Keep a record of these meetings and analyse the findings. Write a report drawing out key conclusions from the discussions, with each supported by bulleted evidence – whether comments from named customers, comments from third parties quoted in the press, data dug up off the Web. Collate them into a short and sharp market research report, which will be an appendix to your strategy report.

If yours is a business-to-consumer product or service, test it on the High St. Get out your clipboard, stand outside an Asda or a Waitrose, depending on your target customer, and talk to people. If you're offering a product, show them. If a service, explain lucidly but swiftly its benefits.

Again, collate the responses, analyse them, draw firm conclusions, support them with quotes and data and stick the market research report in your appendix.

Now, on the basis of those responses, make an estimate of your potential market size. Imagine there were many suppliers of your product or service and that the whole country is aware of its existence. What would the market size be? How does that compare with the market size for products or services not a million miles different from what you'll be offering? Does your estimate make sense?

When to use them

Use them when you feel that the canvassing of others' views would improve the rigour of the HOOF method of demand forecasting.

When to be wary

See above – each of the four survey methods has its limitations.

Statistical methods of demand forecasting

21

The tool

'There are lies, damned lies and statistics' were the famously damning words of Mark Twain. Perhaps, but basic statistical tools may be of help in your market demand forecasting. The main (and simplest) ones are:

- Trend projection
- Regression analysis
- Barometric method (NBER).

This is not a book on the theory of statistics, so the tools are outlined only briefly below.

How to use them

Trend projection

This involves the placing of a line of best fit through points on a chart. The process is as follows:

- Set out market demand data for each year.
- Plot on logarithmic graph paper, with time on the x-axis and demand on the y-axis.
- Visually place a line of best fit through the points.
- Measure the gradient of the line and that will equate to the average annual rate of growth (percentage per annum).

It is an alternative way of deriving compound growth rates to using the moving average approach of Tool 18. Either way should give a similar result – an estimate of historical market demand growth.

Be very careful in going one step further, the trend projecting. Continuing the line and seeing where it crosses future years on the x-axis will give you a set of market demand numbers for future years, but they may well be meaningless as forecasts. They assume that future demand will be subject to exactly the same influences as in the past. This is more often than not unrealistic. Far better to use this approach for working out historical growth rates and the HOOF approach (Tool 17), which was designed to tackle the reality of shifting demand drivers, for forecasting.

Regression analysis

This is a statistical tool which can help you understand how market demand, a dependent variable, will vary in relation to variation in an independent variable, such as GDP or engineering output. The process is as follows (see Figure 21.1):

- Set out market demand data for each year.
- Set out the independent variable: for example, GDP, for each year.
- Plot on graph paper, with GDP on the x-axis and demand on the y-axis.
- Visually place a line of best fit through the points (for linear regression).
- Measure the gradient of the line (m) and the intersect (c) with the y-axis when $x = 0$ and the relationship between demand and GDP will be that of the standard equation, $y = mx + c$.

Figure 21.1 Regression analysis

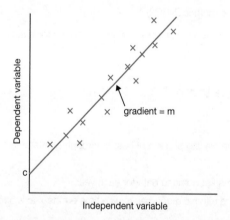

Again you need to take great care in using regression analysis for forecasting. The relationship that was evident in the past may not hold firm for the future. And other drivers may play a greater role in the future. As with trend projection, it is safer to use regression analysis for determining the historical relationship – although this is purely statistical and offers no proof of causality – and the HOOF approach for forecasting.

Barometric method (NBER)

This is a forecasting approach developed by the National Bureau of Economic Research in the US. The barometric method can be used for market demand forecasting as follows:

- Identify a set of economic indicators which influence demand in your market.
- Convert each indicator into a time series of relevant index numbers.
- Weight each indicator according to its influence on market demand.
- Develop a composite index.
- Track the performance of that composite index in the past against an index of past demand in your market.
- Forecast the composite index.
- Derive a forecast of demand in your market.

The barometric method also allows the element of time to be built into the mix. Indicators can be classified as:

- *Leading* – those which vary ahead of others (e.g. new orders ahead of sales)
- *Coincidental* – those which vary apace with economic activity
- *Lagging* – those which vary only after some time lag (e.g. short-term lending after an interest rate change).

The barometric method is a more refined tool than trend projection or regression analysis and incorporates some of the benefits of the HOOF approach. But, in relation to the latter, it has some disadvantages:

- Some people find it difficult to handle the mathematics of indices, let alone weighting, lagging and combining them ...
- ... with probably differing weights (and possibly different lags) in the future compared with the past.
- Most important, many drivers do not translate readily into indices – for example, awareness or fads.

When to use it

Use statistical methods when you suspect that the HOOF approach to market demand forecasting would benefit from greater rigour, especially in the computation of past growth rates.

When to be wary

As stated above, take care not to assume, without specified justification, that the trends, regressions or barometers observed in the past will hold true in the future. You may need to combine your chosen statistical method with the HOOF approach.

[SECTION 4]

Gauging industry competition

Overview

Essential tools

22   The five forces (Porter)

23   Assessing customer purchasing criteria

24   Deriving key success factors

Useful tools

25   Weighing economies of scale

26   Corporate environment as a sixth force

27   Complements as a sixth force (Brandenburger and Nalebuff)

28   PESTEL analysis

Overview

No aspect of strategy development has been so dominated by one person for so long as industry analysis. Michael Porter's Five Forces analysis is the pre-eminent tool in this building block and has been since the early 1980s.

It remains the *sine qua non* of micro-economic analysis for business strategy. Porter was himself an industry economist and much of his work was effectively a reinterpretation of established micro-economic theory.

Porter's genius was in taking some quite difficult economic concepts and presenting them in an Everyman way, with a diagrammatic representation and sets of checklists accessible not just to fellow economists but to every manager.

The analysis of industry supply is the second of the two distinct but interrelated aspects of micro-economic behaviour. You looked at market demand in the previous section. Here you look at industry supply.

Some other useful tools are shown here too – weighing economies of scale, some extensions of Porter's work, putting more emphasis on the environment and complements, redefining segment boundaries and PESTEL analysis.

However, this section also includes two further tools which are essential and could arguably form their own building block – namely, assessing customer purchasing criteria ('CPCs') and deriving key success factors ('KSFs'). They form the basic analysis upon which the study of competitiveness (Sections 5 and 6) can build.

These two tools lead ultimately to the GE/McKinsey Attractiveness/Advantage Matrix (an essential tool in Section 6). This requires an assessment of competitive position by segment, painstakingly built up from CPCs and KSFs.

The process itself greatly assists strategy development. It pinpoints areas of strength and weakness and highlights the strategic gap between a firm's current capabilities and those to which it aspires.

Thus, the assessing of CPCs and deriving of KSFs are treated as essential tools in this building block.

22

The five forces (Porter)

The tool

Competitive intensity determines industry profitability.

That is the basic premise of Michael Porter's work. And he went on to describe in detail what the fundamental forces are which drive competitive intensity.

His Five Forces model made its first appearance beyond his Harvard Business School lecture theatre in his *Competitive Strategy: Techniques for Analyzing Industries and Competitors* in 1980.

Figure 22.1 Five forces shaping competition

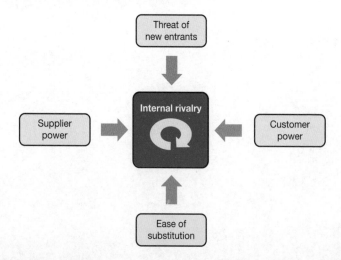

He set out to show that firms in any industry were constrained from maximising profit not just by rivalry with their competitors but by four further competitive forces. These five forces shape competitive intensity:

1 Internal rivalry
2 Threat of new entrants
3 Ease of substitution
4 Customer power
5 Supplier power.

Porter showed how these five forces impact on competitive intensity by means of a simple, memorable diagram – see Figure 22.1.

How to use it

Each of the five forces will be examined briefly below.

Internal rivalry

Internal rivalry is shaped by three main sub-forces: the number of players, market demand growth relative to supply, and external pressures.

The number of players. The more numerous the players, the tougher typically the competition.

Market demand growth. The slower growing the market, the tougher typically the competition.

And what of supply? Are demand and supply in balance? Where there is balance, internal rivalry may well be moderate. Where there is oversupply – where supply exceeds demand – internal rivalry will be intensified. And a dampener placed on prices. Conversely, where there is undersupply (or excess demand), where customers compete for relatively scarce supplies, internal rivalry will be modest – and you and your competitors may be able to nudge up pricing above inflation.

External pressures. External bodies, in particular government and the trade unions, have great power to influence the nature of competition in many industries. Government regulation, taxation and subsidies can skew both market demand and the competitive landscape. Trade unions can influence competition in a number of ways: for example, through restrictive practices which serve to raise barriers to entry.

There are other, lesser factors influencing internal rivalry. Barriers to exit are one such. Where providers have little choice but to stay on competing when they should be withdrawing (for example, a restaurant with many employees, hence potentially high redundancy costs, or a service business with a long lease on office space which is difficult to offload), competition is intensified. Low barriers to exit, such as the minicab business, reduce internal rivalry. Seasonal or irregular overcapacity is another factor. Fluctuating levels of demand (for example, the fruit picking or ice cream industries) intensify competition.

Threat of new entrants

The lower the barriers to entry to a market, the tougher typically the competition. Barriers to entry can be technology, operations, people or cost related, where a new entrant has to:

- develop or acquire a certain technology
- develop or acquire a certain operational process
- gain access to a limited distribution channel
- train or engage scarce personnel
- invest heavily in either capital assets or marketing to become a credible provider.

Switching costs also influence entry barriers. The higher the costs to the customer of switching from one supplier to another, the higher are the entry barriers. A drinks manufacturer may shift from one sugar supplier to another with relative ease, but may require redesign of the factory in switching from one labelling solution to another.

Ease of substitution

The easier it is for customers to use a substitute product or service, the tougher typically the competition.

Consider the impact of the likes of iTunes in the music industry. It was a substitute solution to the sale of CDs in the high street and a contributory factor, along with ecommerce and the supermarkets, to the demise of retailers such as Woolworths and Zavvi.

Customer power

The more bargaining power customers possess, the tougher typically the competition. Ask any supplier to the supermarket chains. Or to automotive manufacturers.

Often this is no more than a reflection of the number of providers in a marketplace, compared with the number of customers. The more choice of provider the customer has, the tougher the competition.

Customer power is also influenced by switching costs. If it's easy and relatively painless to switch supplier, competition is tougher. If switching costs are high, competition is less tough.

Supplier power

The more bargaining power suppliers possess, the tougher typically the competition.

Again it can be just a function of numbers. There are, for example, numerous steel or aluminium converters, but few and increasingly fewer metal producers. When metal converters sell components to automotive manufacturers, they can find themselves in a vice-like squeeze, huge steel or aluminium suppliers at one end, auto giant customers at the other. But the best of them learn how to duck, dive and survive.

Overall competitive intensity

These are the five main forces shaping the degree of competition in a marketplace. Put them all together, and you'll have a measure of how competitive your industry is.

In some industries, such as soft drinks, software, toiletries, all five forces operate benignly to boost profitability – and consistently over the decades. In other industries, like airlines or textiles, the opposite is true – all five forces act against the airlines, and average profitability over the years is dreadful.

How tough is internal rivalry in your industry? And the threat of new entrants or substitutes? How much power do customers and suppliers have over you and your competitors? In short, how intense is competition in your industry? High, low, medium? Or somewhere in between?

And what of the future? Is industry competition set to intensify? Because, however tough it is at the moment, it results in you and your competitors getting an average operating margin of a certain percentage.

But will competitive forces conspire to threaten that margin over the next few years? Or has the industry competition of the past few years been unsustainable and likely to ease off in the future?

In short, what will be the effect of competitive dynamics on pricing in your industry over the next few years?

Will competition intensify and put pressure on prices? Will it stay more or less as is and pricing move as it has been doing in recent times? Or will competition ease off, enabling players to nudge up pricing over the next few years?

When to use it

Always.

When to be wary

Porter's model has had its critics over the years. Some believe that boundary definition – this activity is part of the industry you operate in, that activity is not – can in itself place strategy development in a straitjacket. Pioneering companies succeed by redefining industry boundaries.

But this critique can be addressed by further segmentation – return to Tool 1 and redefine your key product/market segments to allow for shifting boundaries.

Other critics have promoted the corporate environment (government, the regulatory framework, pressure groups, etc.) as a sixth force, still others believe that complements, as distinct from substitutes, should be a separate and sixth force. These proposed amendments are addressed in Tools 26 and 27.

Kevin Coyne and Somu Subramaniam challenged Porter's model on three grounds. They questioned these assumptions:

- An industry consists of a set of unrelated buyers, sellers, substitutes and competitors that interact at arm's length – with little allowance made for co-dependent systems such as strategic alliances, networks and webs, or privileged relationships, whether based on financial interest, friendship, trust or ethnic loyalty.

- Wealth will accrue to companies that erect barriers against competitors and potential entrants: in other words, the source of value is structural advantage – with little allowance made for management, whether through frontline execution or insight/foresight.

- Uncertainty is low, allowing the prediction of competitive response and contingency planning – with little allowance made for differing degrees of uncertainty, ranging from the structural, where the model may be valid, through alternative scenarios and continuous uncertainty to complete ambiguity, where the model is invalid.

The authors make valid points, and the first bullet especially needs to be borne in mind in industry analysis. But they offer a revised industry model, reinforced by a risk-adjusted situation analysis which is so complex that they fail to spot the true genius of Porter's model. It is a starting point for industry analysis and strategy development, not the end point. Its simplicity is its overriding virtue.

Finally, Porter's model has taken some hits from those who point out, conclusively, as in the second bullet above, that industry structure alone tends to be insufficient to explain differences in a firm's profitability. Richard Rumelt, for example, in a 1991 study, found that differences in firms' profitability can be attributed much more to specific 'firm effects' (44 per cent) than to 'industry effects' (4 per cent). (Incidentally the unexplained variance was 45 per cent.) Other studies have shown likewise.

However, this does not invalidate the model. Industry analysis is part of the strategy story and Porter's Five Forces model is a very large part of industry analysis. It is not the final word, but arguably the most critical tool in the strategy development toolkit.

Assessing customer purchasing criteria

23

The tool

'All business success rests on something labeled a sale, which at least momentarily weds company and customer', wrote Tom Peters.

But why does that customer buy from that company? That is the question.

Discovering why customers buy is the first of three tools on how to assess your firm's competitive position in each of your key product/market segments:

- Identify and weight customer purchasing criteria ('CPCs') – what customers need from their suppliers in each segment – that is, from you and your competitors (this tool).

- Derive and weight key success factors ('KSFs') – what you and your competitors need to do to satisfy these customer needs and run a successful business (next tool).

- Assess your firm's competitive position – how your firm rates against those key success factors relative to your competitors (Tool 29 in the next section).

We'll start, as should ever be the case, with the customer ...

How to use it

Start by asking yourself these questions. What do customers in your business's main segments need from you and your competitors? Are they looking for the lowest possible price for a given level of product or service? The highest-quality product or service irrespective of price? Something in between?

Do customers have the same needs in your other business segments? Do some customer groups place greater importance on certain needs?

What exactly do they want in terms of product or service? The highest specifications? Fastest delivery? The most reliable? The best technical back-up? The most sympathetic customer service?

Customer needs from their suppliers are called *customer purchasing criteria* ('CPCs'). For business-to-business (or B2B) companies, CPCs typically include product quality (including features, performance, reliability), product range, timely delivery, technical support, customer service, relationship, reputation, financial stability, and so forth. And of course, price.

For business-to-consumer (or B2C) companies, CPCs tend to be similar, although typically with less emphasis on product range and financial stability. Depending on the product or service being offered, the consumer will place varying importance on quality, service and price.

CPCs can usefully be grouped into six categories. They are customer needs relating to the:

1 *Effectiveness* of the product (or service)
2 *Efficiency* of the product
3 *Range* of products provided
4 *Relationship* with the producer
5 *Premises* (only applicable if the customer needs to visit the supplier's premises)
6 *Price*.

They can be conveniently remembered, with perhaps a faint redolence of a cult science fiction film, as the *E2-R2-P2* of customer purchasing criteria (see Figure 23.1). Let's look briefly at each in turn.

Figure 23.1 The E2-P2-R2 of customer purchasing criteria

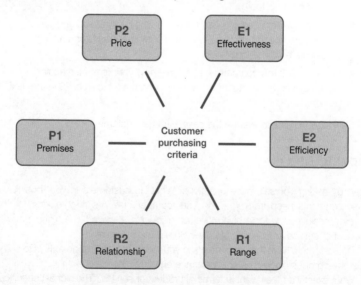

E1: Effectiveness

The first need of any customer from any product or service is that the job gets done. You the customer have specific requirements on the features, performance and reliability of the product. You want the job done. Not half-done, not over-done, just done.

Whether you are the customer of a B2B or B2C supplier, you demand an effective solution. Depending on the nature of the product or service, your criteria may well include:

- Quality
- Design
- Features
- Specifications
- Functionality
- Reliability.

Some of these criteria will overlap. You should select two to four effectiveness criteria which are most pertinent to customer needs in your industry.

E2: Efficiency

The second main customer purchasing criteria heading is efficiency. The customer wants to receive the product or get the job done on time.

All customers place *some* level of importance on efficiency for all types of service. Different customer groups may place different levels of importance on efficiency for the same service.

In most B2B industries, efficiency here translates to delivery – or to customer service at the point of pick-up at the depot. In most B2C industries, efficiency equates to getting the product to the customer or delivering the service to schedule.

R1: Range

The range of products or services provided is an area customers can find important for some products or services, even most important, and for others of no importance at all.

R2: Relationship

Your supplier does the job and does it quickly. But do you like them? Is that important? The relationship component in providing a service should never be underestimated.

P1: Premises

This only applies to those businesses, typically services, where the buying decision can be influenced by the environment of the sale. Do you need a storefront for your business? What do customers expect of your premises?

P2: Price

Price is always an important CPC. Set your prices sky high and you won't have many customers. Set them too low and you won't stay in business.

Think about the buying decisions you make regularly and the influence of price. For non-essential goods or services, we tend to be price sensitive. For essential services, we tend to be less fixated with price. When your central heating system breaks down in the middle of winter, will you go for the cheapest service engineer? Or will you call around to find someone who is reliable, arrives when he says he will, fixes it with no fuss, and charges a price that is not exactly cheap but at least is no rip-off?

You need to find out which of the above E2-R2-P2 of CPCs are important to your customers, in each key product/market segment. How important is each one, relative to others? How does their perception of importance vary by segment? Why?

You must also find out how your customers' needs are likely to change in the future. If they believe one purchasing criterion is highly important now, will it be as important in a few years' time? You need to know.

Finding out CPCs

All this is very well in theory, you may ask, but how do you know what customers want? Simple. Ask them!

It doesn't take long. You'd be surprised how after just a few discussions with any one customer group a predictable pattern begins to emerge. Some may consider one need 'very important', others just 'important'. But it's unlikely that another will say that it's 'unimportant'. Customers tend to have the same needs.

The comprehensive way to find out customer needs is through 'structured interviewing', where you ask a selected sample of customers a carefully prepared list of questions.

In developing a strategy for your business, a customer survey based on structural interviewing is an essential input. If you haven't done one recently, you would be well advised to conduct one. Tool 35 shows how this is done.

When to use it

Always.

When to be wary

Some customers may have a hidden agenda. They see the meeting as an opportunity to get you to nudge down your prices. Or to improve your service offering, incurring extra cost, with no increase in pricing. They may rate price as a most important CPC even though they are primarily concerned with product quality.

Bear this in mind. It is business, and human nature. Such hidden agendas do not negate the validity of the customer survey. But use your judgement.

Deriving key success factors

24

The tool

'Knowledge comes, but wisdom stays', said Alfred, Lord Tennyson. What wisdom do firms in your industry need to succeed? What factors are key to success?

These are Key Success Factors ('KSFs'). They are what firms need to get right to satisfy the customer purchasing criteria ('CPCs') of the previous tool *and* run a sound business.

Typical KSFs are product (or service) quality, consistency, availability, range and product development (R&D). On the service side, KSFs can include distribution capability, sales and marketing effectiveness, customer service and post-sale technical support. Other KSFs relate to the cost side of things, such as location of premises, scale of operations, state-of-the-art, cost-effective equipment and operational process efficiency.

How to use it

To identify which are the most important KSFs for each of your main business segments, you need to undertake these steps:

- Convert CPCs into KSFs:
  - Differentiation-related
  - Cost-related.
- Assess two more KSFs:
  - Management
  - Market share.
- Apply weights to the KSFs.
- Identify any must-have KSFs.

Let's look briefly at each of these steps.

Convert CPCs into KSFs

Here we convert the CPCs we researched in the previous tool into KSFs. In other words, we need to work out *what your business has to do to meet those CPCs*.

KSFs are often the flipside to CPCs. Functionality may be a CPC, so R&D becomes a KSF. Reliability may be a CPC, so quality control becomes a KSF. Delivery to schedule may be a CPC, so spare capacity and/or manufacturing efficiency become KSFs. These are differentiation-related KSFs.

There's one CPC that needs special attention, and that's price. Customers of most services expect a keen *price*. Producers need to keep their *costs* down. Price is a CPC, cost competitiveness a KSF.

Determinants of cost competitiveness in your business could include location of facilities, cost of materials, operational efficiency, use of subcontractors, outsourcing of business processes, overhead control, remuneration levels and IT systems.

And size may be important. Other things being equal, the larger the business, the lower the costs should be *for each unit* of business sold. These are 'economies of scale' (see Tool 25) and may apply not just to the unit cost of materials or other variable costs, where a larger business will benefit from negotiated volume discounts, but also to overheads, such as marketing, where the same expense on, for example, a magazine advertisement or trade show participation can be spread over a larger revenue volume base.

Assess two more KSFs

We have derived two sets of KSFs from the CPCs set out in the previous tool: differentiation-related and cost-related. There are two more sets to be considered: management and market share – see Figure 24.1.

Figure 24.1 Deriving key success factors

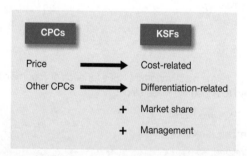

How important is management in general in your industry? Think on whether a well-managed company, with a superb sales and marketing team reinforced by an efficient operations team, but with an average product, would outperform a poorly managed company with a superb product in your industry.

There's one final KSF – an important one – that we need to take into account that isn't directly derived from a CPC: market share. The larger the relative market share, the stronger should be the provider.

A high market share can manifest itself in a number of different competitive advantages. One such area is in lower unit costs, but we've already covered this under economies of scale in cost-related KSFs, so we must be careful not to double count.

Market share is an indicator of the breadth and depth of your customer relationships and your business reputation. Since it is more difficult to gain a new customer than to do repeat business with an existing one, the provider with the larger market share typically has a competitive advantage – *the power of the incumbent*.

The power of the incumbent rises in proportion to the switching costs – not just the financial costs, but the time, hassle and even emotional costs. It's less of a wrench to change your printer than your accountant.

Apply weights to the KSFs

You've worked out which are the most important KSFs in your business. Each one has been ranked in order of importance. Now you need to weight them.

A simple quantitative approach works best. Don't worry, you won't have to compute a weighting of, say, 14.526 per cent. That would be spurious accuracy. But it's helpful to derive a percentage for the weighting, whether to the nearest 5 or even 10 per cent, so that in the next building block you can easily tot up and rate your firm's *overall* competitiveness.

So that 14.526 per cent would become simply 15 per cent. No more accuracy than that is needed. How to do it? There are two ways: methodically or eyeballing.

If you want a systematic approach, take a look at one such in the box. If you would prefer to eyeball it, to get a rough and ready answer, start from this guideline: market share 20 per cent, cost factors 30 per cent, management and differentiation factors 50 per cent. Then, adjust them to what you have found to be critical to success in your business. And make sure that however you jiggle them they still add up to 100 per cent.

A systematic approach for deriving KSF weightings

Here's a step-by-step systematic approach to weighting KSFs:

- Use judgement on the power of the incumbent to derive a weighting for *market share* of i per cent, typically in the range of 15 to 25 per cent.

- Revisit the importance of price to the customer. If you judged the customer need of medium importance, give *cost competitiveness* a weighting of 20–25 per cent. If low, 15–20 per cent. If high, 35-plus per cent. If yours is a commodity business, it could be 40–45 per cent, with a correspondingly low weighting for market share. Settle on c per cent.

- Think on the importance of *management* factors to the success of your business, especially marketing. Settle on m per cent, typically within a 0 to 10 per cent range.

- You've now used up a total of (i + c + m) per cent of your available weighting.

▶

- The balance, namely 100 − (i + c + m) per cent, will be the total weighting for *service* factors.
- Revisit the list of KSFs relating to *service issues*, excluding price, which has already been covered. Where you've judged a factor to be of low importance, give it a KSF score of 1. Where high, 5. Rate pro rata for in between (for example, medium/high would be a 4).
- Add up the total score for these service-related KSFs (excluding price) = S.
- Assign weightings to each service KSF as follows: weighting (per cent)
  = KSF Score * (1 − [i + c + m])/S.
- Round each of them up or down to the nearest 5 per cent.
- Adjust further if necessary so that the sum of all KSF weights is 100 per cent.
- Eyeball them for sense, make final adjustments.
- Check that the sum is still 100 per cent.

Once you've derived the weightings in general, you need to assess to what extent they may differ for each of your business segments. In particular, different customer groups can often place a different emphasis on price, so cost competitiveness may be more of an issue in one segment than in others. Other customers in other business segments may be more concerned about product quality or customer service.

Identify any must-have KSFs

There is one final wrinkle. But it may be crucial.

Is one of the KSFs in your business so important that, if you don't rank highly against it, you shouldn't even be in business? You simply won't begin to compete, let alone succeed? You won't win any business, or you won't be able to deliver on the business you win? In other words, it is a *must-have* KSF, rather than a mere *should-have*.

Must a business in your marketplace have, for example, the right ISO classification to win future orders in a competitively intensifying environment? Must it deploy the new cost-revolutionary range of capital equipment? Must your product incorporate a particular new feature?

Are any of the KSFs in your industry must-haves? Bear this in mind when assessing your competitive position (Section 5).

When to use it

Always.

When to be wary

Don't end up with too many KSFs or you may lose the wood for the trees. Market share, management, two or three cost-related factors and five or six differentiation-related factors should be fine – a total of 10 or so.

Woolworths succumbs to the five forces

Fish and chips, bucket and spade, wool and worth – all quintessential images of the cheap and cheerful end of the British economy. Alas, for the latter pairing, no more.

We grew up with Woolies – we shopped there for toys and Pick 'n' Mix sweets as children, records/cassettes/CDs as youngsters, cheap crockery as students, Ladybird and school clothes as parents, handed out pocket money to the kids to buy sweets there and so the cycle repeated. Its New Cross branch was even the site of one of the most tragic incidents on British soil during the Second World War, when it took a direct hit from a German V-2 rocket.

Yet Woolies is gone. In the very year it was to celebrate its 100th anniversary in the UK, it collapsed. It was still a major force on the British High Street – it was market leader in sweets, number two in entertainment, the same in toys, number four in homeware and number five in children's clothes. It turned over £2 billion and was the UK's eighth biggest retailer. How could it be for sale at £1?

There were a host of reasons, including:

- Abrupt downturn in consumer demand at onset of credit crunch
- Suppliers demanding cash upfront
- Specialist retailers like Toys R Us gaining share
- Direct homeware competitors like Wilkinson gaining share
- Discount stores like Poundland gaining share
- Steep share loss in entertainment sales.

It is the last of these which is of most relevance to this section. Competition in the entertainment retailing sector, formerly a high-margin segment, was intensifying severely, with each of Porter's Five Forces lining up adversely against the likes of Woolworths – see figure below.

- The music downloading substitute was eating into CD share.
- Online competition from the likes of amazon.com, play.com and dvd.com was eroding sales of both CDs and DVDs.
- Supermarket chains were offering loss-leading discounts on chart-listed CDs and DVDs.
- Specialist entertainment stores such as HMV were being forced by the above trends to price competitively.

It was the perfect storm. It was not just Woolworths that reeled in the face of it, but Top Price, Zavvi and independent music stores too. Even HMV was forced to restructure.

Woolies became a poignant memory of yesteryear.

▶

Example: UK High Street entertainment retailing, end-2000s

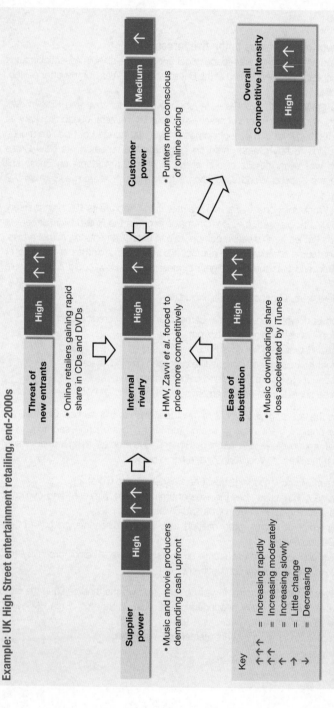

Source: Adapted from Michael E. Porter, *Competitive Strategy: Techniques for Analyzing Industries and Competitors*, The Free Press, (Porter, Michael 1980) page 4, adapted with the permission of Free Press, a Division of Simon & Schuster, Inc., from COMPETITIVE STRATEGY: Techniques for Analyzing Industries and Competitors by Michael E. Porter. Copyright © 1980, 1988 by The Free Press. All rights reserved

Weighing economies of scale

25

The tool

Size is important.

Qualification: size is important in certain sectors, less so in others.

Another qualification: even in sectors where size is important, small players can survive – if they are nimble.

In general a company producing 1000 widgets a day will typically have higher costs *per unit* than one producing 2000 a day. And way higher unit costs than the market leader, which churns out 20,000 a day – see Figure 25.1.

Figure 25.1 Economies of scale

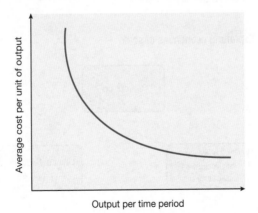

Output per time period

There are four main economies of scale, across the value chain:

1 *Purchasing economies* – the larger the producer, the more likely they will be able to drive a harder bargain with suppliers, such as steel producers, and enjoy volume discounts.

2 *Technical economies* – the machinery needed to produce 20,000 widgets a day is unlikely to be 20 times as expensive as that needed to produce 1000 a day.

3 *Efficiency economies* – the process for producing 20,000 widgets a day is likely to be more highly automated, from handling inputs through manufacturing to handling outputs, and with more advanced or streamlined business processes, for example in R&D, than for the smaller plant.

4 *Indivisibility economies* – some items are beyond the reach of the smaller producer to buy, whether state-of-the-art equipment or a national television advertisement.

Economies of scale apply as much to service businesses as in manufacturing and to small as much as to global businesses.

Think of two hair salons competing on your local high street. One has double the amount of space of the other and serves on average 80 customers a day, compared to its smaller neighbour's 40. They are thus equally productive. They charge similar prices, yet the larger salon has lower rental costs per customer thanks to a deal negotiated with the landlord when the business expanded into double the space. The larger salon also pays lower marketing costs per customer, since advertising space in the Yellow Pages or in the local glossy magazine costs the same per column inch for both salons, irrespective of how many customers the advertiser serves.

Magnify those salon businesses a million-fold and advertising spending by, say, Guinness *per pint sold* will tend to be well below that of a niche brewer such as Cobra (see the example in Section 5).

Nevertheless Cobra survives by offering a differentiated, premium-priced product – see Porter's generic strategies, Tool 45.

Figure 25.2 Exploiting economies of scale

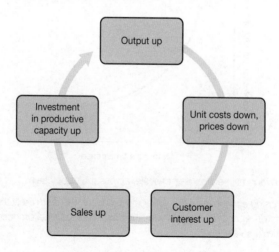

How to use it

How important are economies of scale in your sector?

Are there purchasing, technical, efficiency or indivisibility economies?

In Tool 24, did you place sufficient credence on economies of scale when weighting cost-related key success factors? Should you revisit that weighting?

Will you be able to exploit future economies of scale in your business as it grows – see Figure 25.2?

When to use it

Use it when economies of scale are important in your sector and to your business.

When to be wary

Remember it represents only one of many key success factors. Differentiation may be the name of your game.

26

Corporate environment as a sixth force

The tool

Does government help or hinder your business?

Does government, whether local, central or European, through taxation or regulation, greatly influence profitability in your industry?

Michael Porter's Five Forces (Tool 22) has survived intact for three decades, but not without having to dodge its fair share of sniper fire. Some critics have argued that the importance of certain forces is seriously underplayed in the model, in particular the corporate environment (this tool) and complements (the next one).

How to use it

An approach that gained prominence among many consulting groups in the 1990s, including at my own, was that the corporate environment should be regarded as a sixth force in its own right (see Figure 26.1). The corporate environment is defined as the combined influence of all external organisations, other than Porter's specified competitors, new entrants, substitutes, customers and suppliers, on the firm.

The corporate environment thus defined includes state and industry-wide bodies such as:

- Central (or federal in the US) government, through taxation (tariffs, sales, corporate, value added, labour), subsidisation, trade restrictions, regulation, employment law, health/safety/environment law, industrial restructuring and even the maintenance of political stability

- Local government, whether county, borough, region or province (or state)

- National regulatory bodies, such as Ofcom or Ofgem in the UK

- International regulatory directives, such as the Basel accords on the capital adequacy of financial institutions

- Pressure groups, such as industry associations, trade unions, Greenpeace.

Figure 26.1 Corporate environment as the sixth force?

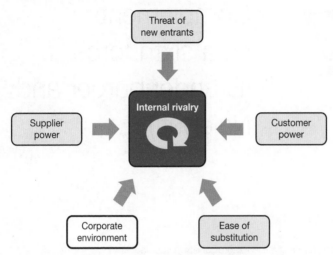

The influence of these bodies can greatly influence both market demand and industry competition. The Common Agricultural Policy of the European Union represents a complete distortion of market forces, operating greatly to the benefit of small farmers, but at a substantial cost to the consumer. Pressure groups can similarly distort demand and supply.

Michael Porter's response has been that the corporate environment is indeed a major 'factor' in driving industry competition, but not necessarily more so than other factors within the major force of internal rivalry – which is where he believes it should reside.

When to use it

When the corporate environment is a determining influence on the profitability in your industry – for example, in sheep farming.

When to be wary

When the corporate environment is one of many factors influencing internal rivalry, such as the number of players or market demand growth, and does not merit recognition as a sixth force.

27 Complements as a sixth force (Brandenburger and Nalebuff)

The tool

Do complements influence profitability in your industry?

The other major claimant to the position of 'sixth force' in industry competition is complements (see Figure 27.1). This arose from the recognition that firm profitability can be greatly influenced by the interactive decision-making of industry participants and from the application of game theory to industry analysis in the

Figure 27.1 Complements as the sixth force?

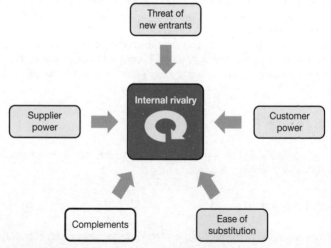

mid-1990s. Complements were singled out in particular in an influential article by Adam Brandenburger and Barry Nalebuff.

How to use it

Complements are more than just supplies to a firm. The value of my Toshiba PC is intricately bound up with the value of its Intel processor – a separate company and one which may extract more value from my purchase than the PC manufacturer itself. This would not be the case were I using an Apple Mac.

Intel's product is a complement to Toshiba's in this product line. Intel is no ordinary supplier to Toshiba. It is an ally. And profit will reside within the party that has the strongest bargaining position.

Complements are broader too than direct supplies. An airline depends for its profitability not just on the five forces, but on the continuity of operations at its complements – airports, air traffic control, suppliers of aviation fuel, inclusive tour operators.

Given the proliferation of strategic alliances since the 1990s, whether formalised joint ventures or loose, de facto, joint marketing agreements, a case can be made for creating a special sixth force for complements.

Again, however, Michael Porter acknowledges the importance of complements, but counters that they tend typically to be no more than a major factor in one of the five main forces, whether supplier bargaining power or internal rivalry.

When to use it

When complements clearly play a major role in driving profitability in a particular industry – for example, again, in airlines.

When to be wary

When complements play a relatively minor role and do not merit identification as a sixth force.

28

PESTEL analysis

The tool

'The business of the American people is business', spake Calvin Coolidge in the midst of the Roaring Twenties, before the Great Depression descended.

Like it or not, since those relatively *laissez faire* days government has become more and more involved with business throughout the Western world.

PESTEL analysis offers a framework for identifying external, often government-influenced issues affecting industry competition. It is an acronym of these six groups of issues: political, economic, social, technological, environmental and legal.

How to use it

PESTEL analysis emerged in the 1990s with just the four factors, as PEST, later evolving into PESTEL with the addition of two further factors (see Figure 28.1). Some recent practitioners have added a seventh factor, ethics, to make it STEEPLE analysis.

Examples of the issues covered in PESTEL analysis are:

- *Political* – government taxation, legal and regulatory intervention in the marketplace (see the corporate environment issues of Tool 26)
- *Economic* – the macro-economic backdrop, including economic growth, inflation, interest rates and exchange rates
- *Social* – the societal backdrop, including population trends, consumption patterns, age distribution
- *Technological* – trends in R&D and innovation, affecting both product and production, and the threat from substitute products
- *Environmental* – trends in weather and climate, and the impact of climate change on your firm's operations and customer preference

Figure 28.1 PESTEL analysis

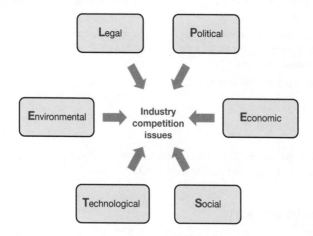

- *Legal* – trends in laws which impact on a firm's operations and decision-making, including employment, health/safety/environment, antitrust, consumer protection, capital adequacy and governance laws.

PESTEL analysis is sometimes used to throw up the range of opportunities and threats needed for SWOT analysis (Tool 6). And therein may lie a problem. Like SWOT, PESTEL analysis can be a rather unstructured and ill-disciplined tool. It tends to generate lists, dozens of issues, some with much relevance to your firm, others with little – though sometimes of much interest and importance in themselves. The issues are unstructured, unlike in the issue analysis of Tool 2, not assessed, unlike those in the Five Forces framework of Tool 22, and unranked for likelihood of occurrence and impact on value, unlike those in the Suns & Clouds chart of Tool 83.

PESTEL analysis also duplicates analyses that are more productively undertaken elsewhere in the Strategy Pyramid process. Thus:

- *Political* – part of the Five Forces analysis of Tool 22, but if especially important in your industry to be pulled out as a sixth force in Tool 26

- *Economic* – no need for an OECD-style review of the country's economic prospects, just for identification of drivers which impact on market demand and how they have been and are likely to change in influence in the HOOF approach for demand forecasting (Tool 17); some macro-economic factors, such as exchange rates, may have negligible effect on demand prospects in your market

- *Social* – again, no need for a sociological survey, just the identification of any key drivers in the HOOF approach (Tool 17)

- *Technological* – potentially vital issues, covered in two of the forces in the

Five Forces model (Tool 22): namely, technological advance in product or production (internal rivalry) and the threat of substitute products enabled by technological advance

- *Environmental* – again, no need for meteorological forecasts, but identification of drivers as appropriate in the HOOF approach to demand forecasting (Tool 17)
- *Legal* – see Political above.

When to use it

PESTEL analysis is an aid to the brainstorming of industry issues. Use it if you are accustomed to it, but be aware of its limitations.

When to be wary

At best, the analysis represents a rather unstructured, non-analytical, unranked identification of key industry issues. At worst, the key issues will be as needles in a haystack.

[SECTION 5]

Tracking competitive advantage

Overview

Essential tools

29 Rating competitive position

30 The resource and capability strengths/importance matrix (Grant)

Useful tools

31 The value chain (Porter)

32 The product/market matrix (Ansoff)

33 Cross, spider and comb charts

34 Benchmarking

35 Structured interviewing

Overview

You have built the foundation of the Strategy Pyramid. The micro-economic context is set. Now you need to place your firm within that context.

You need to set out your competitive position and pinpoint your competitive advantage – for each main business segment.

You need to track your position over time. And assess the strategic importance of your resources and capabilities.

And do the same for all your main competitors.

These are your main challenges in this building block, the tracking of competitive advantage. Two essential tools will be deployed: rating competitive position and Grant's Strengths/Importance Matrix.

We shall then look at other tools which may be useful in helping you track competitive advantage, including Porter's Value Chain and Ansoff's Product/Market Matrix.

Rating competitive position

29

The tool

'A man can't be too careful in the choice of his enemies', said Oscar Wilde. So too, perhaps, with firms and their choice of where and with whom to compete.

Who are yours? And how do you compare with them? Against each key success factor (see Tool 24)?

How is your overall competitive position? And theirs? How do your relative positions differ by product/market segment?

In this tool you will rate your competitive position, against each key competitor, over time and for each main segment.

You could do this right now, at your desk, using feedback you and your sales and purchasing teams have received from customers and suppliers over the years. Or you could do it more methodically, via a structured interviewing programme (see Tool 35).

In this analysis you will assess your strengths and weaknesses and those of your peers. It will pinpoint your source of competitive advantage – as well as that of your most formidable competitor.

How to use it

The process of rating competitive position is straightforward – you have already done most of the work in Tools 23 (assessing customer purchasing criteria) and 24 (deriving key success factors). Now you just rate your firm against each of those key success factors ('KSFs').

Use a 0–5 rating system. If you perform about the same as your peers against a KSF, give yourself a score in the middle, a 3 (*good, favourable*). If you perform very strongly, even dominantly, a 5 (*very strong*). Poorly, a 1 (*weak*). If you perform not quite as well as most others, give yourself a 2 (*tenable*). Better than most, a 4 (*strong*).

Now do the same for each of your competitors against that KSF. Who's the best performer against this KSF? Do they merit a 5, or are they better but not *that* much better than others, for a 4?

And so on against each KSF.

If you've used Excel, your competitive position literally falls out at the bottom of the spreadsheet. Your overall rating is the sum of each rating (r) against each KSF multiplied by the percentage weighting (w) of the KSF. If there are n KSFs, your overall rating will be (r1 * w1) + (r2 * w2) + (r3 * w3) + ... + (rn * wn). As long as the percentage weightings add up to 100 per cent, you should get the right answer.

Figure 29.1 gives an example, one taken from a recent strategy assignment. It shows that the company was the leading player in its niche UK engineering market, but there was no room for complacency. The company had the largest presence in the market, the best engineering service network and a strong cost base, but competitor A had developed a product with enhanced features and functionality that was proving attractive to customers.

Figure 29.1 Competitive position: an example

Key success Factors in UK engineering niche market	Weighting	The company	Competitor A	Competitor B
Market share	15%	5	3.3	2
Cost factors	35%	4	3.5	2.5
Differentiation factors: Product capability and range	15%	4	4.5	3
Product reliability	15%	4	4	2.5
Engineering service network	10%	5	3.5	2.5
Customer service	10%	3	3	2
Competitive position	100%	4.2	3.6	2.5

Key: 1 = Weak, 2 = Tenable, 3 = Favourable, 4 = Strong, 5 = Dominant

Competing by segment

Apply the same process for each key product/market segment: identifying how customer purchasing criteria differ by segment, assessing key success factors for each and deriving competitive position in each. You'll find that some positions will vary because of weighting. Take product quality. Your rating against that KSF may well be the same in each segment relating to a product group. But its weighting may differ by customer group segment, thereby impacting your overall competitive position in each.

Ratings for the same KSF may well differ by segment. For instance, your company may have an enviable track record in service and repair in one segment, but you've haven't long been in another – rating a 5 in the first, but only a 2 in the other. Again that will filter down to the bottom line of competitive position.

Competing over time

So far your analysis of competitive position has been static. You've rated your firm's current competitiveness and those of others. But that's only the first part of the story. How has your competitive position changed over the past few years and how is it likely to change over the next few years? You need to understand the dynamics. Is it set to improve or worsen?

The simplest way to do this is to add an extra column to your chart, representing your position in, say, three years' time. Then you can build in any improvements in your ratings against each KSF. These prospective improvements need, for the time being, to be both in the pipeline *and* likely. In the next chapter we shall assess how you can *proactively and systematically* improve your competitive position. That's strategy. But for now it is useful to see how your competitive position seems set to evolve naturally over the next few years, assuming no significant change in strategy.

Remember, however, that improved competitive position is a two-edged sword. Your competitors too will have plans. This is where analysis of KSF dynamics gets challenging. It's easy enough to know what you're planning but what are your competitors up to?

Try adding a couple of further columns representing your two most fearsome competitors as they may be in three years' time. Do you have any idea what they're planning to do to improve their competitiveness in the near future? What are they likely to do? What could they do? *What are you afraid they'll do?*

Returning to the example of the UK niche engineering company, management was aware that competitor A had plans to outsource certain components and reduce cost and set up a joint venture to enhance its engineering service capability.

Figure 29.2 Future competitive position: an example

Key success factors in UK engineering niche market	Weighting	The company	Competitor A today	Competitor A tomorrow
Market share	15%	5	3.3	4
Cost factors	35%	4	3.5	4
Differentiation factors: Product capability and range	15%	4	4.5	4.5
Product reliability	15%	4	4	4
Engineering service network	10%	5	3.5	4
Customer service	10%	3	3	3.5
Competitive position	*100%*	**4.2**	**3.6**	**4.0**

Key: 1 = Weak, 2 = Tenable, 3 = Favourable, 4 = Strong, 5 = Dominant

A's strategy seemed set to narrow the competitive gap unless my client deployed a proactive strategy focusing on R&D – see Figure 29.2.

Getting past first base

In the last chapter, we introduced the concept of the must-have KSF – without a good rating in this KSF your business cannot even begin to compete.

Did you find a must-have KSF in any of your business segments? If so, how do you rate against it? Favourable, strong? Fine. Okay-ish? Questionable. Weak? Troublesome. A straight zero, not even a 1? You're out. You don't get past first base.

And what about in a few years' time? Could any KSF develop into a must-have? How will you rate then? Will you get past first base?

And even though you rate as tenable against a must-have KSF today, might it slip over time? Could it slide below 2, into tricky territory?

This may be a case of being cruel to be kind. It's better to know. The sooner you realise that you're in a wrong business segment, the sooner you can withdraw and focus resources on the right segments.

Implications for future market share

The tool plays a useful role in business planning (see Market Contextual Plan Review, Tool 82). It gives you an idea of how your firm is likely to fare over the next few years *in relation to the market as a whole*.

If your overall competitive position turns out to be around 3, or good/favourable, you should, other things being equal, to be able to grow business *in line with the market* over the next few years. In other words, to hold market share.

If it is around 4 or above, you should be able to *beat the market*, to gain market share, again, other things being equal. Suppose you forecast market demand growth of 10 per cent a year in Tool 17. With a competitive position of 4, you should feel comfortable that you can grow your business at, say, 12–15 per cent a year.

If your competitive position is around 2, however, you'll be less confident about your business prospects. It's more likely you'll *underperform the market* and, if your boss is expecting the firm to outpace the market, something will have to change!

Implications for strategy development

This tool throws up some facts and judgements highly useful for strategy development:

- How you compete overall in key segments – hence where you are most likely to be most profitable relative to the competition
- Areas of strength in key segments, which can be built on
- Areas of weakness in some segments, which may need to be worked on
- Areas of strength or weakness common to many or all segments, which can be built on or worked on

- Relative competitiveness in each key segment
- Change in competitiveness over time
- In summary, your source of competitive advantage, tracked over time.

This tool will form the basis for identification of the strategic gap in the next section.

When to use it

Always.

When to be wary

Having used this tool for three decades and managed many junior consultants in its use, here are three areas where you may need to take care:

- Too much analysis hinders decision-making – don't do this for too many segments, too many KSFs, too many competitors within each segment or too many years past and future; keep it simple – opt for the main segments, the main KSFs, the main competitors, now and three years' hence; look for the main findings, the key lessons; drill down further only if necessary and potentially illuminating.

- Don't get too scientific – stick to the nearest whole number in the 0–5 range, or when you are torn between a 3 and a 4, go for a 3.5; the exception is for market share, which lends itself to more precise quantification – if competitor A has 60 per cent share, B 25 per cent and C 15 per cent, don't give A a 5, B a 3 and C a 1, be more precise; keep A at 5 and give B a 2.1 and C a 1.2.

- Always have a first shot with or without the relevant research, but if you feel uncomfortable about a rating, type it provisionally into Excel in red or in italics and undertake to do the required research – benchmarking, perhaps (see Tool 34), or a customer survey (Tool 35) – before firming up the rating.

Circumnavigate these pitfalls and the tool is invaluable.

30

The resource and capability strengths/importance matrix (Grant)

The tool

How strategically important is whatever your firm does well?

Rob Grant's essential tool puts your firm's resources and capabilities into perspective. It assesses them by two criteria – how important they are relative to each other and how strongly you are placed relative to the competition.

You should start by differentiating between your firm's resources and capabilities. Resources are the productive assets owned by the firm, whether tangible, intangible or human. Capabilities are what the firm does with its resources, how it deploys them.

Land, buildings, plant and equipment are resources. So too are intangible resources such as brand and intellectual property. How they work together organisationally and operationally, whether in production, purchasing, product development, sales or marketing, are the firm's capabilities.

This tool is more relevant for looking at your business as a whole, the strategic business unit, as opposed to Tool 29's drilling down into each key product/market segment. It can also be used in corporate strategy (Section 8), analysing the shared resources and capabilities of the centre as well as of each business unit.

How to use it

Grant offers a three-step approach on appraising resources and capabilities and thereby guiding strategy development:

1 Identify key resources and capabilities.
2 Appraise them:
  - Assess their relative importance
  - Assess your relative strengths
  - Bring the appraisal together.
3 Develop strategy implications.

In the first step, you need to translate the key success factors you established in Tool 24 into specific resources and capabilities. For this, value chain analysis (Tool 31) may also be of help.

Then you rate them by degree of importance, as defined by which resources or capabilities are the more important in conferring competitive advantage.

Next you assess how your firm stacks up versus the competition in each of these resources and capabilities – as you did in Tool 29. Here, you may find a bench-marking exercise helpful (Tool 34).

This leads us to the Strengths/Importance Matrix, a simple but most revealing chart – see Figure 30.1. Here you can appraise your firm's strengths and weaknesses visually in the context of their strategic importance.

Figure 30.1 The resource strengths/importance matrix

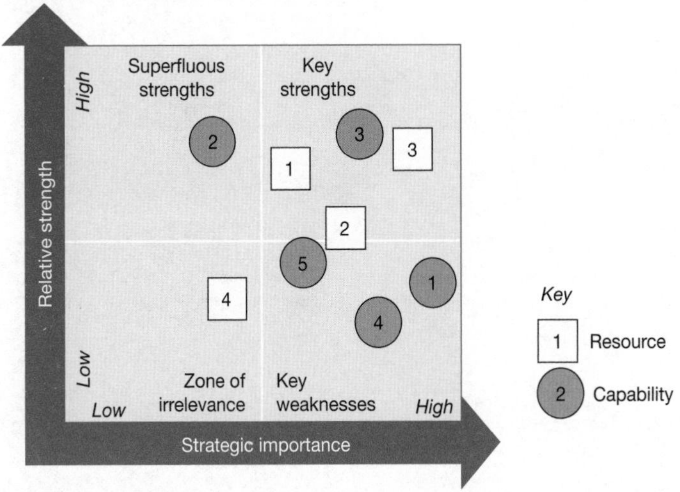

Source: Adapted from Robert M. Grant, *Contemporary Strategy Analysis*, Wiley-Blackwell, 7th edn, 2011

Resources and capabilities that appear in the top-right quadrant are good news and suggest competitive advantage. Those in the bottom-right quadrant are of concern – your firm is potentially weak in those resources or capabilities deemed of strategic importance.

Those in the top-left quadrant are superfluous (you're strong in unimportant areas) and in the bottom-left irrelevant (you're weak in unimportant areas).

Finally, you can develop the strategic implications of the process. How can you exploit the key strengths displayed – perhaps by further targeted investment in developing capabilities? How can you manage the key weaknesses – perhaps through outsourcing? To what extent can the superfluous strengths be deployed to greater effect on shareholder value – perhaps through divestment?

When to use it

Always. The matrix can convey revealing insights.

When to be wary

The strategic implications need care. Successful companies are not necessarily those that possess the greater resources, but those that leverage them (Hamel and Prahalad, see Tool 63). And working on weaknesses may not give as good a return as building on strengths (Section 7).

Cobra Beer's clever competitive advantage

There are few more mature industries than food and beverages. Difficult for a newcomer to find a niche, one might think. But every now and then someone comes along with something entirely new and takes the market by storm. Innocent stormed the fresh juice business, Reggae Reggae the sauce business and Pret A Manger the sandwich business.

But most extraordinary of all was the incursion of Cobra Beer. Beer was one of the industry's most mature segments. Beer consumption in the UK has declined remorselessly since the late 1970s, with per capita consumption falling at around 1 per cent/year (compared to the 3 per cent/year growth of per capita wine consumption), but with the rate of decline accelerating in the late 2000s as alcopops took hold.

Meanwhile, the traditional British 'warm' ale steadily lost share to 'cool' lagers, initially imported, subsequently brewed in the UK and now being imported again as so-called 'premium' beers from all over the world, from Italy to Mexico, Singapore to Jamaica stake their claim.

It was against this background that law student Karan Bilimoria spotted a niche. One of the peculiarities of the British is that when they eat out they like to eat at non-British restaurants (a quirk that amuses the French, Spanish, Italians, Chinese and Thais).

Their favourite is Indian cuisine – with the most popular dish, chicken tikka masala, not even an Indian dish, but one made in Britain.

And with their Indian meal, they like to have a glass of lager beer, its coolness perceived (erroneously) as helping to fight off the flames of a madras or vindaloo curry.

The problem was that lager is gassy. That has two disadvantages: embarrassing eruptions by customers and premature filling up of the stomach.

Hence Cobra Beer – a lager beer low in gas targeted precisely for sale to Indian restaurants. Restaurateurs would be keen to stock it – less gas means more space in the stomach to order a further dish or two.

And punters will be keen to drink it – perceiving it as a beer ideally matched to a curry dish.

The niche worked a treat. Launched in 1990 with a specially commissioned beer brewed in Bangalore, with brewing later switched to the UK, Cobra Beer reached sales of over £125 million by 2012. It was stocked in 90 per cent of Britain's 6000 licensed Indian restaurants. Net profit and cash flow proved more problematic – over-gearing and economic downturn led to a distressed sale by Billimoria of a controlling stake to the Canadian brewer, Molson Coors, in 2009.

But the brand is buoyant. Cobra Beer created a sustainable competitive advantage. And if you're going out for an Indian meal this evening, the chances are you'll be washing it down with a Cobra.

31

The value chain (Porter)

The tool

'You are the weakest link' has entered the realms of memorable, if shrill and irritating, catch phrases in the UK. But are there weak links in your business?

The value chain is a tool for identifying key processes in your business, assessing your firm's competitive capabilities in each and thereby assessing wherein lies the source of your competitive advantage.

It was first introduced by Michael Porter in 1984 and, as with his Five Forces model (Tool 22), has robustly withstood the test of time.

How to use it

Porter divides a firm's activities into primary and support activities – see Figure 31.1. Primary activities involve the conversion of a range of inputs to the production process through to the delivery of the output to the customer and beyond. Or, in the case of a service business, they involve the conversion of personnel and their work tools through the operational processes to service delivery and after-sales service.

Primary activities are:

- *Inbound logistics* – those required to receive, store and disseminate inputs
- *Operations* – those required to transform inputs into outputs
- *Outbound logistics* – those required to collect, store and distribute the output
- *Marketing and sales* – those required to generate awareness of the firm's outputs and their benefits and to stimulate customers to buy them
- *Service* – those required to maintain effective working of the product or service post-sale.

Figure 31.1 The value chain

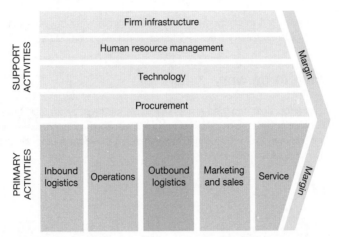

Source: Adapted from Michael E. Porter, *Competitive Strategy: Techniques for Analyzing Industries and Competitors*, The Free Press, (Porter, Michael 1980) Figure 3.3, page 68, adapted with the permission of Free Press, a Division of Simon & Schuster, Inc. from COMPETITIVE STRATEGY: Techniques for Analyzing Industries and Competitors by Michael E. Porter. Copyright © 1980, 1988 by The Free Press. All rights reserved.

Support activities are those which apply across the range of primary activities. They are:

- *The firm's infrastructure* – those required to serve the firm's general needs, typically centred around HQ, such as accounting, finance, legal, planning, PR and general management
- *Human resource management* – those required to recruit, hire, train, develop, compensate and (as necessary) discipline or dismiss personnel
- *Technology* – those required to research and develop the equipment, hardware, software and processes needed in all primary activities
- *Procurement* – those required to acquire inputs needed in all primary activities.

Note that Porter takes technology and procurement as support activities, not primary. In practice, they can be treated as primary activities as long as you recognise that they can be applicable to other such activities.

Thus you can replace technology with 'information technology' as a support activity and insert 'R&D' as a primary activity – or indeed split it into two: 'product R&D' and 'production R&D'. It is up to you – think what will be most illuminating for your business in terms of identifying key success factors.

Procurement used to be treated often as a primary activity, since the term used to be virtually synonymous with the purchasing of raw materials and components. This is no longer the case. The spread of outsourcing and offshoring in the 1990s has meant that procurement activities can now be equally important in operations, even in outbound logistics or post-sale service.

When to use it

When you need to clarify which are the activities in your business that are most important to business success – in other words, which are KSFs.

When to be wary

This is a tool best deployed across the whole business, or strategic business unit. Given that activities such as human resource management or procurement are likely to be common to all product/market segments, it is seldom appropriate to use value chain analysis for each key segment.

The product/market matrix (Ansoff)

32

The tool

'When we're in a peak, we make a ton of money, and as soon as we make a ton of money, we're desperately looking for a way to spend it. And we diversify into areas that, frankly, we don't know how to run very well', mused Bill Ford, great-grandson of Henry.

Ford's story is not unique and not new. Igor Ansoff, author of the first book exclusively on corporate strategy in 1965, created his product/market matrix to illustrate the relative risks of four generic growth strategies – growth though market penetration, market development, product development and diversification.

He argued that diversification, straying too far from what you know best, is by far the riskiest strategy. Ford might agree.

How to use it

Draw a 2 × 2 matrix, with existing and new products along the x-axis and existing and new markets along the y-axis – see Figure 32.1. Take your main sales initiatives planned for the next three to five years and place them in the relevant quadrant – along with their proportionate contribution to the overall forecast sales increase in that period.

Which quadrant shows the greatest uplift in sales? If it is in existing products to existing or new markets, or new products to existing markets, there should be no due cause for alarm. If it is in the quadrant of new products to new markets, that is another story.

Ansoff's main intent was to stress that a diversification strategy, that of growth through launching new products into new markets, operates on a very much higher plane of risk than the other three strategies. Superficially attractive, and practised by many leading companies of his time, it is risky. While the first three strategies built on familiar skills in production, purchasing, sales and marketing, this was unlikely to be the case with diversification. Furthermore, diversification stood the risk of absorbing

Figure 32.1 The product/market matrix

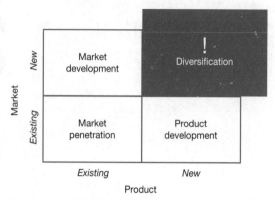

Source: Adapted from H. Igor Ansoff, 'Strategies for Diversification', *Harvard Business Review*, Sep–Oct 1957

a disproportionately high proportion of managerial and engineering resources, due simply to the lack of familiarity with the new venture.

In later years Ansoff came to believe that the matrix was an over-simplification, owing to the different degrees of risk associated with new *market segment* entry and new *country market* entry. So he introduced the third dimension of new geography. Thus, his two dimensional 2 × 2 matrix became 3D, a 2 × 2 × 2 cube.

The extremes of risk were now even more highlighted. The greater the diversification, the greater the compounded risk. The risk of pursuing a strategy of a new product serving a new market segment in a new geographic market was of a very different order of magnitude from a strategy of further market penetration by an existing product in an existing market segment in an existing geographical market.

When to use it

The Ansoff matrix helps to crystallise the riskiness of a proposed strategy. Whether the matrix itself is deployed, or merely the thinking underlying it, the manager should always be conscious of the *compounding* effect on risk from a growth strategy premised on new products *and* new markets *and* new geographies.

When to be wary

Ansoff's complete strategic planning model was complex, too much so in the eyes of some critics. Ansoff himself came to be concerned that it might come to result in 'paralysis by analysis'. But one component of his model, the product/market matrix, has stood the test of time. It is simple, self-evident, and drives home an important message – beware of compounding each element of risk in a growth strategy.

Cross, spider and comb charts

33

The tools

What three items would you take with you to a desert island? How about a cross, a spider and a comb?

No, me neither, but they do have their uses. The three charts by those names are apt tools for displaying key success factors and how your firm rates against them.

Each can also be used for showing customer purchasing criteria or just basic product attributes – and, again, how your firm rates against each.

The cross chart (more formally known as *multi-dimensional scaling*) considers two attributes and compares how your product rates against each of them in relation to its competitors.

The spider chart (also known as a *radar chart* or *web chart*) considers all pertinent attributes and rates your product against the best in class.

The comb chart (sometimes referred to as a *strategy canvas*) shows in a different way the data of the spider chart but gives greater scope for emphasising the relevance of each attribute.

How to use them

They are largely self-explanatory. The product of safari tours to Kenya is taken as an example of a cross chart in Figure 33.1. How the product compares against two attributes, in this case adventure and security, is matched with competing vacation destinations. The chart is indicative only, so please do not rely on it for choosing your summer holiday!

More of the product's attributes can be rated in a spider diagram – see Figure 33.2. Again, the example is for interest only, but the diagram does show immediately attributes of the Kenya safari product which are relatively strong (for example, adventure) and those which are relatively weak (security).

The comb chart is another way of portraying the data of the spider chart and more. Here bar charts can be added easily to highlight the importance of each

Figure 33.1 A cross chart for product attributes: Kenyan safari tours

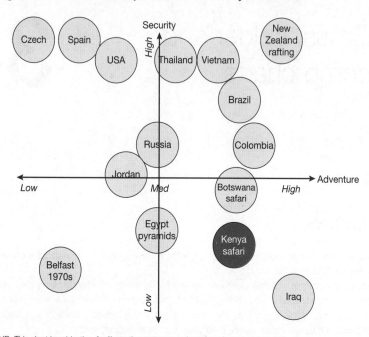

NB: This chart is subjective, for illustrative purposes only and not based on research

Figure 33.2 A spider chart for product attributes: Kenyan safari tours

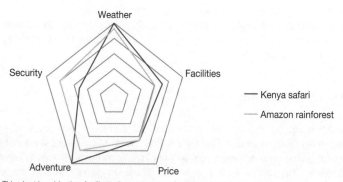

NB: This chart is subjective, for illustrative purposes only and not based on research

Figure 33.3 A comb chart for product attributes: Kenyan safari tours

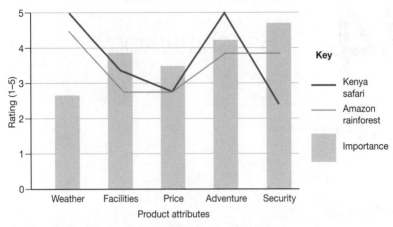

NB: This chart is subjective, for illustrative purposes only and not based on research

product attribute to the customer (see Figure 33.3). In this case, they highlight that the issue of security, which is uppermost in many travellers' minds, is one in which Kenyan safari tours, following Islamist kidnappings, rate less favourably than those in the Amazon rainforest.

When to use them

You can use them for rating and comparing product attributes, but they also work just as well for comparing customer purchasing criteria (Tool 23) or key success factors (Tool 24).

When to be wary

The charts will only prove as reliable as the data fed into them ...

34 Benchmarking

The tool

Here's a question for your pub quiz: 'Which business tool was named after the cobblers' bench, but is anything but a "load of old cobblers"?' (Hint to the latter: think cobblers' awls ...!)

Benchmarking is indeed so derived. It is a systematic approach to measuring key metrics in the operations, systems and processes in your firm against best practice, whether to be found in your industry or, very often, in others.

It can be an invaluable tool in pinpointing areas of strength or weakness in your firm for purposes of strategy development.

Benchmarking developed in the late 1980s in response to the growing realisation that Western companies were being outsmarted by East Asian companies in some key operational areas – not just in well-known areas such as just-in-time purchasing, but even in customer service.

How to use it

One early pioneer, Robert Camp, identified four stages and ten steps in the benchmarking process (see Figure 34.1):

1 Planning
- Identify which parameters require benchmarking
- Identify comparative companies
- Establish data collection methods.
2 Analysis
- Determine the current competitive gap
- Project future performance levels.
3 Integration
- Communicate benchmark findings
- Establish functional goals.

4 Action

- Develop action plans
- Monitor progress
- Recalibrate.

Figure 34.1 Benchmarking

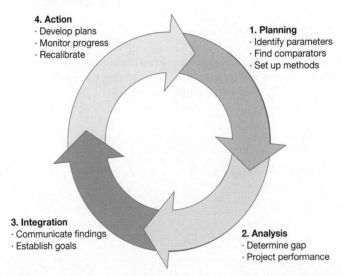

4. Action
· Develop plans
· Monitor progress
· Recalibrate

1. Planning
· Identify parameters
· Find comparators
· Set up methods

3. Integration
· Communicate findings
· Establish goals

2. Analysis
· Determine gap
· Project performance

Source: Adapted from Robert C. Camp, *Benchmarking: The Search for Industry Best Practices that Lead to Superior Performance*, ASQ Quality Press, 1989

Camp's step 2 is the key and is really two sub-steps:

- Identify industries other than yours which use directly comparable processes.
- Identify in those industries, and in yours, in whichever countries, who are the leaders, the very best in those processes.

Camp himself was a logistics engineer in Xerox Corporation, which was losing share in the 1980s as the result of weaknesses across a broad range of processes compared to the Japanese. He encouraged each department to locate best practice wherever it could be found, including the mail order clothing company, L.L. Bean, for its best practice in customer responsiveness.

Another example of benchmarking can be found in the aviation industry. One airline found that routine maintenance on aircraft between flights, such as refuelling, cleaning and tyre checking, was taking too long and incurring too much expense. Benchmarking revealed that the airline was actually the most efficient at such turnarounds in the business, but not as efficient as in motor racing – which uses similar processes in the pits. The airline studied the pit turnaround process minutely, adapted aspects to its own turnaround and managed to reduce aircraft turnaround times dramatically.

When to use it

Use it when you need to drill down to specific operational processes to determine your competitive position, to identify the gap between your firm and its peers, whether in your industry or beyond, and to assess to what extent you should aim to narrow that gap in your strategy development.

When to be wary

It may have its limits. Robert Kaplan has warned of the dangers of ignoring the differentiated output that internal support or shared services provide. Benchmarking is best kept to commoditised processes or services.

Structured interviewing

35

The tool

'Do what you do so well that they will want to come and see it again and bring their friends', advised Walt Disney. Do your customers tell their friends about your firm?

Ask them! And if not, why not? In Tool 29 on rating competitive position, a structured interviewing programme of customers and suppliers was recommended. It is the most methodical and potentially enlightening way to obtain the information needed to derive your firm's competitive position.

How to use it

Here's how to do structured interviewing of customers (see Figure 35.1):

- Select a representative range of interviewees.
- Prepare your storyline.
- Prepare a concise questionnaire.
- Interview them, through email, telephone or face-to-face.
- Thank them and give them some feedback.

The interviewees

The interviewees should represent a broad cross-section of your business, including:

- Customers from each of your main business segments
- Your top six customers in terms of revenue
- Long-standing customers as well as recent acquisitions
- Customers who also use, or used to use, your competitors, so they can compare your performance from direct experience rather than conjecture

- Customers with whom you've had problems
- Would-be customers, currently using a competitor, but on your target list
- Former customers who switched to a competitor – these can potentially yield the most valuable insights of all.

That sounds like a lot, but you'll be selective. Three to six customers for each main segment should suffice, two dozen or so in all.

The storyline

Here's your opportunity to put a positive light on your business. Compare these two storylines:

1 'Sorry to waste your time but can I ask for your help in figuring out how well our firm performs?'
2 'As you know, our firm has been rather busy over the last couple of years. But we thought we should take some time out to ask some of our most important customers how their needs may be changing over time and to what extent we can serve those needs better.'

Guess which line will get the better response *and* put your business in a favourable light? The first storyline conveys a negative impression and is all about your firm and its needs. The second leaves a positive impression and is all about your customer's needs. Stick to the second!

The questionnaire

The questionnaire needs care. It must be taken as a guideline, not as a box-ticking exercise. It stays with you, and it doesn't get handed or emailed to the interviewee. It's a prompter to discussion, no more. It needs to be simple. And concise.

It should be in four parts:

1 The storyline
2 Customer purchasing criteria – which, how important, now and in the future?
3 Performance – how your firm and your competitors rate against those needs
4 The future – how you can better serve your customer's needs.

The storyline. The storyline should be written out at the top of the questionnaire and memorised. It must be delivered naturally and, seemingly, spontaneously. Stick in the odd pause, 'um', or 'er' to make it seem less rehearsed.

Customer purchasing criteria. These are the main questions to put on your questionnaire:

- What are your main criteria in buying this service? What do you expect from your providers?
- How important are each of these criteria? Which are more important than others? How would you rank them?

- Will these criteria become more or less important over time?
- Are any other criteria likely to become important in the future?

You should allow the customer to draw up her own set of criteria, but it's best to prepare your own list to use as prompts, in case your customer dries up, or she misses an obvious one.

Performance. Here are some performance-related questions:

- How do you think our firm meets those criteria? How do we perform?
- How do other providers perform? Do they better meet those criteria?
- Who performs best against those most important criteria?

Again you should allow the customer to select who she thinks are her alternative providers, but you should include a prompt list of your main competitors – which you may or may not choose to use. No need to alert her to a troublesome competitor she's not fully aware of!

The future. What should we be doing to better meet your criteria and those of other customers?

Figure 35.1 Structured interviewing

The interview

Interviews are best done face-to-face. Then you can see the nuances behind the replies – the shifting glance, the fidgeting, the emphatic hand gestures. But they are the most time consuming, unless you happen to be seeing your customer as part of your service delivery anyway.

If the interviews are done over the phone, they are best scheduled in advance. You can do this by email or with a preliminary phone call. After you've delivered the storyline, then add: 'I wonder if you could spare five to ten minutes to discuss this with me. I know you're very busy, but perhaps we could set up a time later in the week for me to give you a call.'

The call itself must be carefully managed. Don't launch into the questionnaire without a warm-up. Ask her how she's doing, how's work, how's the family, whatever. Then gently shift to the storyline: 'Well, as I was saying the other day...'

After you've finished the structured interview, don't forget the warm-down at the closing. Return to one of the topics you discussed at the outset and gently wind down the discussion, not forgetting to thank her sincerely for giving so freely of her valuable time.

The thanks and feedback

A few hours, a day, a couple of days, or a week later – whenever you feel it's appropriate – thank your customer again, officially. By letter is best, but that may feel overly formal for you in this electronic world. Email is probably fine, but use your judgement.

The email should be cheerful and full of sincere gratitude. If possible, it should contain a snippet of information that could be of interest or use to your customer. One or two sentences should suffice. It could pick up on one aspect of the discussion and compare what another customer had to say on the same thing. You could give her an indication of the results of your survey: 'Interestingly, most customers seemed to think that track record was their most important need', or 'Encouragingly, most customers seemed to think we were the most innovative service provider!'

That's structured interviewing. Now, all you have to do is compile the results, whether on a piece of paper, on an Excel worksheet, or simply in your head, and feed them into your ratings against each KSF – for your firm and for each of your main competitors.

The intriguing thing then is to compare these customer-derived ratings with your first draft, do-it-yourself ratings. You may be in for a surprise!

Structured interviewing of suppliers follows the same process – selecting a range of interviewees, preparing the storyline and a questionnaire, interviewing and feeding back.

Here are a couple of tips:

- Supplier interviews can be an important source of information on your competitors; you are not asking them to furnish you with confidential information on their customers, but they may well know of information that is in the public domain but you were unaware of – for example, on the fact that a competitor had shifted production of one product line from plant A to plant B, or that another competitor was now buying in all supplies of one component from the Far East and no longer using national suppliers.

- Choose the list of suppliers to be interviewed not necessarily on grounds of scale of supplies to your firm, but on how much they are likely to know about what is happening in the industry and, in particular, with your competitors.

When to use it

Nearly always in strategy development – though not necessarily if a customer satisfaction survey, whether regular or a one-off, has recently been undertaken. You don't want to overburden your customers.

When to be wary

Take care not to waste customers' time. Try to ensure they too get something useful out of the meeting.

[SECTION 6]

Targeting the strategic gap

Overview

Essential tools

36   The attractiveness/advantage matrix (GE/McKinsey)

37   The growth/share matrix (BCG)

38   Profiling the ideal player

39   Identifying the capability gap

Useful tools

40   The strategic condition matrix (Arthur D. Little)

41   The 7S framework (McKinsey)

42   The opportunity/vulnerability matrix (Bain/L.E.K.)

43   Brainstorming

44   Scenario planning

Overview

'The big gap between the ability of actors is confidence', said Kathleen Turner. As for acting, so with business?

This section is all about confidence. Having assessed your competitive position in the last section, here you target where you want it to be in three to five years' time.

You will identify the strategic gap between where you are now and where the ideal player is, now and in the future. You will then set your sights on the extent to which you aim to narrow that gap.

There are two distinct types of gap:

- In which product/market segments you should compete – the *portfolio gap*
- How you will compete in each of those segments – the *capability gap*.

The portfolio and capability gaps together form the strategic gap. Here you will identify and target the gap. In the next section you will look at the strategic options for bridging it.

You should assume here that you are developing a strategy for a single business, just the one strategic business unit. If your firm has more than one, then you can replicate the tools of this section for each business. In the next section, you will set out to bridge the strategic gap in that business. Following that, you will bridge the gap for your portfolio of businesses, through corporate strategy (Section 8).

Ironically, and a bit confusingly, however, two of the essential tools in this section were designed initially for purposes of corporate strategy. Both the Attractiveness/Advantage Matrix and the Growth/Share Matrix work just as well for – and are essential to – business strategy.

Whether these two tools are used for corporate or business strategy, the axes are the same. The difference comes in the entities analysed and displayed graphically:

- In corporate strategy, the units are businesses (or 'strategic business units').
- In business strategy, the units are business segments, specifically product/market segments within a strategic business unit.

These two invaluable matrices will be your starting point in identifying the strategic gap.

36

The attractiveness/ advantage matrix (GE/McKinsey)

The tool

Where should your business compete? In which segments? Why? How?

Answering those questions is your first step in targeting the strategic gap, optimising your business mix.

You need to undertake a portfolio analysis of your main business segments, and the best tool for this is the Attractiveness/Advantage Matrix.

This matrix originated in the late 1960s, when GE engaged a small army of consultants, including McKinsey, Arthur D. Little, the Boston Consulting Group and Harvard Business School, to advise on how to optimise value from its scores of businesses. From this pioneering effort emerged three innovations which would redefine corporate strategy: namely, the concept of the strategic business unit, the PIMS database (Tool 52) and this portfolio planning matrix.

The matrix will show how competitive your firm is in segments ranked by order of market attractiveness. You should invest ideally in segments where you are strongest and/or which are the most attractive. And you should consider withdrawal from segments where you are weaker and/or where your competitive position is untenable.

And perhaps you should be looking to enter another business segment (or segments) in *more* attractive markets than the ones you currently address? If so, do you have grounds for believing that you would be at least reasonably placed in this new segment? And that you soon could become well placed?

How to use it

First, you need to specify how to define an 'attractive' market segment. This is to some extent sector-specific, and no two strategists will come up with the same list, but over the years I have found these five factors to be both most pertinent and relatively measurable:

- *Market size* – relative to that of other segments (taken from Section 3)

- *Market demand growth* – preferably quantified (again taken from Section 3)
- *Competitive intensity* – allowing for barriers to entry and other forces of industry competition (taken from Section 4)
- *Industry profitability* – average operating margin compared to other segments (again taken from Section 4)
- *Market risk* – cyclicality, volatility for example, exposure to country risk (from Section 3).

The larger the market and the faster it is growing, the more attractive, other things being equal, is the market. Likewise, the greater the industry profitability. But be careful with the other two factors, where the converse applies. The *greater* the competitive intensity and the *greater* its risk, the *less* attractive is the market.

You could argue that taking even just these five factors is effectively double counting certain of them. Market demand growth is a major determinant of internal rivalry, itself one of the five forces in competitive intensity, which is the prime driver of industry profitability. Market risk may be inversely proportional to industry profitability.

Any list will be unscientific, but it should be instructive. You will have to use your own judgement on the composition of the factors, as well as their weighting. Easiest is to give each of the five an equal weighting, so a rating for overall market attractiveness would be the simple average of the ratings for each factor.

You may, however, be risk averse and attach a higher importance to the market risk factor. In this case, you would derive a weighted average.

An example may help. Suppose your business is in four product/market segments and you are contemplating entering a fifth (Figure 36.1). You rate each of the segments against each of the criteria for market attractiveness. Segment D emerges as the most attractive, followed by new segment E. B is rather unattractive. In assessing overall attractiveness, you have gone for a simple average of the

Figure 36.1 Market attractiveness: an example

Segments	A	B	C	D	E (NEW)
Market size	3	2	2	3	3
Market growth	1	2	3	5	5
Competitive intensity	2	2	3	4	5
Industry profitability	3	3	4	2	2
Market risk	5	2	4	4	2
Overall attractiveness	2.8	2.2	3.2	3.6	3.4

Key to rating: 1 = Unattractive, 3 = Reasonably attractive, 5 = Highly attractive
[For competitive intensity, remember that the more intense the competition, the *less* attractive the market. Likewise for market risk, the riskier the market, the *less* attractive it is]

ratings against each factor. You could instead have opted for a weighting system, yielding a weighted average. Or you could, say, have double counted one of the factors – say, risk. More accurate, perhaps, but here you opted for simplicity.

Next you pull out the ratings of competitive position you undertook in the last section, Tool 29, for each segment. Now you can draw up the Attractiveness/Advantage chart, by placing each segment in the appropriate part of the matrix (Figure 36.2). Segment A, for example, has a competitive position rating of 4.0 (out of 5) and a market attractiveness rating of 2.8 (also out of 5).

Figure 36.2 The Attractiveness/Advantage Matrix: an example

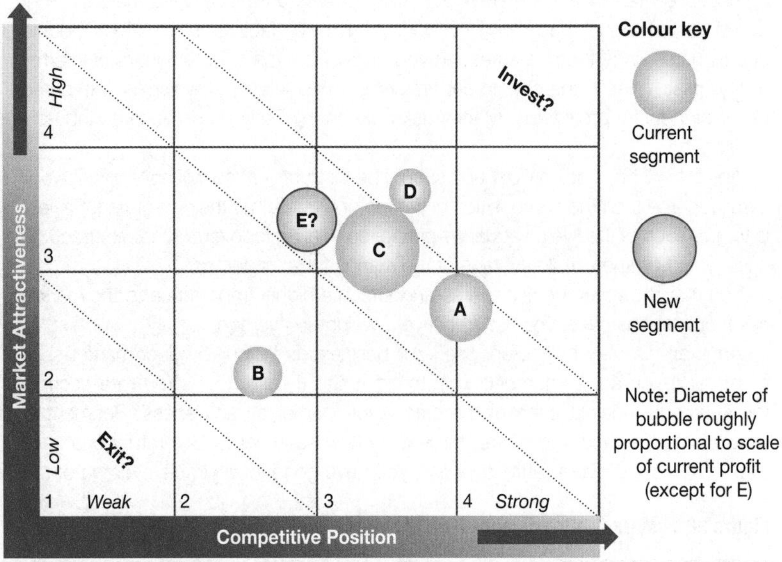

Sources: General Electric, McKinsey & Co. and various

The segment's position in the chart will reflect both its competitive position (along the x-axis) and its market attractiveness (along the y-axis). The size of each circle should be roughly proportional to the segment's contribution to operating profit.

The closer your segment is positioned towards the top right-hand corner, the better placed it is. Above the top-right dotted diagonal, you should invest further in that segment, building on your advantage. Should the segment sink below the bottom-left dotted diagonal, however, you should harvest the business for cash or consider withdrawal. Segments placed along the main diagonal are reasonably placed and should be held, with investment cases carefully scrutinised.

The overall strategic position shown in the example seems sound. It shows favourable strength in the biggest and reasonably attractive segment, C, and an excellent position in the somewhat less attractive segment A. Segment D is highly promising and demands more attention, given the currently low level of profit.

Segment B should perhaps be exited – it's a rather unattractive segment, and your firm is not that well placed. The new segment E seems promising.

You may consider the following strategic options worthy of further analysis:

- Holding and steady development in segments A and C
- Investment in segment D
- Entry to segment E (with competitive position improving over time as market share develops)
- Harvesting or exit from segment B.

How is the overall strategic position in your business? Hopefully your *main* segments, from which you derive most revenues, should find themselves positioned above the main diagonal.

Do you have any new segments in mind? How attractive are they? How well placed would you be?

Are there any segments you should be thinking of getting out of?

Which segments are so important that you would derive greatest benefit from improving your competitive position? Where should you concentrate your efforts?

When to use it

Always.

When to be wary

A major criticism of this portfolio planning tool lies in its subjectivity. Some argue that there are so many subjective calls made throughout the process that deriving strategy from its findings is fraught with danger, thus:

- Factors to derive market attractiveness are chosen subjectively, as is their weighting.
- Key success factors ('KSFs') used to determine competitive position are partially derived from objectively sourced customer purchasing criteria, but the weighting between them and other KSFs, such as market share or management, involves judgement.
- Rating your firm's capabilities against the KSFs to derive competitive position is laced with subjectivity and may be sprinkled with false pride – managers may be reluctant to admit that they are weaker than key competitors against certain KSFs.

The counter-argument to the final bullet is that managers who behave preciously over their fiefdoms are soon brought down to earth at strategy workshops.

The criticism of the tool's reliance on judgement is accepted but misplaced. Strategy is all about judgement, albeit backed up by fact where available. The process of constructing the Attractiveness/Advantage Matrix, taking in work done previously (Sections 3–5), is illuminating, instructive and crucial to strategy development. It forces you to think about what drives success in your business, how your business has fared to date against those capabilities and what you need to do about them in the future. It is not only a portfolio planning tool, but the first step in identifying the strategic gap.

You need to bear in mind, however, two caveats when using the tool. Neither invalidates it, but they merit recognition. They are:

- *Definition of the relevant market*. Your firm may be poorly placed in relation to the whole market, but well placed in a niche corner of that market. Lotus Cars may have an infinitesimal share of the UK automobile market, but it has a significant share of the luxury end of the market and a good share of the luxury performance niche. Any decisions taken on the Lotus business based on an Attractiveness/Advantage Matrix relating to the whole UK automobile market would be misleading.

- *Inter-business synergies*. Your firm may be poorly placed in one business, but it may serve as a loss leader for a strong position in another, better-placed business. This is especially the case when the matrix is used in business strategy, with some product/market segments only persevered with for fear of the potential loss of credibility in withdrawal affecting business in the core segments.

These limitations exist and need to be managed, again using judgement. No strategy tools can obviate the need for judgement. Nor should they be expected to.

Think on military strategy. Sure, there are tomes on classic strategies. But when in the field much will depend ultimately on judgement, often of one general or admiral. Nelson got it right at Trafalgar, Haig not so at the Somme – a gain of five miles in five months at an average loss of 5000 men a day was a terrible indictment of one man's judgement. The strategic alternative, plain, admittedly, only in retrospect, of holding the line for as long as it took for technological advance (the tank) to enable breakthrough might have saved hundreds of thousands of lives.

The growth/share matrix (BCG)

37

The tool

'If you want a friend, get a dog', pronounced corporate raider Carl Icahn. He meant that you don't expect to make friends in his line of business, not that you should go out and buy a dog business.

The latter, as defined by the Boston Consulting Group, is one where you have a low relative market share in a slow-growing market. The Growth/Share Matrix, along with its catchy menagerie, is one of those tools which has held firm over time. It first appeared in the late 1960s and is as widely used today as ever.

Its aims are essentially the same as those of the Attractiveness/Advantage Matrix above (Tool 36), charting the relative position of the entities analysed – whether business units or, in this section, product/market segments within one business unit.

Where it differs is in its choice of parameters:

- Instead of a somewhat subjective assessment of *market attractiveness*, it opts for one measurable parameter, *market demand growth*.

- Instead of a somewhat subjective assessment of *competitive position*, it opts for one measurable parameter, *relative market share*.

The Growth/Share Matrix offers, in essence, an objective, measurable *proxy* for the Attractiveness/Advantage Matrix.

How to use it

Draw up a 2 × 2 matrix, with these axes:

- Relative market share ('RMS') along the x-axis; not market share in itself, but your market share relative to that of your leading competitor; market share on its own is no indicator of relative strength; having a market share of 20 per cent may be a strength in a highly fragmented market where your nearest competitor has 10 per cent and most other main competitors are in single figures, but that 20 per cent takes on a different complexion if you are in a concentrated market where the leader has 40 per cent; in the first market, your relative market share would be 2.0×, but in the second 0.5× – implying very different prospects for sustaining competitive advantage.

- Market growth along the y-axis, taken as the forecast annual average growth rate in real terms over the next three to five years (as derived in Section 3).

Plot your product/market segments accordingly and reveal the following:

- The 'stars': those segments that are in the top-right quadrant, where you have high share in a fast-growing market
- The 'cash cows': those in the bottom-right segment, where you have high share in a slow-growing market
- The 'question marks': those in the top-left quadrant, where you have low share in a fast-growing market
- The 'dogs': those in the bottom-left quadrant, where you have low share in a slow-growing market.

Figure 37.1 The Growth/Share Matrix: an example

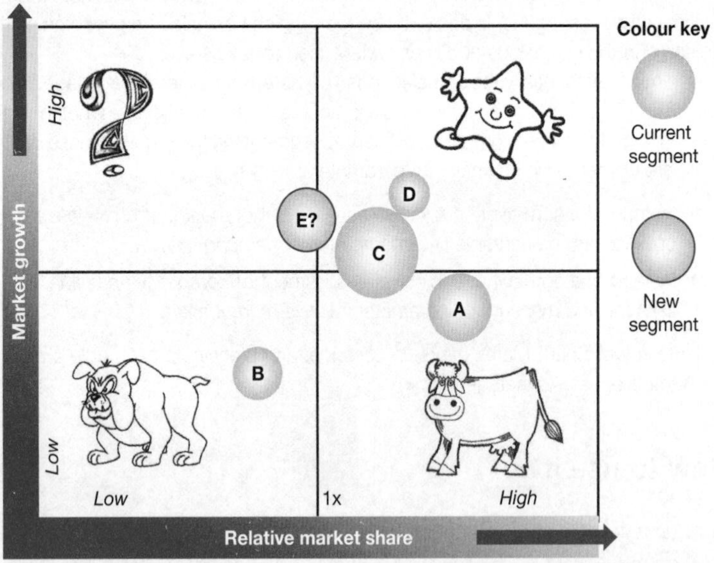

Note: This matrix is often found with the x-axis inverted and relative market share going from high to low. Here it has been taken from low to high, making it more compatible with the Attractiveness/Advantage Matrix

Source: Adapted from the Boston Consulting Group (www.bcg.com)

Other things being equal, you should invest in your stars, harvest your cash cows, divest your dogs and analyse carefully the risks and returns of investing in your question marks.

In Figure 37.1 the example used above in Tool 36 is revisited. The segment circles are left in exactly the same positions as they were in Figure 36.2. This is a simplifying assumption and is unlikely to be the case in practice. A market attractiveness ranking may not be the same as that of market growth. Likewise for relative market share and competitive position – see below under 'when to be wary'.

Again, you may consider the following strategic options worthy of further analysis:

- Milking of cash cow A
- Holding and possible investment in borderline cash cow/star C
- Investment in definitive star D
- Likely entry to borderline question mark/star E
- Harvesting or exit from dog B.

How is the portfolio of segments in your business? With luck your *main* segments, from which you derive most revenues, should find themselves positioned in the right-hand quadrants, the cash cows and stars. Any dogs?

When to use it

Always, but in parallel with the Attractiveness/Advantage Matrix. If the results of the two matrices show up contradictory findings, delve deeper to find out why.

When to be wary

The Growth/Share Matrix shares some of the caveats of the Attractiveness/Advantage Matrix, as discussed in Tool 36:

- Definition of the relevant market
- Inter-business synergies.

Be aware of these limitations but don't let them stop you from using the tool.

A more important critique of this tool stems from its main claim to fame. Unlike those of the Attractiveness/Advantage Matrix, the axes show single, objective, measurable parameters.

Proponents of the Growth/Share Matrix argue that these parameters are genuinely indicative of the parameters of the Attractiveness/Advantage Matrix:

- Relative market share has been shown in many studies to be correlated with profit, hence competitive position, owing to economies of scale on the cost side and perhaps to premium pricing on the revenue side.
- Market demand growth is indicative of market attractiveness, because there

is greater opportunity to gain share in a market where all are growing than in a market which is stagnant and where players are fighting to maintain share.

Opponents, however, believe the parameters on the Growth/Share Matrix represent an over-simplification:

- Relative market share can be an indicator of competitive advantage, but it may not be; equally important is market share change; history is full of examples of companies with formerly high market shares which have since tumbled to earth, and of the converse – companies with little share storming a market; think on the examples of IBM, which fell, and Dell, which rose, in the personal computer market – IBM's relative market share in the early days proved of little competitive advantage against its more nimble rivals; use of the Growth/Share Matrix in the 1970s might have misled IBM, whereas use of the Attractiveness/Advantage Matrix should have pinpointed shortfalls in cost base, product development and distribution.

- Market growth is an equally crude indicator of market attractiveness – again, it may be indicative of relevant industry profitability, or it may not be; unlike in the Attractiveness/Advantage Matrix, it ignores the supply side; the market may be growing fast, but if there is an overdose of suppliers competition will be intense and the market will not be attractive.

Again, though, these limitations should not stop you using the tool. Be conscious of its shortcomings and use it, alongside the Attractiveness/Advantage Matrix. It may well produce some useful insights.

Profiling the ideal player

38

The tool

What will perfection look like in your business?

That may not be your firm, nor may you choose for it to be so. But it can be instructive to think about what that ideal player will look like in three to five years' time.

You have deployed Tool 36, reinforced by 37, and decided in which product/market segments you will compete over the next five years. Here, and in the next tool, you target to what extent you choose to compete in those segments.

First you profile the ideal player.

How to use it

There are three stages in this process (see Figure 38.1):

- Envisioning future scenarios
- Assessing key success factors in each scenario
- Identifying common capabilities.

This tool envisions the future marketplace and the players therein. It suggests that you build scenarios about the future and consider what would be the capabilities of the ideal player under each scenario (see Tool 44 for more detail on scenario planning). Then you can deduce what capabilities are common to these players in all or most of the scenarios. These could become the minimum target capabilities for you to aim for in Tool 39.

Figure 38.1 Profiling the ideal player

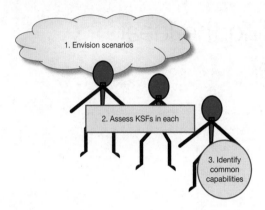

Envision future scenarios

Here you need to envision the future of your marketplace. Will it be more competitive? Will customers have different expectations? Will players need to develop different capabilities?

To answer these questions, it may help to do some brainstorming, thinking a bit more creatively and laterally than you may have done before (in Sections 3 to 5) – see Tool 43. You need to go through and beyond what you have done earlier, to get the right-hand side of the brain working.

Try to develop a range of scenarios on what may happen in your marketplace. Venture beyond the more likely outcomes – you've already drawn those up. Think of those that are less expected but still *quite* likely to occur. Stay clear of fanciful outcomes with only a remote chance of happening. Go for scenarios that could actually happen.

Apply the reasonability test: 'Is it reasonable for me to assume that such and such an outcome could take place over the next five years? Sure it may be less likely to happen than other outcomes, but looking back five years from now would I be surprised that it actually happened?'

Settle on *two to four scenarios*. Give each a name, something that brings the scenario to life.

Assess KSFs in each scenario

You assessed the key success factors ('KSFs') required to meet the needs of customers in Tool 24. Now you should consider what KSFs are required to meet possibly amended future customer needs, under each of the scenarios you have envisioned.

Some KSFs may become more important in one scenario, with therefore a higher weighting. The converse may be true for other KSFs.

Some KSFs may become more important in one scenario, but less important in another.

Some KSFs may be brand new.

Draw up the old, new and re-weighted KSFs for each scenario. The ideal player in that scenario will be the company with the highest achievable rating against each of the KSFs.

You should do this for each of the two to four scenarios you have brainstormed.

Identify common capabilities

The final step in envisioning the ideal player is to investigate what capabilities are common in each of the scenarios.

Some will be pertinent to only one scenario, others to more than one. One or two may be applicable to all scenarios.

You mustn't forget here your original, most likely scenario, the KSFs developed in Tool 24. Those that were identified and weighted there remain the most important, since they are the ones *most likely* to be needed. Those you are now adding or reconsidering may represent just the icing on the cake.

Lack of commonality doesn't necessarily mean that isolated KSFs are unimportant. But it does mean that, in the next tool, you may choose not to take a particular KSF into account. You won't have the time or resources to prepare for every eventuality. Choices will have to be made. You'll need to formulate a strategy and pursue it.

If one or two KSFs are common to most, even all, scenarios, they could become target capabilities on which to set your sights.

You're drawing a picture of the ideal player in your marketplace over the next few years. In the next tool, you'll judge to what extent you should aim to acquire the capabilities of the ideal player.

When to use it

Always, though the brainstorming is optional.

When to be wary

Be careful to keep your feet on the ground. Brainstorming workshops need firm direction, or venturing into the realms of fantasy may prove too tempting. The scenarios must be plausible. There is no point in considering the KSFs needed for a scenario which has a miniscule chance of happening – although you may be wise to think about how your firm would survive in a 'black swan' event (see Tool 87).

39

Identifying the capability gap

The tool

How close to perfection should you aim?

In the previous tool you envisioned the ideal player in your marketplace in three to five years' time. You identified the capabilities needed for competing successfully in the future.

This tool identifies the gap between your firm's capabilities now and those to which you aspire. It asks you to reconsider where you aim to be. Are you sure you've set sufficiently challenging goals?

Should you be stretching your sights and making your plans more ambitious? Should you aim to become the ideal player in your type of service? Should you be 'going for goal'?

You then revisit your assessment of competitive position in Section 5 in the light of the scenarios you've developed and your newly reset sights. And you identify the shortfall between your current capabilities and those to which you aspire.

This is the capability gap. Later you'll select a strategy on how to bridge this gap (Section 7).

How to use it

There are three steps in targeting the capability gap:

- Stretching your sights
- Aiming towards the ideal player
- Identifying the capability gap.

Stretch your sights

Where do you want your business to be in five years' time? What vision of your firm did you create in Section 2? Do you envision doing more or less what you are doing today, serving more or less the same customers, but better?

That's fine. If, however, your firm has greater ambitions, you may want to raise those sights. How about raising the bar on your firm's aspirations? How about raising the return on capital?

How close to the ideal player should you aim to become in your product/market segments of choice?

Aim towards the ideal player

In Tool 29 you identified your firm's strengths and weaknesses and rated them against the key success factors ('KSFs') required to compete in each of your main business segments. You found that there was a gap between your firm's overall rating and that of the ideal player, who realistically would have gained a rating of between 4 and 5 (out of 5) against each KSF.

In the last chapter you envisioned scenarios where new KSFs may be required or existing KSFs gain in prominence. These could further widen the KSF gap – if you were to sit still.

Where do you want to be in tomorrow's marketplace? Do you want to become a good player in tomorrow's marketplace? A strong player?

Or do you want to *lead* in tomorrow's marketplace?

Do you want to get as far as you can towards becoming the Ideal Player of Tomorrow? Do you want to go for goal? – see a chart I developed recently for a client in Figure 39.1.

Figure 39.1 Going for goal

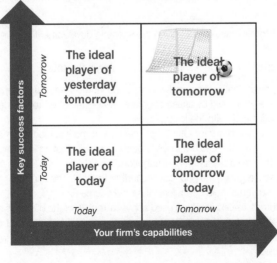

If so, remember that the goalposts may well have shifted by the time you're ready to shoot. Time moves on, and the ideal player in five years' time will have a different mix of capabilities to the equivalent today. Perhaps only with slight differences in nuance, perhaps radically different.

The *Going for Goal* chart highlights three important points:

1 It's fine being the *Ideal Player of Today*, but today only lasts one day.

2 If your firm doesn't develop the extra capabilities required to meet the customer needs of tomorrow, you'll become the *Ideal Player of Yesterday Tomorrow*.

3 There's little point in developing extra capabilities today unless customers need them, or you'll become the *Ideal Player of Tomorrow Today*.

Once you've raised your sights, perhaps to the very top, you need to specify the capability gap and, in the next section, plan how you are going to bridge it.

Identify the capability gap

In Tool 29 you set out your ratings against the KSFs you assessed in Tool 24 for each of your main business segments. These KSFs were in turn largely based on customer needs you identified and ranked in Tool 23.

That assessment was not a purely static exercise. You were encouraged to take a dynamic perspective. You looked not just at customer needs and KSFs today, but how they might change over the next few years. You also considered how your firm might improve its standing against one or more of the KSFs over the next few years. *And* you gave some thought as to how your competitors might enhance *their* standing in the future.

You need to revisit those charts. You should check for any changes in customer needs, KSFs, your firm's competitive position, or that of a competitor, as a result of changes in:

● the external marketplace, given the scenario development you undertook in Tool 38

● your aims, given the resetting of your sights in this tool.

You can now identify the capability gap. You've revisited your competitive position in each of your main business segments and established to what extent there is a gap in each KSF with the ideal player.

You now target that gap. Often that means just the insertion of an active verb, such as 'improve'. There is a capability gap in your distribution in a segment – targeting that gap means improving distribution.

Sometimes targeting the gap requires further thought. The capability gap may be too broad and you should consider exiting the segment.

Let's return to the example we used above in Tool 36 of the business operating in four main segments and contemplating entry to another. As a result of profiling the ideal player in Tool 38 and raising sights as above, you may now target the capability gap as follows:

● Improving margin in segment A

● Withdrawing in segment B, recognising an unbridgeable gap

- Improving distribution in segment C
- Improving product speed to market in segment D
- Entering segment E
- Lowering production costs across all segments
- Improving enterprise resource management ('ERM') systems across the business.

The resultant impact of your targeting the capability gap could be as shown in Figure 39.2. The competitive position of each segment, especially E, should be improved, other than B, which will be exited. The overall strategic position of this business will be greatly improved.

Figure 39.2 Strategic repositioning: an example

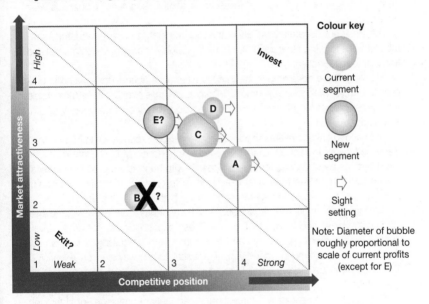

Note that targeting the capability gap does not at this stage specify the *means* of bridging it. That is left for the discussion on strategic options (Section 7).

Improving distribution in segment C is targeting a capability gap. Switching to a new distributor is a strategic option.

Lowering production costs across all segments is targeting a capability gap. Outsourcing or offshoring is a strategic option.

When to use it

Always, but take note of the tool's limitations (following).

When to be wary

This form of gap analysis has had its critics over the years, so much so that you should understand the critique and ensure that you build in such concerns in your own strategy development.

There are two shortcomings to the tool:

- Rectifying weaknesses may be less value enhancing than building on strengths.

- Capabilities are not as easily developed as resources.

The first point is very important. Your competitive position may be favourable in a segment, but investment to upgrade that position towards that of the ideal player may be costly – and unviable. The financial rate of return on the investment may be below the opportunity cost of investing in another segment or business-wide project.

This does not negate the validity of the tool. It merely emphasises that the strategic options to bridge that gap need to be thoroughly analysed, in commercial and financial terms (Section 7).

But the critique does emphasise that the alternative of undertaking smaller projects to bridge small gaps in segments where your firm is strong can be more viable than larger projects to transform competitive position in segments where your firm is weaker.

The second critique relates to the difference between resources and capabilities discussed earlier in Tool 30, Grant's Strengths/Importance Matrix. Grant illustrates the difference by observing that football teams with huge resources, say Chelsea, Manchester City or Real Madrid, are frequently outplayed by those with a fraction of those resources but with superior performance capabilities (on the day).

Success tends to lie with organisations with capabilities that best leverage their resources (Hamel and Prahalad, Tool 63). These capabilities are not easily developed. Creating them organically can be a lengthy and difficult process and may best be acquired through acquisition or alliance. Either way can be expensive. And success in developing capabilities, unlike in deploying resources, cannot be guaranteed.

Thus, in the example above, targeting the capability gap in segment D through improving product speed to market sounds easy enough, but in reality might be a lengthy, expensive, complex, management-intensive challenge.

Again, this critique does not negate the tool, but it stresses that gap analysis is but an intermediate tool in the process of developing a financially viable strategy.

Komatsu targets the cat

There is a popular misconception that the name Komatsu has a sinister meaning. Not at all. The company was named after the town whence it emerged and means, charmingly, 'small pine tree'.

But there could be little doubting the intentions of the banner that was displayed prominently at Komatsu's first warehouses in the US. The literal translation was 'encircle the cat', but became popularly known as 'kill the cat'. Unaware of or unconcerned with the strategic intent of their new adversary, a banner in the Caterpillar plant read: 'think safety'.

This remains a classic example of a company targeting the strategic gap. Sure, many others have done likewise over the years. Think of Tesco in groceries – a byword for cheap and cheerful product in my youth to a leader in quality, own-brand retailing by the 2000s. Or Samsung, a cheap but risky alternative to Japanese electronics goods in the 1990s, now a world leader in mobile phones.

But few have targeted the strategic gap quite so precisely and emotively as Komatsu.

Komatsu's origins were as a producer of military equipment but, in the post-Second World War reconstruction boom, it turned its hand to non-military bulldozers, soon becoming the market leader in Japan. Like its fellow Japanese producers of motorcycles and automobiles, its ambitions soon extended across the Pacific.

Komatsu realised that post-war Japanese products were regarded in the West as being of poor quality, durability and reliability. Phase I was therefore to improve quality of production so that every Komatsu bulldozer shipped to the US would prove as reliable as a Caterpillar. The products would continue to be priced at a discount, but over time the impression of cheap but poor quality would shift to no less than same quality, competitively priced.

Phase II, perceived as many years down the line, would be to narrow the gap in product development – bring product to market faster and compete with Caterpillar on innovation as well as quality.

By the mid-1980s Komatsu had captured 15 per cent of the US market and acquired Dresser to add manufacturing to distribution in Caterpillar's backyard. Caterpillar fought back, through a total-quality-control programme, cost reduction and further strengthening of its dealer network, and regained some lost share.

But Komatsu had targeted the strategic gap and bridged it. It became, and has remained, the second largest manufacturer of construction equipment in the world. The cat lost a couple of lives but remains market leader.

40 The strategic condition matrix (Arthur D. Little)

The tool

'Age is a very high price to pay for maturity', lamented Tom Stoppard. How mature is your business?

The Strategic Condition Matrix was developed by my alma mater, management and technology consultants Arthur D. Little, in the late 1970s. It examines competitive position from the perspective of industry maturity. It remains an insightful tool.

How to use it

The x-axis is competitive position, the same as for the Attractiveness/Advantage Matrix. However, the y-axis addresses not market attractiveness, which is a composite concept, but the one specific aspect of attractiveness: industry maturity.

Industry maturity is categorised in four stages (see Figure 40.1):

- *Embryonic* – with fast market growth, little competition, new technology, high investment and high prices
- *Growth* – with accelerated growth and few competitors
- *Mature* – with slowed growth, stable market share and many competitors
- *Ageing* – with declining market growth, volatile market share and some competitors consolidating or exiting.

Having decided on the industry maturity of each of your product/market segments, you can now plot each segment on the Strategic Condition Matrix – from which you may draw these conclusions:

- If you are well placed in an embryonic or growth segment, invest.
- If you are poorly placed in an embryonic or growth segment, either invest heavily to gain at least competitive parity or exit.

Figure 40.1 Industry maturity

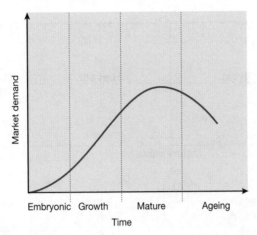

Source: Adapted from Arthur D. Little (www.adl.com)

- If you are well placed in a mature or ageing industry, reinvest selectively to maintain position and harvest.
- If you are poorly placed in a mature or ageing industry, exit – either through divestment or closure.

Figure 40.2 continues the example used earlier in Tools 36 and 39. In this case, you should consider:

- Harvesting in A
- Further differentiating in C
- Preparing for exit in B
- Investing in D
- Entering E with further differentiation.

You should strive to have a balanced position in the Strategic Condition Matrix. Not too many segments in the mature or ageing columns, not too many in the embryonic or growth columns. You need a balance.

In the case of Figure 40.2, that is a reasonable balance – a combination of harvest, divest and invest opportunities.

Figure 40.2 The Strategic Condition Matrix: an example

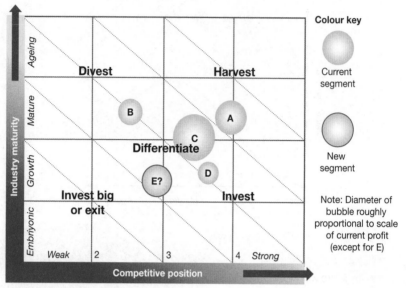

Source: Adapted from Arthur D. Little (www.adl.com)

When to use it

Use this tool when your segments seem to be at different stages of their product life cycles. It will add an extra perspective on the Attractiveness/Advantage Matrix.

When to be wary

This tool is more frequently used in corporate than business strategy. Industry maturity on the y-axis is perceived as a concept more related to a business than a product/market segment.

But the same argument can apply to the Attractiveness/Advantage and Growth/Share Matrices. Yet those tools, and this one, offer useful insights at the level of business strategy.

You may be in the aluminium conversion business, which is generally mature, especially in supplies to the automobile and general engineering sectors. If your business is one of a dozen partially related businesses in a large company, it will be placed high up the y-axis in the Strategic Condition Matrix – mature, bordering on ageing. That in itself will be a useful insight for corporate strategy.

But within your business there will be product/market segments that are mature and some that are in the growth stage. Your widgets to the textile machinery sector may be ageing, but those to a defence sub-sector may be embryonic. Again, that is a useful distinction. The tool can be deployed as validly at the level of business as corporate strategy.

The 7S framework (McKinsey)

41

The tool

'Always aim at complete harmony of thought and word and deed', advised Mahatma Gandhi, not known as a McKinsey consultant, but, who knows, perhaps a source of spiritual inspiration.

McKinsey's 7S Framework proposes that an organisation should have seven different elements working together in harmony to be successful.

It is primarily a change-management or strategy-implementation tool, but it can be used also in performance improvement. In implementation, it highlights the fact that strategy development is just one of many elements needed for success. They specify six others – structure, systems, skills, staff, style and shared values.

In gap analysis, as in performance improvement, it is a useful reminder that you may need to look beyond the evident gap in capabilities between those of your business and the ideal player. Might there also be a gap in organisational structure in your business? Would the ideal player have a different balance of staff? Are your shared values consistent with a winning business?

How to use it

The 7S Framework is in essence a set of three 'hard' elements and four 'soft' (see Figure 41.1), thus:

1 Hard elements
   - Strategy – as being developed in this book
   - Structure – who reports to whom in which organisational structure
   - Systems – IT and other systems and processes.
2 Soft elements
   - Skills – the effective competence of the personnel and their processes
   - Staff – the educational, training and experience background of employees

- Style – the leadership style and collaborative culture
- Shared values (or 'subordinate goals') – what the organisation stands for, its *raison d'être*.

Figure 41.1 The 7S Framework

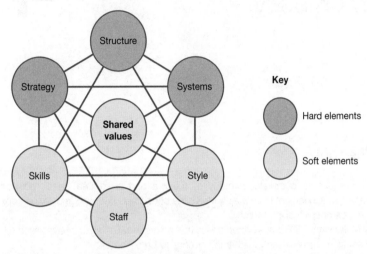

Source: Adapted from the McKinsey 7S Framework by Robert H. Waterman, Jr. and Tom Peters

The model sees the shared values element as the fulcrum of the seven elements. Strategy, staff, style *et al*. are all influenced and ultimately determined by the organisation's shared values.

Key questions to be asked include, for example:

- *Strategy* – how does your strategy differ from that of the ideal player?
- *Structure* – will your organisational structure support the implementation of your strategy in the way that the ideal player's structure would?
- *Systems* – are your systems aligned with your strategy or would the ideal player's systems improve the chances of implementing your strategy?
- *Skills* – do you have the right skills to implement your strategy and to what extent do these differ from those of the ideal player?
- *Staff* – do you have the right calibre of staff to implement your strategy and what calibre of staff would the ideal player have?
- *Style* – is your leadership style compatible with strategy implementation in the way it would be with the ideal player?
- *Shared values* – are your firm's values consistent with implementing the strategy in the way it would be with the ideal player?
- *All* – to what extent do the answers to these questions depend on each other – how are they interrelated?

When to use it

When you need to ensure that you have taken all factors into account in identifying and targeting the strategy gap – both hard and soft elements.

When to be wary

The framework is useful for asking the right questions, less so for answering them. Strategies are easier to change than organisational culture, values and people.

42 The opportunity/ vulnerability matrix (Bain/L.E.K.)

The tool

Is one of your businesses performing well above the norm? Might it be vulnerable? Or is there one performing well below the norm? Can you revamp it?

The Opportunity/Vulnerability Matrix is a useful derivative of the BCG Growth/ Share Matrix, developed by Bain & Co and further by L.E.K. in the late 1980s.

Figure 42.1 The Opportunity/Vulnerability Matrix

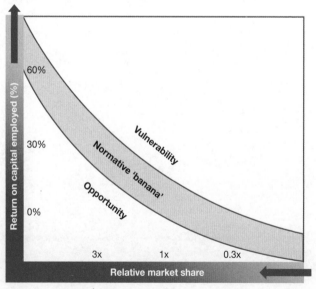

Source: Adapted from Richard Koch, *Financial Times Guide to Strategy*, FT Publishing, 2011

The basic premise of the BCG matrix was that the higher the relative market share ('RMS') of a business (or segment), the higher is its profitability. Indeed RMS was taken as a measurable, proxy indicator for profitability.

Studies carried out by Bain showed that RMS was indeed a reliable indicator, with 80 per cent of observations falling within the narrow, normative band shown in Figure 42.1, termed the 'banana'.

But what about performance in those businesses constituting the 20 per cent whose results fall outside the banana? What if a business has a high RMS but low profitability? Or vice versa?

The former have potential, the latter are vulnerable.

The former business is crying out for a winning strategy. Its results should be within the banana. Its managers should read this book! Almost certainly its strategy should be to:

- nudge up pricing to reflect the status and customer appreciation accorded by its high RMS, or

- drive down costs to improve profitability within the same pricing umbrella, or

- a bit of both.

If you were a private equity player, you would want to buy this business. It could be a steal.

The latter business is a cause for concern. It is making good profit, but unexpectedly. It does not seem to have a high enough RMS to justify such a return.

What is behind this return? Does the business have a clear differentiation advantage which boosts its profitability? If so, is it sustainable?

Or is industry pricing set at a high and unsustainable level, either through an industry leader keeping it artificially high or due to structural distortions in the market, for example government regulation? If so, what happens when industry competition returns to normality? This business will see profitability return to where it should belong in the banana.

It may be vulnerable. A private equity player would be tempted to sell this business pronto.

How to use it

Data permitting, plot your businesses on a chart as in Figure 42.1. Do the same for your competitors.

Are any of your businesses lying below the banana? That is good news – you have the opportunity to transform profitability there.

Are any lying above the banana? They may be vulnerable. Think about:

- investing in your differentiation advantage to make it more robust

- merging with another player to enhance RMS, enter a new range of normative profitability in the banana and reduce the potential drop in profitability should industry structure return to normality

- exit.

When to use it

Use it when you want to assess whether your businesses or segments are achieving results consistent with their industry standing. Can they be classified as having potential, being vulnerable or doing fine?

There is another use for this chart. If you find you have a business with a low RMS which is performing as expected, within the banana, is there scope for improving profitability by acquiring one or more players to raise profitability to within a higher norm in the banana?

This runs counter to the standard BCG matrix ethos. A business with low RMS is at best a question mark, at worst a dog. But could that business become less canine if you merged it with others to claw its way up the banana?

When to be wary

This tool is all about the data. It can be difficult enough to get return on capital employed ('ROCE') data for each of your businesses, but for product/market segments you may have to make some cavalier assumptions.

And as for data on the competition ...

Nevertheless, it can be worth the effort. Make some assumptions and see where they take you. Then do some sensitivity testing. Be careful with the results, remember where they came from, but they may prove illuminating.

Brainstorming

43

The tool

'Great minds discuss ideas; average minds discuss events; small minds discuss people', asserted Eleanor Roosevelt. Be great: brainstorm!

Brainstorming is a structured process for the generation of ideas. It can be done individually or in a group setting.

How to use it

Individual brainstorming is different strokes for different folks. I like to brainstorm while walking – preferably on a cliff top above the Cambrian Sea, with jagged rocks and swooping cormorants to one side and lush pastures and baaing sheep to the other. Others find inspiration in yoga or the flotation tank.

In the corporate setting, it works best if you escape from the premises. A country hotel setting, with brainstorming in the morning, group activities such as archery or drama improv in the early afternoon, followed by more brainstorming and wrap-up in the late afternoon.

The idea is to try to get people to think 'out of the box', using the imagination, stimulating the right side of the brain. Encourage plenty of use of visuals, whether through projectors, flip charts or Post-It notes (see Figure 43.1).

Alex F. Osborn, who popularised the concept in the 1950s, had four main rules for brainstorming:

- *Focus on quantity* – get as many ideas into the melting pot as possible.
- *Defer judgement* – any criticism of ideas should be put on hold while the ideas are being generated – all ideas can be dealt with later, but, for the time being, the focus must be on generating as many ideas as possible.
- *Welcome unusual ideas* – don't dampen people's creativity, encourage divergent, 'left of field' thinking.
- *Build on ideas* – combine or improve ideas as they come along.

Figure 43.1 Brainstorming output

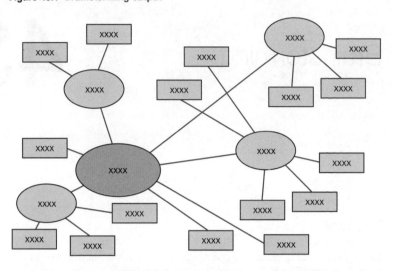

Only later on, whether in a group or individual setting, should the ideas be grouped, appraised and, for those most promising, evaluated.

When to use it

Use it to generate scenarios when you are profiling the ideal player. How could the market develop over the next five years? How tough could competition get? What could a competitor do, what are you afraid they might do? How would you respond?

When to be wary

Brainstorming is not a panacea. It is one tool to be tossed into the mix. Research into its efficacy is inconclusive. It is no substitute for quiet, solitary, individual, deep thought and analysis in the strategy development process.

Scenario planning

44

The tool

What's your best case scenario? And your worst?

Scenario planning is a structured process for envisioning the future of an industry and its players, technologies, markets, customer needs, key success factors and the like – and the implications of this evolution on the competitive environment for your firm and its competitive advantage.

It is an integrated part of the strategy planning process of some companies, most notably at Royal Dutch Shell since the 1960s.

Scenario planning is not just a set of predictions of the future. Its utility lies in the *clustering* of interrelated events – if this happens, then that is likely to happen, and that other too, and maybe even another event.

It can be done quantitatively or qualitatively. If the former, it begins to blend with sensitivity analysis and expected value tools (Section 9), with the main difference that scenario planning takes into account multiple, interrelated variables, in combinations of uncertainties, whereas sensitivity analysis typically focuses on one at a time.

If done qualitatively, your output will effectively tell a story. It will be a researched and well-thought-through narrative, but it will be at best 'factional'. It will be your story of how the things that matter to your business may play out.

How to use it

Here is a four-stage framework for scenario planning (see Figure 44.1):

- *Select and predict key value drivers* – identify the most likely and influential future value drivers, whether related to customer behaviour and market demand, to industry competitive intensity or to the competitiveness of key players, and predict (possibly through brainstorming – see Tool 43) how these may change over the next five years (or longer in some industries: e.g. oil and gas).

- *Plot linkages and clusters* – examine which of these future value drivers will be linked to others: for example, declining market demand and intensifying competition; this stage is typically carried out using Post-It notes on flip charts around the room.

- *Develop mini-scenarios, combine and name them* – use these groupings to develop mini-scenarios, fleshing them out and making them more coherent; then combine these dozen or so mini-scenarios into two, three, four major scenarios and assign a name to each.

- *Assess strategic implications* – think through what your firm would need to do to sustain competitive advantage under each of the scenarios; which issues, especially those which are potentially critical, need specifically to be addressed to make your strategy more robust?

Figure 44.1 Scenario planning

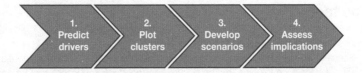

When to use it

It can play a key role in profiling the ideal player – see Tool 38 in this section.

When to be wary

Scenario planning has taken flak from some academics, owing to the scarcity of academic theory or research underpinning it. It is a tool developed in the field, largely by Shell.

But so too are many of the tools in this book and that in no way invalidates them. They work. If they are so obvious that academics have not got round to 'proving' them, that's tough.

A more serious criticism concerns the failure of typical scenario planning, or at least the plans and budgets that emerge from the process, to predict and mitigate events such as the 1973 oil price shock, 9/11 or the credit crunch of 2008. This will be revisited in Tool 87 on 'black swan' events.

[SECTION 7]

Bridging the gap: business strategy

Overview

Essential tools

45 Three generic strategies (Porter)

46 The experience curve (BCG)

47 Strategic repositioning and shaping profit growth options

48 Making the strategic investment decision

49 Blue ocean strategy (Kim and Mauborgne)

Useful tools

50 The tipping point (Gladwell)

51 Price elasticity of demand (Marshall)

52 PIMS (GE/SPI)

53 The 4Ps marketing mix (McCarthy)

54 Product quality and satisfaction (Kano)

55 The hierarchy of needs (Maslow)

56 The bottom of the pyramid (Prahalad and Leiberthal)

57 Business process redesign (Hammer and Champy)

58 Outsourcing

Overview

'Don't be afraid to take a big step. You can't cross a chasm in two short jumps', exhorted David Lloyd George. It is time for your big step.

You have identified and targeted the capability gap in your business (Section 6). If yours is a multi-business company, you did that for each business.

Now you need to bridge the strategic gap. This has three distinct but interrelated aspects:

- Bridging the capability gap in each business – using the tools of business strategy
- Optimising your business portfolio – using the portfolio planning tools of corporate strategy
- Leveraging your resources – using the resource-based tools of corporate strategy.

Together the tools will enable you to bridge the gap between where you are strategically today and where you aim to be in five years' time.

This section will address the tools of business strategy, the next those of corporate strategy.

In business strategy you will encounter five essential tools – Porter's three generic strategies, BCG's experience curve, strategic repositioning and shaping profit-growth options, making the strategic investment decision and Kim and Mauborgne's blue ocean strategy – plus a range of useful tools, from PIMS and the 4Ps to BPR and outsourcing.

45 Three generic strategies (Porter)

The tool

Clowns to the left, jokers to the right, Stealers Wheel were 'stuck in the middle...'. Not the place to be in business either, according to Michael Porter.

This is another area of business strategy where Porter's mastery of the synthesis of industry economics has been influential and long-lasting. As with his five forces in industry analysis (Section 4) and value chain (Section 5), his three generic strategies have been with us since the early 1980s and still form the base camp whence strategists ascend to the peak.

His three generic business-level strategies are:

- Cost leadership
- Differentiation
- Focus.

Any one of these strategies can give sustainable competitive advantage. Pursue two or all three of these strategies in the same business and you will in all probability end up 'stuck in the middle' – a recipe for long-term underperformance.

How to use it

What is the primary source of competitive advantage in your business? Is it cost? Or is it the distinctiveness of your product and/or service offering?

Think back (Section 5) to where you rated your business in its key product/market segments against their key success factors ('KSFs'). Did your business get higher ratings against the cost KSFs or the differentiation KSFs?

And go back one stage further. You identified and weighted KSFs in each key segment (Section 4). Did you give a higher weighting to differentiation factors than to cost factors? Or the other way round?

There is little to be gained in being a cost leader in a segment which is not price sensitive. Likewise in being a highly differentiated producer in a segment where customers are interested in price above all else.

If cost factors are most important in your business and you rated well or at least promisingly against them, then you should opt for a strategy of cost leadership.

If differentiating factors are more important and you rated well or at least promisingly against them, you should pursue a strategy of differentiation.

Either strategy can yield a sustainable competitive advantage. You supply a product that is at lower cost to competitors or you supply a product that is sufficiently differentiated from competitors that customers are prepared to pay a premium price for it – where the incremental price charged adequately covers the incremental costs of supplying the differentiated product.

For a ready example of a successful, low-cost strategy, think of easyJet or Ryanair, where relentless maximisation of load factor enables them to offer seats at scarcely credible prices compared with those that prevailed before they entered the scene, and still produce a profit. Or think of IKEA's stylish but highly price-competitive furniture.

A classic example of the differentiation strategy would be Apple. Never the cheapest, whether in PCs, laptops or mobile phones, but always stylistically distinctive and feature-intensive. Or Pret A Manger in fresh, high-quality fast food.

These two strategies were well recognised before Porter introduced his generic strategies. He identified a third, the focus strategy (see Figure 45.1). While acknowledging that a firm can typically prosper in its industry by following either a low-cost or differentiation strategy, one alternative is to not address the whole industry but narrow the scope and focus on a slice of it, a single segment.

Under these circumstances, a firm can achieve market leadership through focus and differentiation leading over time to scale and experience-driven low unit costs (see Tool 46) compared to less-focused players in that segment.

Figure 45.1 Three generic strategies

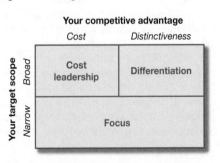

Source: Adapted from Michael E. Porter, *Competitive Strategy*, Free Press, 1980

The classic example of a successful focus strategy is Honda motorcycles, whose focus on product reliability over decades yielded the global scale to enable its differentiated, quality products to remain cost competitive.

When to use it

Always.

When to be wary

Any generic strategy is vulnerable to shifting customer needs and preferences. No strategy should be set in stone.

If you pursue a low-cost strategy, beware of a shift in customer needs putting a greater emphasis on quality or service, for which customers are prepared to pay a higher price. An example is the cinema industry. For years many chains followed a policy of shoving customers into their 'fleapits', keeping costs down to a minimum. Customers deserted in droves, opting for the comfort of their living rooms and the ease of the video recorder. Today some cinemas offer reclining seats and waiter service – the diametrically opposite concept to the fleapit, and a service many customers will pay for.

Likewise, if you pursue a strategy of differentiation, beware of changing customer preferences. Customers may be prepared to shift to a new entrant offering a product or service of markedly inferior quality to yours, but good enough and at a significant price discount. The classic example is that of low-cost airlines, originating in the US and spreading rapidly to the UK, Europe and Asia, and forcing the full-service national carriers to radically rethink their business model.

The canny business will spot the emergent trend and open a new business, often under a new brand, so as not to blur the image of the brand in the eyes of the customer. They will pursue one generic strategy in one business and a different one in another.

There is, however, no guarantee of success in the new business, given that it will operate in an entirely different culture – for example, the short-lived airline Go, launched by British Airways to address the booming low-cost market and eventually swallowed up by easyJet. Likewise, attempts by Ford Motor Company to move into more differentiated businesses via acquisition proved not to be value enhancing, and the Jaguar and Land Rover divisions were soon resold.

But it is especially inadvisable to mix strategies in one business, even if you are doing so in different segments. By definition, a strategic business unit operates in product/market segments that are interrelated – whether by offering the same or similar products or services or addressing the same or similar customer groups. One strategy in one segment coupled with another strategy in another segment may not only confuse the customer, but again land you 'stuck in the middle'.

The experience curve (BCG)

46

The tool

Albert Einstein said that 'the only source of knowledge is experience'. So too with cost competitiveness.

In the previous tool, a focus strategy was shown to combine elements of both the differentiation and low-cost strategies. This was largely due to the effects of the experience curve.

A 'learning curve' effect had long been recognised in industry before the Boston Consulting Group got in on the act. Managers understood that the more often a manufacturing task was performed, the less labour time it took to complete the next similar task. Initial quantification at a US airforce base in the 1920s suggested that each doubling of cumulative production of First World War aeroplanes led to a decrease in the total labour time to build one unit of 10–15 per cent.

Figure 46.1 The experience curve

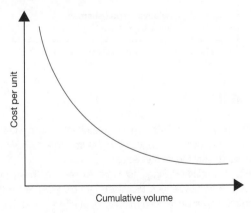

Source: Adapted from the Boston Consulting Group (www.bcg.com)

Forty years on, BCG transformed this thinking. In a series of studies on a broad range of industries, from beer and toilet paper to machinery and industrial components, they found that a similar relationship existed across the board. Their 'law of experience' found that 'the unit cost of value added to a standard product declines by a constant percentage (typically between 20 and 30 per cent) each time cumulative output doubles' – see Figure 46.1.

BCG ascribed to their law of experience a range of causes, in particular:

- *Labour efficiency* – workers learn the tricks of the trade, what works, what doesn't, what short-cuts to take – and managers too.

- *Process efficiency* – processes become optimised and more standardised.

- *Technology efficiency* – process automation displaces labour inputs.

BCG's research was broad and comprehensive, but not new. Where they broke new ground came in their interpretation of the research and its implications for strategy. If the player with the largest cumulative experience would have the lowest unit costs of production, then strategy should be aimed at maximising sales and production, hence market share, rather than maximising profit.

This was the theoretical underpinning of BCG's Growth/Share Matrix (see Tool 37). Thanks to the experience curve, relative market share should be a firm indicator of relative cost position. Indeed, BCG created a table setting out a typical relationship (see Figure 46.2).

Figure 46.2 Relative market share and the experience curve effect: an example

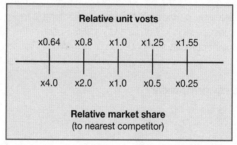

Source: Adapted from Bruce Henderson, *The Experience Curve Reviewed*, Boston Consulting Group, 1973 (reprint No 135)

How to use it

Building on your analysis in Tool 45, consider a strategic option whereby you invest heavily in market share gain in a segment where you already have a high market share – and are preferably the market leader.

By gaining further market share, to what extent will the experience curve effect enable you to further reduce unit costs? If this were to be translated into reduced pricing rather than increased margin, what effect would that have on your competitors?

Would they retaliate? Could they? Could your strategy force some weaker competitors to withdraw from the segment?

When to use it

Always consider it as a strategic option.

When to be wary

Bruce Henderson was aware of its main strategic limitation – namely, shared experience in the industry. Referring to Figure 46.2, he wrote: 'characteristically, a normal experience curve slope will produce cost ratios to the largest competitor like these; where the cost differential is less than this, it is usually because of shared experience … [or] by inadequate investment or poor management'.

Shared experience between competitors can come about a number of ways – through papers, seminars, conferences, supplier briefings, but perhaps most of all through consulting promiscuity and labour mobility. If you know that your competitor has developed a better production process, you would be wise to either engage the same consulting group that advised your competitor or recruit one or two of your competitor's former employees.

Also, even if your unit costs are lower because your relative market share is high, cost factors remain only part of the story. Differentiation factors may prove critical. If a competitor comes to market with a product that is technologically superior, your lower unit costs on your technologically inferior product will be of little comfort as customers switch to the new product.

47

Strategic repositioning and shaping profit growth options

The tool

What next, beyond the generic?

In the previous two tools, you set your generic strategy. Now you need to develop a series of profit improvement options consistent with that strategy to bridge the strategic gap (identified in Section 6).

In Tool 36 you applied the Attractiveness/Advantage Matrix to your business and concluded that you should invest in certain product/market segments, hold in others and perhaps exit one or two – and, conversely, perhaps enter one or two new ones.

In Tool 39 you targeted the capability gap that needs to be bridged for your firm to achieve your target level of competitiveness in selected segments.

You must now determine how to bridge the capability gap in each key segment to be invested in. You will also consider profit growth options in segments to be held – and even those to be exited. And you will consider the business as a whole and how it can be reshaped in line with your strategy to generate sustained profit growth.

Finally, you will differentiate between actions you can take now to increase profit in the short term (next 12 months) and those which will improve strategic position and grow profits in the long term.

Having drawn up a range of profit growth options in this tool, you will evaluate them in the next tool to decide which investment alternatives will yield the greatest return towards the goals and objectives of your firm.

How to use it

Start by taking one product/market segment at a time. Take those segments identified in Tool 36 as to be invested in, and then move on to those for holding, exit and entry. Finally look at profit growth options which apply to all segments.

Segments for investment

Take your largest segment, the one that gives the greatest contribution to overhead.

You have identified the capability gap in this segment in Tool 39. What are the options for bridging it?

The gap may be in new product speed to market. Bridging it may require stream-lined processes. You may need to invest in expert advisers.

The gap may be in product reliability. Bridging it may require investment in new equipment, whether in production or testing.

The gap may be in customer service. Bridging it may require investment in staff and training, even a cultural shift, achievable only through a controlled change-management programme.

In each of these examples, bridging the capability gap is a long-term process. That is often the case, but some profit growth options have faster results.

Indeed, you should be on the look-out for short-term profit growth options. There is nothing like a quick win or two following a strategy development process to gladden the boss's heart, justify the investment in time and energy, and build team morale.

The quick win could come from a new angle in marketing, in its broadest sense – product, promotion, place, price (see the 4Ps in Tool 53), revealed in the strategy development process.

One such angle could be to lower prices. But that would reduce profit, not grow it, you might think. Perhaps, but maybe not for long:

- Volumes sold should increase (depending on the price elasticity of demand for the product – see Tool 51), holding or growing revenue.

- Market share will be gained, enhancing your presence in the market and potentially stimulating further volume growth.

- Economies of scale may kick in, lowering your unit costs and restoring your operating margin (and even gross margin, if your greater volumes enable you to drive down the unit costs of bought-in materials, components and sub-assemblies).

These are some of the profit growth options, both short and long term, for bridging the capability gap in segments you will invest in. They are summarised in Figure 47.1.

Next, you consider the profit growth options for those segments which you have chosen for holding – probably not to invest in, but definitely not to withdraw from.

Figure 47.1 Strategic repositioning and profit growth options

Strategic repositioning by segment	Profit growth options to bridge strategic gap	
	Short-term	Long-term
Invest	• Marketing • Lower pricing to gain share?	Bridge capability gap, invest in: • Fixed and curret assets • Business processes • Staff and training
Hold	• Reduce variable cost • Tweak pricing?	• Reduce variable cost • Recompete? • Alliance?
Exit	• Improve financials?	• Withdraw (sell?)
New	• Prepare project plan	• Leverage strengths
Whole business	• Benchmark overhead • Marketing	• Reduce overhead • BPR, outsourcing, etc. • Resource-based investment

Segments for holding

Holding on in a segment does not mean doing nothing, taking no strategic action. You need to actively manage your segment position and preferably strengthen it.

In the long term there are three profit growth options you should consider:

1 *Reduce variable cost* – if you stand still on cost, you run the risk of a competitor under-cutting you over time; an ongoing programme of cost reduction would be wise, whether in purchasing or operational efficiency.

2 *Recompete* – change the rules of the game in some way, so that you effectively create a new segment out of the old; easier said than done, but it can be done – think of a specialist retailer like Pets at Home, which has stolen share from traditional pet shops, supermarkets and DIY chains through offering not just a vast range of pet supplies but a destination in itself, with its rabbit, guinea pig and tropical fish displays captivating customers young and old; or in manufacturing, look for inspiration to the iPhone, so much more than a mobile phone.

3 *Alliance* – you have a favourable competitive position in a segment which is moderately attractive; perhaps by allying with a competitor you could jointly have a stronger position in that segment and enable superior profit growth prospects for both parties – see Tool 60 on creating value from mergers, acquisitions and alliances.

In the short term there are other options for you to consider. Cost reduction is both a short- and long-term option, but you may also consider tweaking your pricing in the segment, whether up or down:

- Nudging pricing up may change customer perceptions and give the impression that you are a premium player, though again you should think carefully on the price elasticity of demand (Tool 51); there are many examples of this strategy, such as the plethora of 'premium' lager brands in the UK, in reality bog-standard, mass-market beers in their home countries of Belgium, Germany, France, Italy, Mexico, Singapore, China – the list is endless, with so many playing the same game.

- Nudging pricing down, again depending on price elasticity, may gain you some extra volume and share, but beware of competitive retaliation.

Segments for exit

Profit growth options in those segments you have chosen to exit are limited. In corporate, as distinct from business, strategy, exiting a business unit can generate value through a structured sale process, including preparing the business for sale ('dressing the bride') and improving the financials pre-sale. In business strategy your presence in the business segments you choose to exit may have no sale value.

But there may be elements of value in that segment that may find a buyer. There may be some physical assets to sell or even some intangibles such as use of the brand name in that segment.

Segments for entry

Previously you have identified new segments your firm should consider entering (Section 6). These should be segments where you can leverage your existing strengths.

The new product/market segment should preferably be synergistic with your existing business, having one or more of these characteristics:

- It is a new product (or service) related to your existing products and sold to the same customer group.

- It is the same product and sold to a related customer group.

- It is both a new product and to a new customer group. This is highly risky and would require a much tougher degree of substantiation – see the Ansoff matrix of Tool 32.

- It is a segment where key success factors, both in cost and differentiation, mirror the relative strengths of your business.

- It is one in which some of your direct competitors are prospering and so might you.

- It is one in which some players in other countries are prospering and there seems no reason why the same should not apply in your country.

In the short term, there is little you can do to improve profit, other than prepare a robust project plan for new segment entry and improve the odds on securing long-term profit growth.

All segments

Finally you need to consider profit growth options that apply across all segments in your business.

Long-term options may include:

- Reducing overhead costs, having benchmarked them in the short term (see Tool 34)
- Improving key business processes, perhaps through business process redesign (see Tool 57)
- Outsourcing business processes, perhaps offshoring, such as IT, technical support, customer services (see Tool 58)
- Investing in the core competences of your business, whether they be in R&D, operations or sales – see resource-based strategy (Section 8)
- Marketing – leveraging the name of your business across all segments, which is also a potential profit growth option in the short term.

Strategic alternatives

By now you may have a whole range of profit growth options. It may look like a laundry list.

You may choose to group them into two or three strategic alternatives. Each will represent a defined and coherent strategy for bridging your strategic gap. One alternative may reflect investment primarily in one segment, another may reflect investment spread across a combination of segments and business-wide processes.

They should be mutually exclusive – you can follow one or another, but not both (or all). You can follow just the one alternative.

This will make the next tool more manageable – evaluating the options available. Rather than evaluating 20 profit growth options, you will be evaluating two or three strategic alternatives.

When to use it

Always.

When to be wary

Take care with the drawing up of profit growth options. The list should not get out of control.

Each option should satisfy two fundamental criteria:

- It should be consistent with your strategy.
- It should seem like a sound investment in itself.

Grouping the options into strategic alternatives further helps manage the process.

Making the strategic investment decision

48

The tool

'I shall be telling this with a sigh / Somewhere ages and ages hence / Two roads diverged in a wood, and I / I took the one less traveled by / And that has made all the difference', wrote Robert Frost.

In the previous tool you derived two or three strategic alternatives aimed at bridging the strategic gap. They were mutually exclusive, so you can only take one road. How do you evaluate the roads and select which one to travel on?

The answer is straightforward in theory. Assuming your main goal is to maximise shareholder value, and subject to goals relating to other stakeholder interests (see Section 2), you should choose the alternative that gives you *the highest return for the lowest risk*.

How you get there is not so straightforward. There is a spectrum of methods, ranging from the dangerously complex – real option valuation – to the dangerously simple – impact on earnings.

For the purposes of this book we shall take two methods somewhere in the middle of the spectrum – the rather complex discounted cash flow ('DCF') analysis and the rather simple payback method.

But, before starting, there are three fundamentals in making the strategic investment decision that need to be borne in mind whatever the method chosen.

The first is the nature of making an investment. It usually means a cash outlay today that should give you cash, or other benefits, flowing in for years to come. Investment tends to be a one-time, upfront cost, leading to recurring annual benefits.

Second is 'sunken costs'. When you're comparing the viability of strategic alternatives, any cash you've already spent has to be forgotten about. It's history. You must only take into account what *extra* cash you need to spend on an alternative from this day forward to generate the benefits expected.

Finally cash today and cash tomorrow are different things. Cash invested today in a strategic alternative has a higher value than cash generated in future years, not just because of inflation, but because of the 'opportunity cost of capital' – cash today could have been invested elsewhere to generate a real return until tomorrow.

How to use DCF analysis

The use of DCF analysis for strategic investment decision-making is one aspect of what is known as *value-based management*. Proponents believe it introduces quantification and rigour into the strategy development process, taking the process beyond the bubble charts and into the real, measurable world of financial performance.

Opponents assert such quantification is based on too many dubious, ultimately compounding assumptions, especially down the line on product development, competitive response, pricing, etc. Strategy should be about direction of travel, not the nitty gritty of the itinerary.

I am a proponent. Generic strategy can indeed be evident from the bubble charts. But when it comes to the selection of two seemingly viable strategic alternatives, quantification helps eradicate woolly thinking. And it lends itself perfectly to risk analysis (Section 9).

In DCF analysis you translate each strategic alternative into forecast cash flows, via revenue and cost projections, discount the cash flows back to Year 0 and add them up to get the net present value ('NPV'). The alternative with the highest NPV should be the most promising.

Sounds simple enough? It is anything but. I have seen it done poorly so many times, leading to wildly off-the-mark valuations and wayward investment decisions. Done correctly though, it works well.

If you are to attempt it, seek guidance from a dedicated manual such as *Valuation: Measuring and Managing the Value of Companies* by McKinsey & Co. Inc.

In the meantime, here are some common user concerns, along with some tips, many of them learnt the hard way along the road:

- *How can five-, even ten-year forecasts be remotely realistic?* They can't, but they can be rational, consistent and coherent; and they can be used to highlight the *differences* between the strategic alternatives in terms of impact.

- *How can some aspects of the strategy be converted into cash flows, when they are so general, like improving quality or customer service?* Make realistic assumptions as to their impact on sales or costs and always consider the two basic scenarios, *with* and *without*; what would revenues and costs look like with the alternative, what without? the difference yields the NPV impact of the alternative.

- *How can distant revenue forecasts be credible?* They must be consistent with your market demand, competitive position and market share assumptions – see Tool 82, the Market Contextual Plan Review.

- *How can distant segment margin forecasts be credible?* They must be consistent with your competitive intensity and performance improvement assumptions – see the same tool.

- *How can overall operating margin forecasts be credible?* If yours are showing 40–50 per cent, they aren't! Assuming you have forecast sales volumes and operating costs sensibly, you may have made insufficient allowance for competitive intensification, possibly through new entrants, and declining unit pricing and margins.

- *How do I know what capex needs will be in, say, Year 8?* They should be consistent with your sales volume forecasts.

- *What to do after the end of the forecast period?* Use a conservative terminal value calculation; assume the final year's cash flow continues ad infinitum, but with no further growth, giving a terminal value equal to the final year's cash flow divided by the discount rate – then consider halving it for extra conservatism (who knows, a disruptive technology may have arrived?) and discount it back to Year 0; alternatively, assume flat cash flows to, say, Year 15 and zero thenceforth.

- *Which cash flow line do I discount?* You should use the free cash flow line: that is, operating cash flow (operating profit plus depreciation less change in working capital less capex) before interest and before corporation tax.

- *How do I go about discounting?* Apply a discount factor to each year's cash flows; in Year n you should discount by a factor of $1/(1+r)^n$, where r is the discount rate; cash flow in Year 0, the year of the investment, need not be discounted (theoretically cash should be assumed to flow midway through the year, thereby meriting a half year discount, but this can usually be ignored when comparing strategic alternatives).

- *What discount rate do I use?* Use the cost of equity (you are not trying to value the company, so there is no need to consider the cost of debt and derive a weighted average cost of capital); according to the capital asset pricing model, the cost of equity is equal to the risk-free return on capital (yield to maturity on long-term gilts) plus the market risk premium (the premium expected from investing in equities as a whole, historically around 4–5 per cent) times the Beta coefficient (the relative volatility of your sector, typically a value between 0.5, for relatively steady utilities, and 1.5, for relatively volatile capital goods producers).

- *What if one alternative seems riskier than the others: should I use a different discount rate?* Possibly, but better to use the same cost of equity, which is a measure of systematic (non-diversifiable) risk not specific risk; deal with the riskier alternative through the cash flow forecasts, using appropriate probabilities and expected values – see Tool 86.

- *What if I still don't feel comfortable with that discount rate?* You're not alone, no one ever does! Apply sensitivity testing in the range of +/– 2 per cent to see if the impact on NPV affects the relative ranking of the strategic alternatives and your strategic investment decision; if so, why?

If that all sounds a bit daunting, you could try the simpler payback method.

How to use the payback method

Work out the cost of the investment, say £I. Assess the annual benefits from the investment, namely the difference between the extra cash inflow (from revenues) and the extra cash outflow (from expenses) generated each year as a result of the investment. If the annual benefits are different each year, take their average over the first five years, £B/year. Divide B into I, and this gives you the 'payback', the number of years taken for the cash costs of the investment to be recouped.

If payback is *four years* or less, that could well be a sound investment. (That is equivalent to a 9 per cent/year rate of return over a five-year period, assuming – conservatively – no benefits beyond five years, due to obsolescence, competitive response, etc.) But don't jump on it. Work out the payback on the other strategic alternatives as well. They may have an even lower payback.

If you believe your investment is going to give you a longer-term advantage, and could last all of ten years, then an investment with a longer payback may still be beneficial. You might give serious consideration to an investment with a payback of six to seven years. It'll be riskier, of course, because all sorts of things could happen to your competitive position over time.

Next, work out the 'net benefits' of the strategic alternative, the total benefits over the five years less the investment cost. If the alternative has a longer-term horizon, with benefits taking a few years to kick in and only blossoming after five, six, seven years, you should opt for DCF analysis.

There are, however, other elements. The above has focused on one side of the story, the financial. What are the benefits of pursuing an alternative in terms of meeting your firm's non-financial goals? These may need to be factored into the evaluation.

Figure 48.1 The payback approach to evaluating strategic alternatives

	Unit	Strategic alternatives		
		A	B	C
Financial benefits Investment costs = I	£			
Average annual cash benefits over 5 years = B	£/Year			
Payback = I/B	Years			
Total cash benefits over 5 years = TB × 5	£			
Net benefits = TB – I	£			
Risk	L/M/H			
Non-financial benefits		• .... •	• .... •	• .... • ....
Non-financial dis-benefits		• .... •	• .... •	• .... • ....

Then there is risk. Each alternative will be more or less risky than the other. The alternative that promises the highest returns for the lowest investment outlay may be unacceptably risky. Another alternative that offers modest payback for a modest outlay may be virtually risk-free. How risky are your proposed alternatives?

It may be helpful for you to lay out the strategic alternatives in a table, along with their investment cost, annual benefits, payback, net benefits, non-financial benefits and risk, as shown in Figure 48.1.

The table will guide you on which of the three alternatives is the most financially beneficial. It should be the one with the highest net benefits and with an acceptable payback – subject to the three fundamental provisos above concerning the time value of money.

Note that the alternative with the fastest payback is not necessarily the best – net benefits may be too small, even though they are the most rapidly achieved. But if the alternative with the fastest payback is not mutually exclusive with the one that has the highest net benefits, perhaps you could do both?

The most financially beneficial alternative from the table, however, may be the riskiest. In this case you may choose to opt for an alternative with a lower return but commensurately lower risk.

When to use them

Use the payback approach only if you are uncomfortable with the complexities of DCF analysis.

When to be wary

The payback approach to evaluating investment alternatives is a short cut, a simple approach. Or should that read simplistic?

It has serious drawbacks. It doesn't take into account the time value of money, nor the possible lumpiness or risk of annual cash flows. And it ignores cash flows beyond the payback period, thereby favouring investments with short-term returns.

If your strategic investment decision is complex, and especially if benefits are late developing, do it properly through DCF analysis. If you don't feel comfortable with that, engage a specialist.

Finally, whichever approach you use, the most financially beneficial alternative may not be the most beneficial to your firm overall. It may have the most negative implications for your non-financial goals.

A chart may help. In the example of Figure 48.2, strategic alternative A has the highest NPV (or net benefits if using the payback approach). But it is also of medium to high risk and the least beneficial in meeting the non-financial goals of the company – perhaps in terms of maintaining employment or meeting environmental targets. Alternative C, which is less risky and more in keeping with the firm's non-financial goals, but promises lower financial benefit, may be the preferred option.

Figure 48.2 The strategic investment decision trade-off: an example

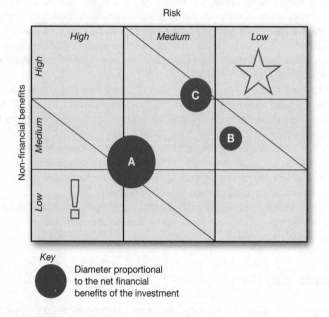

Key

Diameter proportional
to the net financial
benefits of the investment

The strategic investment decision is seldom clear cut. The financials are often hard to evaluate, and even then there may be a trade-off between financial return, risk and meeting non-financial goals.

The decision is yours.

Blue ocean strategy (Kim and Mauborgne)

49

The tool

What if Porter is wrong?

One of the criticisms long aimed at Michael Porter's Five Forces industry analysis (Tool 22) is that it is too confined, too narrow in focus. The delineation of industry boundaries for analysis of the five forces and the shaping of a competitive strategy within that industry may constrict the strategist so rigidly that the opportunity for genuine value innovation *beyond current industry boundaries* may be lost.

Two INSEAD academics, Chan Kim and Renee Mauborgne, argue that competing head-on in today's overcrowded industries results in nothing but a 'bloody red ocean of rivals fighting over a shrinking profit pool'. Using a study of 150 strategic moves over a 100-year period, they argue that tomorrow's winners will succeed not by battling in red oceans but by creating 'blue oceans of uncontested market space ripe for growth'.

In a red ocean you fight competitors with tooth and nail in an existing market space. In a blue ocean you swim jauntily in an uncontested market space – new demand is created and competitors become irrelevant.

Such strategic moves create genuine 'value innovation', or 'powerful leaps in value for both firm and buyers, rendering rivals obsolete'.

They quote examples such as Apple's iTunes and Cirque du Soleil. Apple created a new market space by teaming up with the music companies to offer legal online music downloading, thereby consigning pioneer Napster (and bane of the music companies) to history. Cirque du Soleil reinvented the circus industry by blending it with ballet to create a new market space.

They further argue that the conventional choice of generic strategy between differentiation and low cost is also sub-optimal. Such is, the traditional choice faced by competitors in a red ocean. Blue ocean strategy enables the firm to do both, offering a differentiated product to a new market space at a cost sufficiently low to deter further entrants.

The holy grail of blue ocean strategy is to create: Differentiated Product + Low Cost = Value Innovation.

They put forward six principles for creating and capturing blue oceans:

- Reconstruct market boundaries.
- Focus on the big picture.
- Reach beyond existing demand.
- Get the strategic sequence right.
- Overcome organisational hurdles.
- Build execution into strategy.

They have developed a framework supported by a range of tools to put these principles into effect – see www.blueocean.com. Two in particular will be elaborated on below.

How to use it

Their Pioneer-Migrator-Settler chart is a stimulating start point. Try plotting your portfolio of addressed product/market segments on a matrix as in Figure 49.1.

Settler segments are those where you are a me-too player, migrators are where your competitive position is strong and pioneers are where you offer distinctive value.

If your current portfolio consists mainly of settlers, you are playing in a red ocean with dim prospects for sustainable, profitable growth. In your planned portfolio you need to push into migratory or, best, pioneer segments.

Figure 49.1 The pioneer-migrator-settler matrix

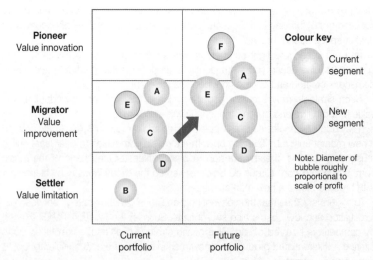

Source: Adapted from W. Chan Kim and Renee Mauborgne, *Blue Ocean Strategy: How to Create Uncontested Market Space and Make the Competition Irrelevant*, Harvard Business School Press, 2005

If your current portfolio consists of settlers and migrators, your growth prospects may be reasonable but you are at risk to losing out to a pioneer competitor.

In the example shown, the firm is reasonably placed, with mainly migratory segments and just a couple of settlers. For the future, the firm is planning to exit segment B, differentiate further and improve value in the other segments, and enter a new segment F, where they will be a pioneering value innovator.

The second of Kim and Mauborgne's tools highlighted here tackles what you should do about a sub-optimal Pioneer-Migrator-Settler portfolio. They set out how to go about searching for pioneer segments – see Figure 49.2.

Figure 49.2 Rethinking key success factors for value innovation

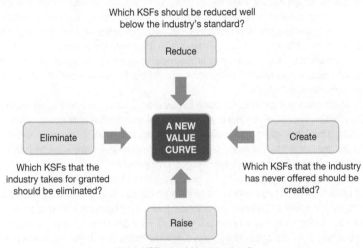

Source: Adapted from W. Chan Kim and Renee Mauborgne, *Blue Ocean Strategy: How to Create Uncontested Market Space and Make the Competition Irrelevant*, Harvard Business School Press, 2005

Kim and Mauborgne challenge you to rethink fundamentally the rules of the game in your industry. The key success factors you drew up in Tool 24 and revisited in your brainstorming sessions of Tool 38 need to be radically rethought, perhaps even, and this is their first port of call, eliminated:

- Which KSFs that the industry takes for granted should be *eliminated*?
- Which KSFs should be *reduced well below* the industry's standard?
- Which KSFs should be *raised well above* the industry's standard?
- Which KSFs that the industry has never offered should be *created*?

In short, how can these KSFs be revised so that a new value curve is created, one that breaks the trade-off between differentiation and low-cost strategies?

When to use it

When your 'red ocean' strategy seems set to lead to unexciting growth prospects.

When to be wary

Kim and Mauborgne's work has received much criticism, some of it ill-founded and perhaps not unrelated to the phenomenal success of their book. Some say that there is little that is original in their work, with the concept of seeking uncontested market space not much different from that, say, of Gary Hamel and C. K. Prahalad in *Competing for the Future* and their 'competing for industry foresight' (see Tool 63).

But similar criticism was levied at Michael Porter, whose genius was in synthesising the formerly ivory tower world of industry economics and repackaging it to make it more pertinent to the business world. In this case, Kim and Mauborgne have built a coherent structure and toolkit around how to look for and exploit uncontested market space – and made it more accessible to the business world than many of their predecessors' efforts.

Others criticise the model for being largely retrospective. Successful companies are, with the benefit of hindsight, shown to have deployed a blue ocean strategy, though when they did so they were unaware such a strategy existed. Kim and Mauborgne admit this: 'although blue ocean strategists have always existed, for the most part their strategies have been largely unconscious'.

Yet the critique is misplaced. It is like saying that Marshall's pioneering work on the price elasticity of demand in the nineteenth century was invalid because it was what market traders had been doing for centuries – chopping the price of an apple towards closing time, less so on a loaf of bread. Post-Marshall, business strategists were wiser. They adjusted prices, aware of likely elasticities. Likewise, in the post-Kim and Mauborgne era we can search for blue ocean strategies through changing the KSF rules of the game.

A more significant criticism concerns the usefulness of the model for the average business, whether small, medium or large. Nine times out of ten, strategy development will be about improving strategic position in red ocean markets. Blue ocean markets may exist, but they are riskier – often greatly riskier. For every Apple iTunes and Cirque du Soleil, there must be scores of attempted blue ocean strategies that have foundered.

As Ansoff highlighted in the 1960s (see Tool 32), new products to new markets carry a degree of risk orders of magnitude higher than new products to existing markets or existing products to new markets. iTunes was a new product to the new market, for Apple, of online downloading. It worked. Many such don't.

Risk, however, is no argument for debunking Kim and Mauborgne. It is an argument for embracing their blue ocean thinking and subjecting it to the rigours of risk analysis and sensitivity testing (see Section 9).

Could Facebook be undone the way it undid MySpace?

It is said that 'the early bird gets the worm, but the second mouse gets the cheese'. There were plenty of cheesey smiles on the faces of Facebook staff on IPO launch day, May 2012.

In all the hype, and a valuation in excess of $100 billion, one existential question seemed to have been sidelined: will someone come to do to Facebook what it did to MySpace?

The Facebook success story can be interpreted in two ways pertinent to this book. Facebook succeeded either because it implicitly followed a winning strategy or because there was no strategy, just a bunch of techies winging it in the 'whitespace' (see below).

In the dot-com boom time of the late 1990s, there was a common misconception that whoever gets there first wins – the so-called 'first mover advantage'.

This certainly did not apply in pre-Internet days. Excel did not always rule the personal computer spreadsheet world. When I was at business school in the early 1980s, the state-of-the-art software was Visicalc. That was overtaken by Lotus 1-2-3, then Lotus Symphony, which offered integration with word processing. Excel, and its integration within Office, eventually won because it was on a par functionally and could be packaged with the Microsoft operating system. But it was not the first.

Even in the world of cyberspace, amazon.com was not a first mover – that was bookstacks.com. Google.com came well after altavista.com, yahoo.com and others – it was started as an academic exercise, with a capability (ranking search items according to back links) so distinctive and powerful that the earlier movers were soon to melt away.

Jim Collins, whom we met in the tool Built to Last (Tool 14), was one of those who debunked the theory of first mover advantage with an article in *Forbes* magazine, 'Best Beats First', in August 2000 and later in his book *Good to Great: Why Some Companies Make the Leap ... and Others Don't* of 2001. First movers tend to win only if they can erect patent protection, a proprietary industry standard (like MS-DOS or Windows) or switching barriers – thus, we all stay with QWERTY keyboards, despite there being better options, because we don't want the hassle of learning to type all over again.

Otherwise, the odds are stacked against first movers. Followers learn from first mover mistakes. They take short cuts. They target and focus resources on sustainable competitive advantage. De Havilland launched jet-powered commercial aircraft, but its Comets suffered from metal fatigue and too many fell out of the sky. Boeing followed with an ultra-safe alternative design and went on to dominate the industry for three decades.

Facebook can be seen in this context. Like Boeing and Google, as in the words of Ralph Waldo Emerson, they set out to 'build a better mousetrap, and the world will beat a path to your door' – perhaps in four ways:

▶

- *Multi-generational* – Facebook was redirected from its initial student market to include those older, those much older and those younger – appealing now to the whole family, from primary schoolkid to granny.
- *Multi-purpose* – Facebook has targeted not just the leisure but the business user, overlapping with the target market of LinkedIn.
- *Multi-functional* – Facebook has moved way beyond messaging to profiling, user groups, music sharing, live meetings, social games, movies.
- *Multi-corporate* – Facebook has attracted businesses, public and other non-profit organisations to set up profiles and fan clubs.

In short, 'best beat first'. But how did Facebook get there? Did the founder and his colleagues set out to produce a multi-generational, multi-purpose, multi-functional and multi-corporate alternative to MySpace? Or did it evolve as it went along, reshaping itself dynamically in response to user feedback within an unplanned, semi-anarchic environment?

That is very much what Adam Hartung believes. Author of *Create Marketplace Disruption: How to Stay Ahead of the Competition*, he is an unabashed proponent of the 'whitespace' school of strategy – see Mintzberg and Maletz and Noria in Tool 69. And Facebook is a shining example: 'The brilliance of Mark Zuckerberg was his willingness to allow Facebook to go wherever the market wanted it. Farmville and other social games – why not? Different ways to find potential friends – go for it. The founders kept pushing the technology to do anything users wanted.'

That's whitespace management, says Hartung:

'No rules. Not really any plans. No forecasting markets. Or foretelling uses. No trying to be smarter than the users to determine what they shouldn't do. Not prejudging ideas so as to limit capability and focus the business toward a projected conclusion. To the contrary, it was about adding, adding, adding and doing whatever would allow the marketplace to flourish. Permission to do whatever it takes to keep growing. And resource it as best you can – without prejudice as to what might work well, or even best. Keep after all of it. What doesn't work stop resourcing, what does work do more.'

Meanwhile, MySpace had been acquired by News Corp and absorbed into the mega-corporation's planning process – with smart MBAs presenting smart PowerPoint decks on smart investment plans and ROIs to professional managers. Whether their plans were inadequate, inflexible or just too slow, MySpace's market share tumbled exponentially. News Corp sold it in 2005 for $35 million, having lost $545 million on the deal.

Facebook's multi-everything strategy was extraordinarily successful. The extent to which it evolved through constant piloting, in true Mintzberg or whitespace fashion, or whether new ideas were quickly tested and summarily planned pre-pilot, is difficult to deconstruct in such a rapidly growing environment.

Certainly the example suggests that the faster moving the environment, the more progress a firm is likely to make if it has a flat, entrepreneurial, relatively unplanned and rule-free, innovative, Mintzbergian environment. But that's assuming they make the right calls ...

The question remains: will someone do to Facebook what it did to MySpace?

Where will Google+ be in a couple of years' time? Could Yahoo or AOL make a comeback? Could someone new come in with something slightly different, something fresher? Something cooler? Could Facebook's original student base defect? The barriers to switching are minimal.

Should a usurper arrive, the tipping point (see Tool 50) could be sudden and catastrophic. The risks are high. To many, the IPO valuation of Facebook defied economic logic.

50 The tipping point (Gladwell)

The tool

'If at first you don't succeed, try, try again. Then quit. There's no point in being a damn fool about it', quipped W. C. Fields.

That, of course, is the conundrum, in business as in life: when to quit. When to realise it's a dead horse you're flogging.

Or when to carry on persevering, because with one more heave you may reach a tipping point – when all you have strived to achieve happens, and more. When your profit growth option (see Tool 47) becomes a winner.

Malcolm Gladwell's book of 2000, *The Tipping Point: How Little Things Can Make a Big Difference*, became an immediate best-seller because it seemed appropriate to so many of our situations – see Figure 50.1.

Figure 50.1 The tipping point

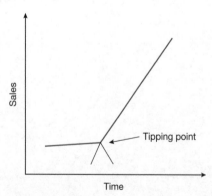

Source: Adapted from Malcolm Gladwell, *The Tipping Point: How Little Things Can Make a Big Difference*, Little Brown, 2000

It sought to explain how ideas, products or social norms, which had been around for a while, suddenly caught alight and spread like wildfire. He used a wide range of examples, from the TV series *Sesame Street* to the New York City crime rate (though his conclusions were later disputed convincingly by Steve Levitt in the book *Freakonomics*), the athletic shoe company Airwalk to syphilis in Baltimore, to show that 'social and commercial epidemics' depend on the 'Law of the Few', the involvement of 'people with a particular and rare set of social gifts':

- Connectors – those with exceptional social (or commercial) networks
- Mavens – those 'information brokers' who are prepared to share and promote what they know
- Salesmen – those whose communication skills are such that people *aspire* to agree with what they say.

How to use it

To reach tipping point, Gladwell recommends three courses of action:

- *Focus* – concentrate resources on a few key areas and on the Law of the Few.
- *Test* – do not just do what you think is right, test your intuition in the market.
- *Believe* – have a bedrock of belief that change is possible, that 'people can radically transform their behaviour or beliefs in the face of the right kind of impetus'.

Gladwell takes the example of Airwalk shoes as a classic case. Stimulated by his young son's frustrations with dull, white sports shoes which soon wore out at his Los Angeles skate park, founder George Yohn designed a set of skate shoes that were durable and flashy, yet economical. He focused on the skate market, tested them with top skaters and believed passionately in his tailor-made product. Within a few years he had a thriving niche business, turning over $10–15 million.

But he had ambitions to expand, to break out of his skate niche into other cool sports such as surfing, snowboarding, mountain biking. With the help of a dynamic advertising agency and an international network of youthful, innovative trendsetters, Airwalk launched wave after wave of inspired ranges, from James Bond villain to Tibetan monk themes. Within two years turnover had exploded tenfold. The epidemic had taken root, the market had tipped.

Airwalk later made serious strategic errors – easing off on the fad marketing, thereby denting the cool image, and failing to protect the marketing and distribution exclusiveness of its original skate business – but it remains one of the largest global sports shoe brands – though well behind leaders Nike and Adidas.

When to use it

Use it when you are approaching that awful dilemma in business – to persevere, or not to persevere, with a product or market. To invest further, or withdraw.

If you need inspiration, here are Gladwell's final words of the book: 'With the slightest push – in just the right place – (the world) can be tipped.'

When to be wary

That horse you are flogging may have reached a similar stage in life to that famed parrot in the Monty Python sketch ...

Price elasticity of demand (Marshall)

51

The tool

There is a popular saying on the Malay peninsula about harvesting time for their malodorous but amatory regional fruit: 'When the durians come down, the sarongs go up.' Likewise prices and volumes.

Some of the short-term profit growth options discussed in Tool 47 related to the adjustment of product pricing in key segments, whether up or down. In each case you were advised to take into account the price elasticity of demand in that segment before embarking on the adjustment.

The price elasticity of demand is a measure which addresses the relationship between change in price for the product or service in that market and the resultant quantities of the product purchased. A high price elasticity of demand means that volumes purchased will rise or fall greatly in relation to a change in price. A low price elasticity of demand means the opposite – that volumes will be little affected.

The measure was introduced by the economist, Alfred Marshall, in 1890 and has remained a most useful concept ever since. It is defined as the percentage change in quantity demanded divided by the percentage change in price.

The price elasticity of demand ('PED') is almost always negative – if it were positive, consumers would demand greater volumes the higher the price, which is the case only with certain luxury or premium products ('Veblen goods') or inferior products ('Giffen goods'). If PED is less than minus one, the product is said to be *price elastic*. If it is greater than minus one, it is *price inelastic* – see Figure 51.1.

If PED is zero, it is perfectly inelastic – in other words, there is no change in volumes demanded irrespective of price. If PED is infinitely negative, it is perfectly elastic – an increase in price would see demand drop to zero, only conceivable in a perfectly competitive market.

The prime determinant of price elasticity of demand is the availability of substitute products, ones which convey similar benefits to the consumer but where pricing is independently determined. If the price of pork goes up, but that of chicken does not, some consumers may well switch from pork to chicken. Pork is price elastic.

Figure 51.1 Price elasticity of demand

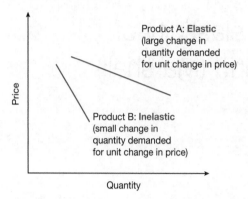

But chicken is a cheaper meat, and a staple for many low-income families. If the price of chicken goes up, but that of pork does not, some people will switch to pork, but many will stay with chicken. Chicken will be less price elastic than pork.

Other determinants of PED are:

- *Substitute pricing* – the pricing of products which are the closest substitutes to the product; as with chicken and pork above, or with many types of industrial components.

- *Timing* – the longer the consumer has to consider the purchase of substitute products or services, the more elastic the product; thus, package tour holidays are highly elastic, with the consumer typically having months to plan an alternative way of spending the two-week summer vacation; likewise, the longer the duration of the price rise, the more likely it is that consumers will opt for substitutes.

- *Necessity* – the greater the degree of necessity, the less elastic the product; thus men's visits to the barber are price inelastic, while ladies' visits to the stylist less so; at the extreme, most luxuries, such as visits to the opera or concert hall, are highly price elastic.

- *Importance* – the higher the proportion of the consumer's income spent on the product, the more elastic it typically is; at one extreme, motor cars are price elastic, with yachts even more so; at the other extreme, nails and screws are price inelastic.

- *Brands or fads* – the higher the degree of emotional attachment to the product, or the higher the lifestyle component of the product, the less elastic the product; thus, for example, the pricing of the Hollister brand of youth clothing in the early 2010s.

How to use it

In appraising opportunities for short-term profit growth through price adjustment, bear in mind the price elasticity of demand for that product or service.

If you are planning to lower prices to gain market share, think how reasonable are your share gain assumptions. What are the implied assumptions on the price elasticity of demand in that segment? Do those assumptions ring true?

If you are planning to raise prices, whether to milk cash flow from that segment or to give consumers an impression of a premium product, what reduction in volumes sold have you budgeted for? What are the implied assumptions on the price elasticity of demand in that segment? Do those assumptions ring true?

Gauge your assumptions against the benchmarks in Figure 51.2.

Figure 51.2 Typical price elasticities of demand

PED range	Type	Examples
< –1.5	Highly elastic	Spirits, sports cars, long-haul leisure tours
< –1.0, but > –1.5	Elastic	Wine, theatre tickets, saloon cars
< –0.5, but > –1.0	Inelastic	Cinema visits, soft drinks, low-cost air tickets
< 0, but > –0.5	Highly inelastic	Petrol, beer, bread
> 0	Giffen good Veblen good	Kerosene, potato, moonshine Champagne

If your price/volume assumptions do not seem in accord with the known elasticities of similar products or services, you may need to revisit them.

When to use it

Use it whenever you are taking a major initiative to adjust your pricing against competitors, whether up or down.

When to be wary

If your firm produces high-tech widgets for specialised capital goods manufacturing equipment, or any other such niche product or service, you won't find any estimates of PED on the Web for your product. You will need to use common sense and judgement. Look at products as similar as possible and Google them along with the phrase 'price elasticity of demand'. You never know, someone somewhere may have done some research on it.

For example, if you want to know the PED for the civil aircraft industry, you can find a document from 1994 on the Web by the US National Bureau for Economic Research, which reveals that the PED is around −1.5. The value of PED in your industry may likewise reside somewhere on the Web.

PIMS (GE/SPI)   52

The tool

What financial impact can you expect from your profit improvement options?

If your firm gains market share of 10 per cent, what impact *should* that have on your return on investment (ROI)? If the market grows by 10 per cent, what impact *should* that have? And what about if your employees raise productivity by 10 per cent? And how about the impact of the above on return on sales (ROS)?

All these questions and many, many more can be answered by the PIMS database – or Profit Impact of Market Strategy. This was set up by General Electric in the mid-1960s to measure internal performance, later extended to other companies, developed by Harvard Business School and shifted to the Strategic Planning Institute, a non-profit institution which was set up to operate it.

It now represents the 'real world business performance experiences of more than 3000 businesses representing 16,000+ years of data'. Subscribers range from Alcoa to Sandoz, Bertelsmann to TRW, Campbell Soup to Xerox.

The PIMS database is

'a collection of statistically documented experiences drawn from thousands of businesses, designed to help understand what kinds of strategies (e.g. quality, pricing, vertical integration, innovation, advertising) work best in what kinds of business environments. The data constitute a key resource for management tasks as evaluating business performance, analyzing new business opportunities, evaluating and reality testing new strategies, and screening business portfolios.'

It has ambitious aims for users. It

'helps managers understand and react to their business environment by assisting them in developing and testing strategies against various strategic and financial measures. It allows for the identification of those critical strategic factors that enable a business to achieve an improved sustainable position.

Those businesses that position themselves to win the strategy game through a sustainable advantage also win the performance game.'

How to use it

Subscribe and follow the PIMS process:

1 Define the business and identify key issues, choosing between these reports:

- *Return on Investment Report*. What level of profitability is 'expected' for comparable businesses (see Figure 52.1)?
- *Market Share Change Report*. What level of share gain/loss is 'expected' for comparable businesses?
- *Marketing Budget Report*. What level of marketing expenses is 'expected' for comparable businesses?
- *Market Attractiveness/Competitive Strength Report*. How attractive is the market/competitive position of comparable businesses?

2 Develop a quantitative profile of the business.

3 Enter values for sample variables and run the program to select sample of comparable PIMS businesses.

Figure 52.1 PIMS: Return on investment report

Name of variable	Your input data	PIMS sample mean	PIMS standard deviation
Return on investment			
Market share			
Market share rank			
Relative quality			
Capital intensity			
Market growth			
Number of immediate customers			
Accounting for 50% of sales			
Served market concentration			
Market differentiation			
Relative market share			
Relative direct cost			
Capacity utilisation			

Source: Adapted from www.pimsonline.com

4 Review results.
5 What outcome is 'expected' for PIMS businesses comparable to this business?
6 What is the potential of this business?

When to use it

Use it when you need to sense-test your strategy or financial forecasts against those achieved by peers in your and related industries.

When to be wary

Subscription costs make the service less suitable for small and medium-sized enterprises, who may also struggle with the required data provision. Most subscribers are large, multi-business, multi-national companies, with the output reflecting this. The sample is also more heavily weighted towards manufacturers than service providers.

In the words of Henry Mintzberg (see Tool 69), the PIMS service is more suitable as a technique for assessing the state of 'being there rather than getting there'.

53 The 4Ps marketing mix (McCarthy)

The tool

'It will work. I am a marketing genius', proclaimed Paris Hilton modestly. Sales spiel goes a long way in marketing.

If your chosen generic strategy is one of differentiation, you had better get the marketing right. And the best place to start, as it has been for over four decades, is with the 4Ps.

A product or service may be special, but does not sell itself. The product itself is but one of four key components in the marketing mix developed by E. Jerome McCarthy in the 1960s, the 4Ps (see Figure 53.1):

- Product
- Place (distribution)
- Price
- Promotion.

Marketing to McCarthy, and to generations of marketers since, is about putting the right product in the right place at the right price and with the right promotion. Then the product will sell.

But if you get one of the 4Ps wrong, your product may not sell. You may have the right product at the right price and with the right promotion, but if it is distributed in the wrong place, customers can't buy it.

Or you may have three Ps right, but the price too high, so customers won't buy it. Or the price may be too low – you'll sell plenty, but won't make much of a margin.

Or you may, like me with my initial venture into writing and self-publishing, have the right product (*Backing U!*, a book on career development and change using crossover tools of business analysis), at the right price (US $24.95), in the right place (Barnes & Noble, Amazon, etc.), but with rather pathetic promotion. It sold poorly.

All 4Ps must be firing to sell.

Figure 53.1 The 4Ps marketing mix

Source: Adapted from E. Jerome McCarthy, *Basic Marketing. A Managerial Approach*, R. D. Irwin, 1960

How to use it

Some of your profit growth options may have marketing implications. You may be planning to enter a new segment or strengthen your position in an existing segment. You may intend to adjust your pricing in a segment.

If so, you should touch base with each of the 4Ps. You should ask yourself some leading questions, for example:

1 *Product (or service)*

- Is your product delivering what the customer actually needs?
- What attributes could meet customer needs better, whether in size, features, colours, functionality?
- Can these attributes be developed cost-effectively?
- Should the product range be trimmed?
- Should it be rebranded, repackaged or sold in a package with other products or services?
- What can you learn from your competitors' best practice?

2 *Place*

- Is your product available at the places where most customers buy your kind of product?
- Is it there in sufficient quantities and delivered to meet customer needs?
- What are the inventory and transport cost implications of meeting customer needs?
- If your product is in the supermarkets, should it also be available at specialist stores? In catalogues? Online?

- What are the implications for your salesforce?
- What can you learn from your competitors' best practice?

3 *Price*

- What are the benefits to the customer from the product, hence what value does the customer perceive from the product?
- Is there scope for nudging up pricing to take a greater slice of customer benefits?
- How sensitive would the customer be to a change in pricing (see price elasticity of demand, Tool 51)?
- How would any price change affect your price positioning relative to your competitors?
- How would competitors respond?

4 *Promotion*

- How can you best get your message across to your target customers of the benefits of your product?
- How will you split your promotional budget between sales-time-efficient/ broad audience advertising, whether in the press, TV, radio, billboards, internet or social media, or in sales-time-intensive/narrow audience one-on-one selling, or in activities in between – see the promotion pyramid in Figure 53.2 (a construct I developed in the early 1990s to illustrate promotional options in management consulting services, but which can be adapted to many product and service sectors)?
- What can you learn from your competitors' best practice?

Figure 53.2 The promotion pyramid: management consulting, an example

Breadth of audience

Ask yourself these and other questions about your profit growth options. Will you be deploying an optimal marketing mix in each option?

Will the customer receive the right product in the right place at the right price – and will enough customers be aware of the product through promotion?

When to use it

Use it for thinking through the marketing implications of a profit growth option.

When to be wary

There have been several variants and developments on the 4Ps over the years. Some critics saw McCarthy's approach as being product and producer led, a reflection of business strategy of a bygone age. In the age of market-driven organisations (see Tool 72), Robert F. Lauterborn *et al.* in 1993 argued for a more customer-focused categorisation.

They proposed a 4Cs approach:

- *Consumer* – viewing *product* as something that meets consumer needs
- *Cost* – viewing *price* as the total cost of ownership to the consumer, including ongoing maintenance as well as purchase cost
- *Communication* – essentially *promotion*
- *Convenience* – essentially *place*, but with the emphasis on online presence, with its greater convenience to the consumer.

Others perceive the 4Ps as being more relevant to the marketing of product, rather than service. The Chartered Institute of Marketing propošes 7Ps, having usefully added these three for the marketing of services:

- *People* – customer-facing staff must be in sufficient numbers, of the right quality and with the right training to do full justice to the service offering, including those in after-sales support.
- *Process* – the process of delivering the service and the behaviour of the service deliverers are crucial, including in such areas as waiting times and communication of information.
- *Physical evidence* – from the appropriateness of the firm's premises to the service offered to testimonials from satisfied customers.

Other extensions to the Ps have included these from Brian Tracy:

- *Packaging* – the dressing-up of the product or service, as exemplified by the blue suits and white shirts of the IBM salesmen of yesteryear
- *Positioning* – how you reside in the hearts and minds of your customers.

Proponents of the 4Ps approach might counter that most of these extensions are sub-sets of the original four. But whether 4, 7 or 9Ps, or indeed 4Cs, the tool is evergreen in its discipline of dissecting the marketing mix.

54

Product quality and satisfaction (Kano)

The tool

Does your product excite your customers?

Noriaki Kano's model of product development and customer satisfaction develops this theme extensively. It is a most useful tool if you are pursuing a strategy of differentiation.

'Product' is one of the 4Ps in the marketing mix. In some of your profit growth options, you will address whether your product delivers what the customer needs and whether characteristics of your product can be developed cost-effectively to better meet those customer needs.

Kano classifies product attributes into five categories:

- *Attractive* – those which provide satisfaction to the consumer when present, but do not create dissatisfaction when absent – also translated and known as *exciters*

- *One-dimensional* – those which are inessential but provide satisfaction to the consumer when present, and create dissatisfaction when absent – also known as performance attributes or *satisfiers*

- *Must-be* – those which are taken for granted when present and create dissatisfaction when absent – also known as *threshold* attributes

- *Indifferent* – those which create neither satisfaction nor dissatisfaction when present, likewise when absent

- *Reverse* – those which create dissatisfaction when present – also known as *dissatisfiers*.

The relationship between product quality and customer satisfaction, along with the five categories, can best be portrayed diagrammatically – see Figure 54.1.

Figure 54.1 Product quality and customer satisfaction

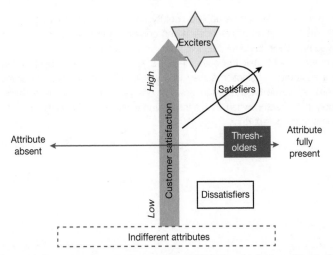

Source: Adapted from N. Kano, N. Seraku, N. Takahashi and S. Tsuji, 'Attractive Quality and Must-be Quality', *Hinshitsu: The Journal of the Japanese Society for Quality Control*, April 1984

How to use it

Identify those attributes of a key product that are to your customer's benefit and place each attribute into one of Kano's five categories.

Rate your product's performance against each of the attributes. This product is sold in one of your key product/market segments and represents one of your profit growth options, so it must surely meet adequately all the threshold attributes.

But how does it rate against the performance attributes, the satisfiers, those in the top-right quadrant of the chart, yielding high levels of customer satisfaction when present?

And does your product display the attractive attributes, those giving greatest satisfaction, the exciters? If not, why not? This is a target segment.

To what extent can you boost customer satisfaction by eliminating indifferent attributes or cutting back on performance attributes in order to focus on exciters?

What are the cost implications of developing exciters? Will you be able to adjust pricing? If not, will you still make a healthy margin?

When to use it

Use it when a profit growth option involves product development.

When to be wary

Often Kano's model can be applied usefully via internal brainstorming – gathering your sales team in an offsite location and comparing the views of the assembled team on how their customers benefit from product attributes.

When in doubt, ask the customer. This kind of analysis is best undertaken after a customer satisfaction survey. You would not want to invest in developing one bell or whistle based on the views of one forceful, opinionated salesperson, possibly the director, when that attribute turns out to be important only to one customer-cum-golf-partner.

The hierarchy of needs (Maslow)

55

The tools

'Consumers are statistics. Customers are people', perceived US retailer Stanley Marcus.

The last couple of tools have looked at product attributes and the extent to which they satisfy and meet customer needs.

It may be useful to pause and think further about customers as people, with real human needs, the same as for you and me – not just their functional needs, but their social and psychological ones too.

A good starting point is often the work done by Abraham Maslow in the 1940s, where he set out a hierarchy of needs which rings true to this day (see Figure 55.1).

Figure 55.1 The hierarchy of needs

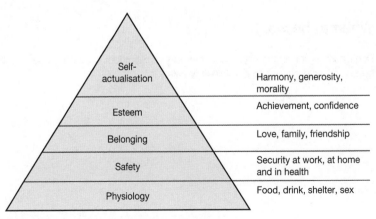

Source: Abraham H. Maslow, 'A Theory of Human Motivation', *Psychological Review* 50, 1943

The more basic the human need, the broader is it represented at the bottom of the pyramid. Thus, someone whose physiological or safety needs are not met is unlikely to be overly concerned with self-actualisation.

How to use it

At what level does your product meet your customer's needs? At the very least it should satisfy their needs of *physiology* (for example, food, shelter) or *safety* (for example, air transport, medicine, clothing or, in business-to-business sales, the customer's job security).

But can you also appeal to their needs for *belonging*? The canniest consumer brands attempt this. Think on the ubiquity of Levi jeans in the 1970s and 1980s, creating a sub-culture identified readily by trousers worn and creating a sense of global community.

Tailoring your product's attributes or marketing to appeal to a customer's need for belonging could magnify your sales greatly.

Even better, can you appeal to their needs for *esteem*? Luxury brands exploit this human failing mercilessly. It never ceases to amaze me that people pay more, much more, to display the name or logo of a top brand on their clothing when you would expect the brand owner to have to pay them for promoting the brand!

Appealing to esteem implies a price premium on your product. Think of the iPod or iPhone – good products, but not necessarily superior in attributes to their competition. Yet they are priced at a premium because they boost the consumer's esteem – and also the sense of belonging to an elite, techno-savvy, hip sub-culture.

When to use it

Use it for thinking about your product or price positioning.

When to be wary

Don't push up pricing until you are confident your product is meeting needs well beyond those pertaining to physiology or safety.

The bottom of the pyramid (Prahalad and Leiberthal)

56

The tool

Do you sell to, not just buy from, China or India?

In 2012 the editors of the *Harvard Business Review* combed their magazine archives to select the five charts that they believed had most changed the shape of strategy. Each chart 'so deftly captures an important strategic insight that it becomes an iconic part of management thinking and a tool that shows up in MBA classrooms and corporate boardrooms for years to come'. Four of their charts came as no surprise:

- The Five Forces (Porter) – see Tool 22
- The Growth/Share Matrix (BCG) – Tool 37
- The experience curve (BCG) – Tool 46
- Disruptive technologies (Christensen) – Tool 74.

The fifth, perhaps nudging aside contenders such as Porter's Value Chain (Tool 31), GE/McKinsey's Attractiveness/Advantage Matrix (Tool 36) or Kim and Mauborgne's Blue Ocean Strategy (Tool 49), was C. K. Prahalad and Kenneth Lieberthal's Bottom of the Pyramid (see Figure 56.1).

In 1998 this chart was a revelation. Today it is accepted wisdom. Managers now know well that the most attractive growth opportunities lie outside the OECD countries and in the emerging markets – in the noughties it was the BRIC countries (Brazil, Russia, India and China), in the tens it is these four again, plus diverse countries such as Poland, Turkey, Indonesia and Nigeria.

What Prahalad and Lieberthal highlighted was that there was a demographic of immense purchasing power – those emerging market consumers earning in the US$5–10,000 year range. They constituted an attractive market for OECD companies selling in particular food, housing or energy.

In his subsequent book, *The Fortune at the Bottom of the Pyramid*, Prahalad zeroes in on the vast untapped buying power of the world's 5 billion poor. Companies

Figure 56.1 The bottom of the pyramid

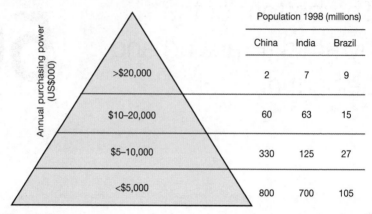

Annual purchasing power (US$000)	Population 1998 (millions)		
	China	India	Brazil
>$20,000	2	7	9
$10–20,000	60	63	15
$5–10,000	330	125	27
<$5,000	800	700	105

Source: Adapted from C. K. Prahalad and Kenneth Lieberthal, 'The End of Corporate Imperialism', *Harvard Business Review*, Jul–Aug 1998

which provide them with what they need 'create a win-win situation – not only do corporations tap into a vibrant market, but by treating the poor as consumers they are no longer treated with indignity; they become empowered customers'.

Companies which address this market create an 'economic infrastructure which creates real jobs for the poor and finally an end to the vicious cycle of poverty'.

How to use it

Perhaps you already outsource certain products, components or processes to India or China. Try a reverse perspective. Think on them as customers not just suppliers.

When to use it

Use it when you are looking for left-field growth opportunities.

Also don't forget the bottom of the pyramid in your own country. The likes of McDonald's have prospered and recruited greatly in the US in the post-financial crisis recession, Aldi has entered the market strongly and Mexican and Indian telecoms, heathcare and automotive companies are tailoring their offerings to address the bottom of the US pyramid.

When to be wary

Remember Ansoff (Tool 32) – think twice of selling new products or services to these markets, think more of selling existing ones or lower-cost variants.

Criticism of the hype has come from those who say that there is nothing new here. Capitalism has always been about the bourgeoisie becoming enriched by selling basic goods to the proletariat. In a famous poster of the early 1910s parodying the capitalist system, workers are shown underpinning a wedding-cake shaped societal structure. In the layers above, the middle class diners are saying 'we eat for you', the military 'we shoot at you', the clergy 'we fool you' and the aristocracy at the top of the cake 'we rule you'. Meanwhile the more numerous workers underneath toil to support the structure and humbly state 'we work for all, we feed all'.

Ashish Karamchandani, Mike Kubzansky and Nishant Lalwani found in 2011 that

'despite the extent of the markets and the volume of the hype, few multinational firms have built sizable businesses serving people who survive on just a few dollars a day. Companies sense that profits in this market are elusive, and the evidence backs them up. Apart from some successes in industries such as telecommunications, fast-moving consumer goods and pharmaceuticals, global corporations have been largely unable to reduce costs and prices enough to serve poor consumers.'

Their research showed that only a minority of corporations that have engaged with poor populations have created businesses with 100,000 or more customers in Africa or 1 million in India. Procter & Gamble, for example, invested more than $10 million in its PUR water purification powder for bottom-of-the-pyramid markets – but eventually had to shift the product to its philanthropic arm because take-up struggled to exceed 5 per cent.

They conclude that the bottom of the pyramid isn't for everyone: 'Burgeoning middle classes in developing countries often provide targets that are less com- plicated to reach and require less alteration to corporations' usual ways of doing business.'

57

Business process redesign (Hammer and Champy)

The tool

Are you poised to obliterate?

Business process redesign (BPR, also known as business process *reengineering*) was the big thing of the 1990s – whole consulting groups were spawned to meet the booming demand, while existing groups hastened to offer their own take on the theme.

It offered an attractive solution to difficulties caused by the deep construction-led recession of 1989–92. Instead of the standard cost-reduction strategies, chopping out people and units through restructuring or downsizing, it proposed reinventing the operational processes that go towards the crafting of a product or service. This would lead both to lower unit costs of production and improved service.

Michael Hammer and James Champy were at the forefront of this push. Hammer's provocatively entitled article, 'Reengineering Work: Don't Automate, Obliterate', in the *Harvard Business Review* took aim at processes which failed to add value. Technology, and especially IT, was being used to upgrade and streamline all organisational processes, including those that were of no value. This they termed 'paving over cowpaths'.

Processes needed to be redefined, rethought from a 'zero base' (i.e. start from scratch), justified and reengineered. Redundant processes should be axed.

How to use it

There are numerous tomes written on BPR. You would do well to start with Hammer and Champy's 1993 book, *Reengineering the Corporation*. They define BPR as 'the fundamental rethinking and radical redesign of business processes to achieve dramatic improvements in critical contemporary measures of performance, such as cost, quality, service and speed'.

They identify principles which are common to all BPR projects:

● Several jobs are combined into one.

- Workers make decisions.
- The steps in the process are performed in a natural order.
- Processes have multiple versions.
- Processes are performed when it makes the most sense.
- Checks and controls are reduced to the point where they make economic sense.
- Reconciliation is minimised.
- A case manager provides a single point of contact at the interface between processes.
- Hybrid centralised/decentralised operations are prevalent.

A BPR project should follow a standard cyclical process (see Figure 57.1):

1 Align the BPR project with your firm's strategy, nascent or developed.
2 Identify all pertinent operational processes and rethink them from first principles:
   - What are they for?
   - How did they come into being?
   - What value do they add?

Figure 57.1 Business process redesign

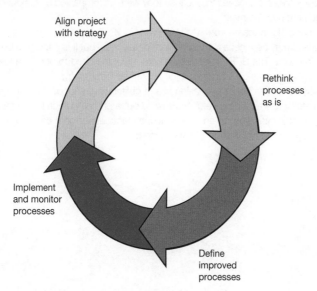

Source: Adapted from Michael Hammer and James Champy, *Reengineering the Corporation: A Manifesto for Business Revolution*, Nicholas Brealey, 3rd edn, 2001

- How can they be improved to add further value?
- Would they add more value by being axed or combined?

3 Define a set of improved processes, which are:
   - Value adding in their own right
   - Yet more value adding when combined with other processes.

4 Implement and monitor the redesigned processes.

5 After a while, start again ...

When to use it

When benchmarking suggests that your business is underperforming in cost, quality, service or speed.

When to be wary

Critiques of the 1990s BPR fad came from a number of directions. Because a BPR project often resulted in redundancies, it came to be associated with downsizing. They are very different projects, but management of perceptions is important, especially in labour relations.

More substantial are the concerns over implementing BPR projects. Many projects failed to produce the aspired results, often due to employee resistance. Some BPR projects succeeded because they were accompanied by major change-management programmes.

Another criticism came from Michael Porter in 1996. Improved efficiency from a BPR project may be a necessary condition for success, but it is unlikely to be a sufficient condition. The BPR project should not mask the need to pursue a low-cost or differentiated strategy. Efficiency is no substitute for strategy.

Finally, Hammer's headline-chasing title of obliterating redundant processes can also create problems – be careful of throwing out a process which has in fact contributed subtly, over time, to an organisational capability or core competence (see Tool 63) you would not wish to see weakened.

Outsourcing

58

The tool

Can someone else do parts of what you do better than you?

Outsourcing is the name given in the 1990s to the process of buying in business processes from independent, specialist providers as opposed to performing them in-house.

It is not a new concept. The venerable economic and business philosopher Peter Drucker was a great proponent of outsourcing. He believed that a company should focus exclusively on 'front room' activities, those closest to the customer and which are core to the business. 'Back room' activities should be outsourced to other companies, for whom these are their front room activities, and so on.

It is a variant on the 'make or buy' decision faced by all manufacturing companies through the ages – produce the component in your factory or buy it in from a more focused supplier – but one now faced by all companies, manufacturers or service providers, on a whole range of business processes. This trend is sometimes referred to as 'vertical de-integration', giving rise to 'virtual firms' whose added value is the buying in, repackaging and marketing of the goods and/or services of their suppliers.

Four main reasons that manufacturers have long bought in components, and some now buy in whole product lines, also apply to the outsourcing of processes:

- *Lower costs* – the outsourcer specialises in that component and should enjoy economies of scale.

- *Focus on core business* – no further need to invest in R&D or capital equipment in making that component; instead investment (and managerial time) can be focused on the core business.

- *Higher quality* – the specialist outsourcer will invest in state-of-the-art product and production technology to stay ahead of its competitors.

- *Faster speed to market* – you focus on your new product, the outsourcer on their component.

The first processes that turned to outsourcers in the 1980s were IT services. Companies had become frantic trying to keep up with rapid and costly change in IT hardware and software and welcomed the opportunity to offload such decisions to large, fast-growing, well-resourced outsourcers whose very *raison d'être* was to keep ahead technologically and operationally.

Since then, outsourcing has spread to a whole range of services, from technical support to customer service, payroll to training, debt collection to claims management.

It is useful to differentiate between three types of outsourcing:

- *Specialist providers* – the original outsourcing, where cost advantages were to be gained from the economies of scale and scope of specialist operators
- *Low-cost providers* – operators in a lower-cost location, typically in the regions, who may or may not be specialists
- *Overseas low-cost providers* – otherwise known as offshoring, with operators often based in Eastern Europe, South Asia, South-East Asia or China (or South America serving US companies).

If your main reason for outsourcing is to improve the quality of that process, you may well choose a specialist provider with operations in your home country, rather than opt for offshoring.

How to use it

The outsourcing decision is often prompted by shrinking margin. You find that pricing in a major segment is becoming ever tighter. You have kept good control on costs, but still the margin is unsatisfactory compared to other product lines. To what extent could margin be improved with outsourcing production of a component, or the whole product line, or all production?

Or it may be prompted by an investment decision. Your production director wants to buy the latest machine to make a key component. Your IT director wants to invest in some new exclusive, expensive software. Your logistics director wants to replace his fleet of vans.

Or perhaps by a customer satisfaction survey. Customers may be insufficiently happy with product quality. Or delivery. Or service at your help desk.

Or ... you find out your competitor is offshoring.

Consider the options for outsourcing (see Figure 58.1). Should you go for specialist, low-cost or offshore providers? What emphasis should you put on quality versus cost?

Get some quotes and sample contracts. Test the water in initial negotiations.

Consider the impact on your employees. If you decide to outsource, will the provider take your employees? If not, what provision will you make for them? Can they be redeployed? If not, what would be the cost of redundancy? And what effect would that have on the morale of the remaining workforce?

Figure 58.1 Outsourcing

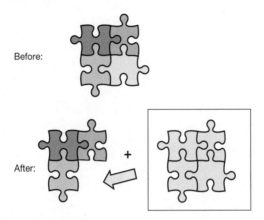

Before:

After:

+

When to use it

When you need to drive down unit costs or improve service standards. It is an option, increasingly used throughout the 2000s and 2010s – including by government.

When to be wary

As with business process redesign in Tool 57, one of the main dangers is that of losing a core competence. By the time you have offloaded a whole bunch of services and processes to outsourcers, you may find you have little left on which to place your distinctive stamp.

Or you may be taking the risk of falling behind in your performance against a key success factor. Your in-house production may enable you to be flexible and nimble compared to your competitors. If you outsource, you may lose this advantage. How important is this purchasing criterion to your customers?

Or you may become vulnerable to competitive inroads. Many Internet service providers shifted their technical help desks to India and other low-cost countries in the 2000s. Nowadays, some of their competitors are specifically marketing user-friendly help desks in the UK and successfully charging premium pricing.

[SECTION 8]

Bridging the gap: corporate strategy

Overview

Essential tools

59 Optimising the corporate portfolio

60 Creating value from mergers, acquisitions and alliances

61 The corporate restructuring hexagon (McKinsey)

62 Creating parenting value (Goold, Campbell and Alexander)

63 Core competences (Hamel and Prahalad)

64 Strategically valuable resources (Collis and Montgomery)

Useful tools

65 Strategically distinctive resources (Barney)

66 Distinctive capabilities (Kay)

67 Distinctive competences (Snow and Hrebiniak)

68 Dynamic capabilities (Teece, Pisano and Shuen)

69 Deliberate and emergent strategy (Mintzberg)

70 Stick to the knitting (Peters and Waterman)

71 Profit from the core (Zook)

72 The market-driven organisation (Day)

73 Value disciplines (Treacy and Wiersema)

74 Disruptive technologies (Christensen)

75 Co-opetition (Brandenburger and Nalebuff)

76 Growth and crisis (Greiner)

77 Good strategy, bad strategy (Rumelt)

78 Innovation hot spots (Gratton)

79 Strategy as orientation or animation (Cummings and Wilson)

80 The knowledge spiral (Nonaka and Takeuchi)

81 The eight phases of change (Kotter)

Overview

Is yours a multi-business firm?

If so, this chapter applies to you. Earlier you sought to bridge the strategic gap through improving competitiveness in each of your businesses (Section 7). That was business strategy. Now for corporate strategy.

There are two schools of thought in corporate strategy, each with their corresponding sets of tools and analysis:

- *The market positioning school* – where strategy should be focused at the level of the business, where all meaningful competition resides, and corporate strategy limited to portfolio planning

- *The resource-based school* – where strategy should be focused on leveraging the resources and capabilities (or 'competences') of the corporation as a whole.

Both schools have their merits and this section sets out how to extract the best from each. Six essential tools have been chosen:

- Three from the market positioning school – optimising the corporate portfolio, creating value from M&A and McKinsey's Corporate Restructuring Hexagon

- One, which has proved the most influential, from the resource-based school (Hamel and Prahalad's core competences)

- One which seeks to blend the two schools (Collis and Montgomery's Strategically Valuable Resources)

- And one which embraces both schools by emphasising the role of the centre or parent in creating value through both its resource and portfolio management (Goold, Campbell and Alexander's Creating Parenting Value).

This section also buzzes with an array of other stimulating tools of corporate strategy, ranging from four further takes by Barney, Kay *et al.* on the resource-based view to Christensen's explosive Disruptive Technologies, and from Mintzberg's venerable Deliberate and Emergent Strategy to Gratton's innovative and still hot Innovation Hot Spots.

Optimising the corporate portfolio

59

The tool

In the early 1980s the new CEO of General Electric, Jack Welch, asked management guru Peter Drucker for advice. He responded with two questions that arguably changed the course of Welch's tenure: 'If you weren't already in a business, would you enter it today? And if the answer is no, what are you going to do about it?'

This led directly to Welch's corporate strategy that every one of GE's businesses had to be either No 1 or No 2 in its sphere. If not, it would fixed, sold or shut.

The strategy was effective, if brutal. 'Neutron Jack' slashed GE's workforce by a quarter in his first four years, and famously culled underperforming managers each year. But he presided over a thirty-fold increase in market capitalisation over 23 years, by which time GE had become the highest-value company in the world.

Corporate strategy is seldom that extreme. But the central objective is often the same – optimising the corporate portfolio to maximise group shareholder value.

Corporate strategy tools address different questions to business strategy. Whereas the latter seeks to determine how a business can gain a sustainable competitive advantage, corporate strategy asks three main questions:

- Which businesses should you be investing (your scarce resources) in?
- Which businesses should be subtracted from or added to your portfolio?
- Which resources or capabilities common to all businesses should you focus on?

The second question will be looked at in the next tool on adding value in mergers, acquisitions and alliances. The third on the resource-based view of strategy will follow. Here the focus is on which businesses you should invest in.

You have already met the tools to do just that. Earlier, you used these tools to determine the optimal balance of product/market segments within a business (Section 6). Now you can use these same tools to determine the optimal balance of businesses within a corporation.

These are they (as re-displayed in Figure 59.1):

- The Attractiveness/Advantage Matrix (GE/McKinsey) – see Tool 36
- The Growth/Share Matrix (BCG) – Tool 37
- The Strategic Condition Matrix (Arthur D. Little) – Tool 40.

Figure 59.1 Corporate portfolio planning tools

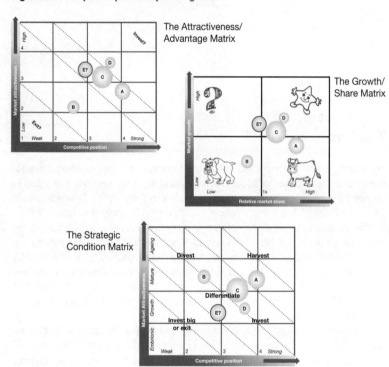

These tools should give you a clear picture on:

- Which businesses you should invest in
- Which businesses you should hold and improve performance in
- Which businesses you should divest
- Which businesses you should enter organically, or via acquisition.

How to use them

You should use these tools as set out previously (Section 6), substituting the word 'business' for 'segment' all the way through.

But there is one aspect that differs in corporate strategy – the option of buying and selling businesses. Specific tools for mergers, acquisitions and alliances ('M&A') are set out in the next tool, but here it is useful to review the corporate strategic rationale behind M&A activity.

There are three main types of M&A strategy:

- *Horizontal integration* – where you link up with a fellow producer, whether a direct or indirect competitor, to improve your collective competitive position

- *Vertical integration* – where you link up with an operator further up (a customer) or further down (a supplier) the value chain, to give you greater control of the market

- *Diversification* – where you link up with a player in a different market altogether, but where there is sufficient compatibility in resources or capabilities between the two of you for synergistic benefits.

Horizontal integration is the most common M&A option. Vertical integration works for some (e.g. mobile phone operators setting up as retailers), not for others (e.g. kitchen furniture producer Magnet, which ventured almost fatally into the High St in the late 1980s). Diversification was a fad of the 1970s and 1980s, with the likes of Hanson and Tomkins, but was proven to be a short-lived strategy, found to be dependent on taking over firms with sub-par financial planning systems.

How to assess the relative benefits of different types of M&A option is discussed in Tool 60.

Finally, each of the above options has a converse. That of acquisition is divestment, which may well be a viable option – your unwanted business may find a home in another corporation where it is more wanted and so worthy of a healthy exit price.

Likewise, vertical de-integration is common today – not just the selling-off of businesses at different parts of the value chain, but the outsourcing of processes (see Tool 58).

When to use them

These corporate portfolio planning tools are essential in corporate strategy.

When to be wary

Again, the value of these matrices is only as good as the data and analysis put in. Your assessment of market attractiveness and competitive position in the Attractiveness/Advantage Matrix must be rigorous and dispassionate. Your data on market growth and share in the Growth/Share Matrix must be well researched – and relate to the right, specific markets. Likewise for the Strategic Condition Matrix.

Remember the old adage of management information systems: garbage in, garbage out. This applies with equal validity to portfolio planning tools.

60

Creating value from mergers, acquisitions and alliances

The tool

Eat or be eaten.

This old saying may have pejorative undertones, but it does serve as a reminder of the dangers of corporate underperformance.

Mergers, acquisitions and alliances (together 'M&A') have been with us since the dawn of capitalism. They form an important, if on occasion controversial, component of the Anglo-Saxon business model.

M&A are frequently deemed to be successful when the merged entity survives, yet all too often they have in reality failed, as defined in the only truly meaningful manner: the creation of incremental shareholder value.

At the very least the shareholder value of AB should be greater that the standalone pre-merger value of A plus the standalone pre-merger value of B.

But studies are regularly carried out, since well before I started working on M&A activities in the mid-1980s, which show, again and again, that in the majority of cases shareholder value is destroyed by M&A, not enhanced.

The reason is simple: acquirers pay too much to gain control.

And the reasons behind that over-payment are also well known:

- Managers are often hell-bent on closing the deal – they have made up their minds this is what they want to do, for whatever reason, genuinely strategic or personal empire building, and they will not permit prolonged negotiations and an ever-rising price tag to prevent them from getting the deal done.

- Managers do insufficient strategic analysis pre-deal along the lines set out in this tool.

- Managers do inadequate due diligence.

- Managers underestimate the difficulties of post-deal integration and the inevitable delay in achieving aspired merger benefits.

The theory behind M&A value creation is simple. We start with the premise that the acquisition of company B by A will be of strategic benefit to A. Then:

- The acquisition will create synergies, i.e. benefits in cost saving or revenue enhancement, that will be tapped by the joining forces of A and B.
- The value of AB will exceed the standalone values of A and B by the value of the synergies.
- A will be unable to buy B at its standalone value – shareholders of B will demand a premium to the pre-bid price to cede control.
- The acquisition will be successful, as defined by creating, not destroying, value for the shareholders of A, if the synergy value is greater than the premium paid by A for B.

The challenge of this M&A tool, therefore, is to work out the synergy value.

How to do it

There are six tasks in the acquisition assessment process:

- Confirm strategic rationale
- Select the right target
- Assess the risks
- Value the standalone entities
- Value the net synergies
- Ensure added value.

More detail follows.

Confirm strategic rationale

Very often the opportunity to acquire a business happens opportunistically, so the temptation is to move straight to due diligence.

The temptation should be resisted. Acquisition is a time-consuming and resource-hungry business. You can't be doing half a dozen at a time.

Take a step backwards and confirm the strategic rationale – and in the light of that rationale, assess whether this potential target really is the most promising candidate.

There are three steps in the task of confirming strategic rationale:

- What are your strategic objectives?
- Is acquisition the appropriate route?
- What are your transferable strengths?

Taking one at a time ...

What are your strategic objectives? Reviews of the rationale for acquisitions are frequent and tend to point to these main objectives:

- Access new markets/products
- Acquire skills/technologies
- Achieve economies
- Spread risk
- Reduce competition.

Motivation, for acquisition can be offensive, defensive (e.g. if your objective is to reduce competition) or a mix. What are yours?

Is acquisition the appropriate route? There are four broad alternative routes to achieving your business objectives, with pros and cons for each – see Figure 60.1. Is acquisition the best route for you?

Figure 60.1 The strategic rationale for acquisition

Route	Pros	Cons
Organic	• Strategic clarity • Control	• Investment • Time
Acquisition	• Time • Control	• Investment premium • Integration
Merger	• Time • Little investment	• Shared control • Integration/management
Alliance	• Time • Little investment	• Shared control • Integration/management

What are your transferable strengths? Here you should identify your transferable strengths – and any constraining weaknesses. This should be a guide to identifying and assessing realisable synergies later on in the process.

Your transferable strengths may be in R&D, operational efficiency, marketing, distribution coverage, financial control. One classic example a good few years ago was in the application of Nestlé's marketing and distribution strengths to the quality product range of Rowntree, a rationale repeated, albeit more controversially, by Kraft in its acquisition of Cadbury in 2010.

Select the right target

The second task is to select the right target, for which there are four steps:

- Set criteria for strategic fit.

- Prioritise the criteria.
- Screen the candidates rigorously.
- Rank the candidates.

Taking one at a time ...

Set criteria for fit. These are best divided in two – hard and soft criteria – to ensure that the soft criteria get adequate attention.

Examples of hard criteria are size, product/market segments, technologies, competitive capabilities and financial standing.

The criteria need to reflect your objectives for the acquisition. If your main rationale is to acquire skills, for example, you will be looking for a target that is strong in those skills you want to acquire. To enhance your bargaining position, however, you will probably want a target that is weak in those skills where you are strong. If, on the other hand, your rationale is to achieve economies of scale, you will want to be sure that the target has a strong competitive position in key segments.

The soft criteria for strategic fit may be equally important. These may include orientation towards customers or employees. Or the firm's culture concerning innovation, or cost control.

Remember, the greater the difference in the 'cultural map' between the two organisations, the more difficult the post-transaction integration is likely to be. Ideally, you and your target will share a common business philosophy. If you don't, you may need to factor the differences into your later assessments on synergy benefits.

Prioritise the criteria. Now you need to set priorities. The essential criteria, the ones the target has to meet if there's to be any point in going ahead with the deal, will be your 'screening criteria'. Applying them to all potential targets will allow you to eliminate the non-starters quickly. The 'nice to have' criteria will help you rank the companies that pass through the initial screening in order of attractiveness.

This two-stage process is important if you are to end up with the right target. In a one-stage ranking process, there is a danger that you could end up with a target that scores high on all but one criterion, which might be a screening criterion in a two-stage process. It is better to have a two-stage process and find a target which ranks resonably in the ranking criteria but passes through the screening.

Figure 60.2 Screening acquisition candidates for fit

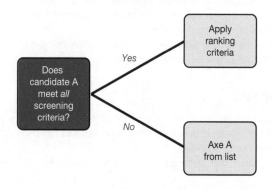

Differing criteria may have differing weighting depending on the precise nature of the deal. In an outright acquisition, a common business philosophy can be helpful, but not necessarily essential. In a transaction with an ongoing relationship component, i.e. a form of alliance, a common business philosophy may well be critical, hence a screening criterion.

Screen the candidates rigorously. The first stage in finding the right target is to screen all the potential candidates. Be ruthless. If any candidate fails to meet every one of your screening criteria, drop it from your list. Those that pass through the screen move on to the ranking stage – see Figure 60.2.

Rank the candidates. Suppose you have four candidates which have passed through the screening stage, A, B, C and D. Now you rank them – see Figure 60.3.

Figure 60.3 Ranking acquisition candidates for fit and availability

			Candidates			
Criteria for fit		**Weight**	**A**	**B**	**C**	**D**
Hard	Segment attractiveness	20	3	3	4	3
	Segment strategic fit	10	4	3	3	3
	Business strategic fit	30	3	3	2.5	4
Soft	Business cultural fit	40	3	4	2	3
Overall rating for fit (0–5)		100	3.1	3.4	2.6	3.3
Overall ranking for fit			3	1	4	2
Availability			X	Y	YY	Y

First you weight the ranking criteria in relative importance – in the example, cultural fit is given a high weighting.

Next, you rank the candidates by each criterion, with B emerging as the best bet.

Then you compare the ranking with an assessment of availability: in the case above, it seems a toss-up between the preferred candidate B and the more available D. It's probably best to start talking to both.

The same process *must* be applied if you are approached out of the blue by an interested potential target: be careful, it may be candidate C!

Assess the risks

There should be no substitute for the process of due diligence. Many acquisitions have succeeded without it, or without much of it, but that has been down to luck. They could have been disasters.

Without financial due diligence, the target's management accounts may be misleading. Without legal due diligence, don't be surprised if you receive a letter from a lawyer representing some aggrieved claimant soon after signing. Without environmental due diligence, how can you be sure of the target's compliance with regulation?

Above all, though you could argue I would say this, since I have specialised in the field since the mid-1980s, it is strategic due diligence which will give you the answers to the fundamental question: will this deal create or destroy shareholder value?

To be able to value the synergies, you need to know at what rate the market is growing, how competitive forces are impacting on pricing, how the target is positioned relative to competitors, how positioning is set to change – not least as a result of this merger, what will be the impact of recent and planned business initiatives by the target, and so forth. All this needs to be done for each major product/market segment (if the target is a business) or each business unit (if the target is a multi-business corporation) – see Tool 82 on strategic due diligence.

The risks and opportunities identified by the due diligence need to be assessed by likelihood of occurrence and impact on value should they occur – see the Suns & Clouds chart of Tool 83.

You then need to build key risks and opportunities into your cash flow forecasts for the target. By attaching probabilities against each key risk or opportunity occurring, you can derive expected value (see Tool 86) cash flow forecasts, hence the standalone value of the target.

Value the standalone entities

Discounted cash flow ('DCF') analysis is by far the best tool for this task, but, as noted in Tool 48 on making the strategic investment decision, there are many pitfalls awaiting the novice user and you may prefer to use more rough and ready valuation techniques, such as these three:

- *Net asset value* – but this is a book (historic), not market, valuation and typically understates value, often by some distance.

- *Comparable trading multiples* – you can find relevant multiples of publicly traded companies operating on the Web; sales, EBITDA, EBIT or P/E multiples are most frequently used – but they all suffer from the same shortcoming, in that they are multiples of the trading performance of one company during one period of time, which may or may not be indicative of trend performance.

- *Comparable transaction multiples* – you can search various databases for sales or earnings multiples on deals completed in the last few years, where the targets have operated in the same or similar industry sectors, but again these multiples will refer to specific time points in history, when both trading performance and the appetite for acquiring stock in that sector might differ from today.

My advice is to use all three techniques above to value a company to around a certain range, hopefully not too broad and within +/− 15 per cent of the central point.

Then try DCF analysis on the company, forecasting revenues and costs to get profits and fixed and working capital expenditure to get cash flow, before discounting back to values of today. Tweak assumptions within reason and try a range of (reasonable) discount rates before you reach a new present value around and about the central point derived from the three rough and ready valuation techniques.

This will give you a set of cash flows with which you can do some sensitivity testing in step 3 to derive synergy values. They will be estimates, but should be usable – and very much better than nothing.

Value the target on a standalone basis. Using the target's financial information disclosed to you in the confidential information memorandum, or in greater detail in the online data room, draw up a base case set of cash flow forecasts for the target.

The forecasts should show revenues and direct (and preferably variable overhead) costs for each major product/market segment.

Derive a central value for the target using the techniques outlined above.

Value your firm on a standalone basis. Do the same for your firm, or at least for those product/market segments, or business units, that will be interrelating with the target following acquisition. Use the same discount rate as for the target.

Value the net synergies

First you need to identify the synergies to be gained from merging two companies, then you need to value them.

Identify the synergies

M&A synergies are best identified under three areas:

- Revenue enhancement synergies
- Operating cost savings
- Capital cost savings.

Revenue enhancement synergies typically come from these areas:

- The target selling your product (or service) to its customers
- You selling the target's product to your customers
- You and the target combining to sell new product to both sets of customers
- Your combined capabilities enabling you to sell more or different product to your customers or to reach new customers
- Net of the customers you will lose due to them switching to a new supplier independent of the merged entity.

Operating cost savings are often the main rationale for acquisition. Savings can come from one or many of these areas:

- Lower cost of raw materials or components due to greater purchasing power
- Likewise of outsourced services, such as IT or payroll

- Economies of scale in production
- Economies of scope
- Rationalisation of overhead staff, whether in sales, marketing or administration
- Rationalisation of physical assets – buildings, land, factories, offices, plant, equipment.

Finally, capital cost savings can often be realised on acquisition. Instead of building an extension to your factory, acquisition of a competitor with spare capacity can provide you with the space and hopefully the right equipment to maintain growth. Likewise, capital cost savings can be in the field of IT, head office or the like.

Value the net synergies
You have a DCF model of the target. Now make specific assumptions on each of the revenue enhancement synergies identified above. By how much will sales of product X grow each year with promotion to the target's customers?

By how much has the target's NPV increased? That is the value of that particular synergy.

And how about product Y?

And what about selling the target's product Z to *your* customers? By how much has the NPV of your firm increased from the standalone valuation you did earlier?

Work out the value of each revenue enhancement synergy.

Then do the same for each cost-saving synergy.

Add them up and you have a number for total synergy value. But wait! There are two big caveats:

- Managers tend to overestimate the magnitude of synergies, often wildly so; it is in the nature of the M&A process – the thrill of the chase; apply a 50 per cent probability factor to your revenue enhancement synergies (say, R), to give an expected value (see Tool 86) of 0.5R; likewise, apply a 80 per cent probability to all cost savings – which are more in your control and ability to influence – to give an expected value of 0.8C.

- Don't forget the transaction costs pre-deal and the costs of integrating the two companies post-deal – not just in redundancies, but in such items as early lease termination.

You now have a base estimate of the value of the net synergies from this transaction.

Ensure added value

You now have three sets of data:

- A base estimate of the standalone value of the target
- A base estimate of the synergy value of the acquisition
- An assessment of risk and opportunity.

Acquisition premia tend to be in the range 30–40 per cent. If that is what you are likely to have to pay and if your base estimate of the synergy value of the acquisition is less than 40 per cent of that of the standalone value of the target, you should walk away.

If synergy value is higher than that, you need to consider the risks and opportunities identified and assessed during due diligence. If any risks are sufficiently likely to make a big dent in either the standalone value of the target or in the synergies (or both), you may need to walk away.

Again, remember: more than half of all acquisitions destroy value. This is because the acquirer overpaid.

You don't want to be part of that statistic.

When to use it

Always in a merger, acquisition or alliance.

When to be wary

Be wary of every merger, acquisition or alliance. One last time: most fail!

Alliances have an even higher failure rate. An alliance, whether a simple marketing relationship or a full joint venture, is an inherently unstable vehicle. The partners need to work together in harmony for the good of the alliance, but sometimes to the detriment or neglect of the parent company's interests.

They require even more pre-deal strategic analysis than in an acquisition. The process is very similar (differences are in italics):

- Confirm strategic rationale
- Select the right *partner*
- Assess the risks
- Value *each partner's contribution*
- Value the net synergies
- Ensure added value.

Unlike in an acquisition, *both parties* need to emerge from the pre-deal process believing they have secured a reasonable deal. Otherwise the alliance will be off to a lop-sided start and its prospects for longevity minimal.

But they can work to add shareholder value and they can be long-lasting. The alliances that are Unilever and Royal Dutch Shell are their embodiment, but a clear example of a successful, more recent joint venture is Cereal Partners Worldwide ('CPW'). From its formation in 1990, as a full-frontal assault on the pre-eminence of Kelloggs in Europe, it looked like a winning, almost obvious strategy – the realisation perhaps of Kelloggs' worst nightmare. The combination of General Mills, the other cereal giant in the US, with the marketing clout of Nestlé and, two decades on, CPW has become, all but inevitably, a formidable player in the European cereal market.

The corporate restructuring hexagon (McKinsey)

61

The tool

Might you be prey?

As set out in the preceding tool, the objective of M&A activities is to create incremental shareholder value to the corporate entity – by buying businesses to which you can add more value than can your competitors, by selling businesses for which the converse applies and by joining forces with other companies where value can be created for all parties involved.

But others are doing the same thing. Might you be in their sights?

The process of creating incremental corporate value is put into interesting perspective in McKinsey's corporate restructuring hexagon – see Figure 61.1. It highlights that there are five distinct ways of raising corporate market value:

- Communicating to shareholders information and data which highlight the company's competitiveness and narrow the gap, frequently believed, not always with justification, between your perception of the firm's value (promoted market value) and that of investors (current market value) – in other words, boosting your P/E ratio through targeted communication

- Putting into effect operational performance improvement measures, perhaps along the lines of business process redesign (Tool 57) or outsourcing (Tool 58), leading to an internally driven enhanced market value

- Disposing of businesses which are worth more to prospective bidders than they are to the group, having first taken care to 'dress the bride' and improve operational and financial performance in these businesses, leading to an internally driven potential market value

- Conceiving and exploiting growth opportunities, whether organic or acquisitive, following perhaps selected tools from this book, leading to an externally driven potential market value

- Judicious deployment of financial engineering, perhaps raising the debt ratio through issuance of bonds, to maximise the equity value without taking on undue risk of financial distress, leading to maximum potential market value.

Figure 61.1 The corporate restructuring hexagon

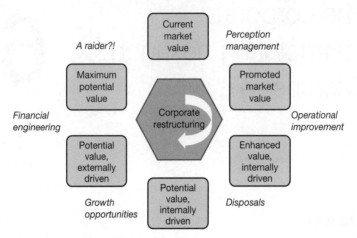

Source: Adapted from Tim Koller, Marc Goedhart and David Wessels (all McKinsey & Co), *Valuation: Measuring and Managing the Value of Companies*, 5th edn, 2010

As highlighted in the diagram by the conjoined question and exclamation marks, the gap between the current market value and the maximum restructured market value can be regarded as the 'maximum raider opportunity'.

In other words, if you cannot lift your market value beyond its current lowly level, by means of better communication with the City, improved operational performance, a winning organic strategy, a value-enhancing M&A strategy and measured financial engineering, someone else may do it for you – a corporate raider.

Whether the raider is a leveraged buy-out house or a competitor, a downstream integrating supplier or upstream integrating customer, or a player in the diversification game, no matter – you may be vulnerable to takeover.

How to use it

Use the valuation techniques of Tool 48 to derive these hexagonal values of your firm:

- Current market value
- Promoted market value following communication of value-defining data and information to shareholders
- Potential incremental value following a performance improvement programme – or, better, from each major strategic initiative as well as the overall impact (as in value-based management – Tool 48 again)
- Potential incremental value following M&A activity – or, likewise, from each major divestment or acquisition

- Potential incremental value following pursuit and achievement of strategic growth opportunities
- Potential incremental *equity* value through adjustment of capital structure.

What lessons can you draw from these differential values concerning your operating performance, your organic strategy, your M&A plans and their implementation, and communication to the investment community?

Are investors buying into your story? If not, why not? What evidence can you produce to give it greater credence?

Do they lend encouragement to a raider?

When to use it

Is the current market value of your firm below its maximum potential value? Well below?

If so, break down the differential into its constituent parts. Which part contributes most of the differential? How can these part's value be boosted? What can be done to improve probabilities, hence expected values (see Tool 86), in that part?

Even if your firm is not quoted on a stock exchange, it is instructive to consider to what extent the notional value of your firm lies below its maximum potential value.

When to be wary

The tool is a bit confusing. The hexagon implies a circular process, but there is a disconnect between the end point of restructured market value and the start point of current market value. The process may better have been displayed using bar charts.

But, never mind. It is a useful, stimulating prompt that the purpose of strategy development is value creation, whether internally or externally driven, and that shareholder communication and financial engineering are important extra components in keeping those prowling predators at bay ...

62

Creating parenting value (Goold, Campbell and Alexander)

The tool

'To lose one parent may be regarded as a misfortune; to lose both looks like carelessness.'

The success of management buy-outs since the mid-1980s suggests that the converse of Oscar Wilde's quip can apply in the world of business. Losing a parent has often been far from unfortunate – it can liberate the offspring and spur them to thrive.

The Ashridge Strategic Management Centre has led the field in researching the management of multi-business companies. The 1994 book, *Corporate-Level Strategy: Creating Value in Multi-Business Companies,* written by three of their academics, Michael Goold, Andrew Campbell and Marcus Alexander, found that Head Office, or the corporate centre, more often than not failed to create value in a multi-business company. It destroyed value.

Goold *et al.* encourage the strategist to think of the centre as the intermediary between the investor and the business unit. The centre can add value to the business unit if there are net synergies between them. These should offset inherent dissynergies such as:

- Wrong decision-making by the centre due to distance from the frontline and often unfamiliarity with the business unit's market environment and key success factors
- The demotivating aspect of distancing frontline managers from their investors
- The overhead expense of HQ, often high
- The acquisition premium, where the business was bought rather than organically built, and which is all frequently way too high (see Tool 60).

They believe that multi-business companies can create synergistic value by developing the right 'parenting skills', exploiting the right 'parenting opportunities' and establishing a 'parenting advantage' by owning the business.

In essence the centre, or 'parent', should view its business units using the same lens as the acquirer of Tool 60 – to create value, there should be synergies not just between business units but between centre and each business unit. That will create a parenting advantage.

They go further. If a parent's ownership of a business creates an advantage but a competing parent would create a bigger advantage, the parent should consider selling the business at a healthy sale premium and invest the proceeds in a business where its own parenting advantage is maximised.

Successful parents know where to look to add value. They have special resources or capabilities and have a feel for each business. More specifically, they possess:

- *Value creation insights* – they have identified a mechanism for adding value common to many of their businesses – thus the identification of a common technology base by leading electronics manufacturers or the sprinkling of Virgin's stardust brand.

- *Distinctive parenting characteristics* – they are leaders in certain resources or capabilities that help deliver the value creation insights and are transferable from parent to business – thus, the corporate R&D functions of many pharmaceutical groups or Virgin's centre leveraging brand promotion across all its businesses by, for example, sponsoring the London Marathon.

- *Presence of 'heartland' businesses* – ownership of those businesses which are best placed to exploit the parent's value creation insights and its distinctive parenting characteristics – thus the presence in Virgin Group of mobile phone or banking businesses rather than a business-to-business engineering business.

Thus do Goold *et al*. blend the two schools of corporate strategy. The concept of the parent's distinctive parenting characteristics is akin to a company's transferable resources and capabilities (see Grant, Tool 30) – or core competences (Hamel and Prahalad, Tool 63) – and reflects the resource-based view. While the management of the portfolio, once armed with distinctive parenting characteristics, reflects the portfolio optimisation view (Tool 59).

How to use it

Ask these questions of the businesses in your firm's portfolio:

- Do the parenting opportunities in a business fit with the firm's value-creating insights and distinctive parenting characteristics?

- Do the key success factors ('KSFs') in the business have any clear misfit with the firm's parenting characteristics?

See where each of your businesses sits on Goold *et al*.'s Parenting-Fit Matrix (Figure 62.1). They suggest five categories:

- *Heartland business* – where there is a strong fit between parenting characteristics and opportunities and also with the KSFs in the business.

- *Edge of heartland business* – partial fit between parenting characteristics and opportunities and also KSFs, some fit, some don't; net value creation is marginal and you should consider how you could better boost performance against KSFs.

- *Ballast business* – little fit between parenting characteristics and opportunities but no serious misfit with KSFs, a typical portfolio business which may well do better under a more synergistic parent; too many ballasts in your firm and you'll be a takeover target.

- *Alien territory business* – a total misfit, from every perspective, your firm is destroying value there – you should exit, and fast!

- *Value trap business* – a red flag business, where there is strong fit between parenting characteristics and opportunities, but a misfit with the KSFs of that business; the danger here is in you mistaking this business for an edge of heartland business – it is not, because your firm is not best placed to exploit the KSFs in this business.

Figure 62.1 The parenting-fit matrix

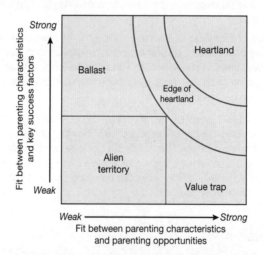

Source: Adapted from Michael Goold, Andrew Campbell and Marcus Alexander, *Corporate-Level Strategy: Creating Value in Multi-Business Companies*, Wiley, 1994

Your portfolio should ideally consist of heartland businesses, or those on the edge, poised to be nudged into the heartland.

When to use it

It forces you to think through the strategic rationale of why your firm's portfolio of businesses is as it is, how you add value to each business as a parent, building on your distinctive parenting characteristics. And where is the next parenting opportunity? Where next can you apply those value-creation insights?

When to be wary

Don't fall into the trap of redefining your parent characteristics to justify a parenting opportunity – or even of asserting that you plan to strengthen the former to justify the latter. Parenting characteristics are harder to build than opportunities. It may be wiser to let the opportunity pass, or divest a business, than attempt to build a characteristic. It is easier to change the portfolio to fit the characteristic than vice versa.

63

Core competences (Hamel and Prahalad)

The tool

Does your firm have 'the right stuff', 'the goods'? Are these goods the ones needed to compete in the marketplace of tomorrow?

If strategic thought was dominated in the 1970s by BCG's experience curve and Growth/Share Matrix and in the 1980s by Michael Porter's Five Forces, the 1990s can be viewed in retrospect as the time of the resource-based school of corporate strategy.

Chief trumpeters of this school were Gary Hamel and C. K. Prahalad, culminating in their influential book, *Competing for the Future,* in 1994, but other business academics made arguably as important contributions. One encountered already (Section 5) was Grant's Resources and Capabilities Strengths/Importance Matrix. Others were Barney's synopsis of preceding resource-based thought and encapsulation in the VRIN model (Tool 65), Kay's Distinctive Capabilities (Tool 66), Snow and Hrebiniak's Distinctive Competencies (Tool 67) and Teece, Pisano and Shuen's Dynamic Capabilities (Tool 68). Finally, Collis and Montgomery's work on Strategically Valuable Resources (Tool 64) blends the resource-based view with the market-based views of Porter, BCG *et al.,* and can be taken as a summary, balanced view of the resource-based school.

Hamel and Prahalad believed fervently that there was more to corporate strategy than just portfolio planning. Corporate HQ had a major role to play in areas such as developing strengths in key operational processes (termed 'core competences') and conveying a sense of vision throughout the firm (termed 'strategic intent').

Instead of the downsizing or reengineering prevalent at the time, companies should be 'reinventing their industry' or 'regenerating their strategy'. They proposed a new, radically more ambitious strategy paradigm.

Figure 63.1 shows just six of the 13 strategic challenges they set out, six that have arguably had much impact on subsequent strategic thinking. Of these, competing for leadership in core competences (or 'competencies' in their language) has been the most influential.

Figure 63.1 Getting to the future first

Not only	But also
Competing for market share	Competing for opportunity share
Strategy as positioning	Strategy as foresight
Strategy as fit	Strategy as stretch: intent
Strategy as resource allocation	Strategy as resource leverage
Competing within an industry	Competing to reshape industry
Competing in products	Competing in core competences

Source: Adapted from Gary Hamel and C. K. Prahalad, *Competing for the Future*, Harvard Business School Press, 1994

The authors define a core competence as an 'integrated bundle of skills and technologies'. It represents the 'sum of learning across individual skill sets in individual organizational units'. It is unlikely to reside in a single individual or small team, and may not reside in a single business unit.

Core competences in financial services, for example, are quoted as relationship management, transaction processing, risk management, foreign exchange, financial engineering, trading skills, investment management, tele-service and customer information capture.

How to use it

Hamel and Prahalad see the key to competing for the future as the building, deploying, protecting and defending of your core competences.

They suggest you should draw up a chart of the core competences needed to compete in the market, distinguishing between those of today and of tomorrow – see Figure 63.2.

These are the key questions which emerge from the chart:

- In the lower-left quadrant, 'fill in the blanks', representing your current portfolio of competences for your current businesses (or product/market segments – this tool can be used for business strategy too); what is the opportunity to improve your position by better leveraging your current core competences?

- In the lower-right quadrant, 'premier plus 10', to become the premier provider in five to ten years' time (a similar aspiration to profiling the ideal player and 'going for goal' in Tool 38); what new competences will you need to build to protect and defend your franchise in current markets?

Figure 63.2 Acquiring core competences

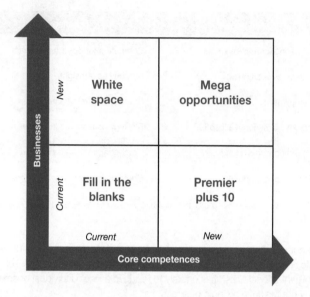

Source: Adapted from Gary Hamel and C. K. Prahalad, *Competing for the Future*, Harvard Business School Press, 1994, 'Establishing the Core Competence Acquisition Agenda'

- In the upper-left quadrant, 'white space'; what new businesses could you create by redeploying or recombining your existing core competences?

- In the upperish right quadrant, 'mega opportunities'; what new core competences would you need to build to participate in the most exciting businesses of the future?

The more distinctive, the more unique or the more defensible is your core competence, the more value it has.

How can you strengthen your core competences and thereby build value?

When to use it

Use it in corporate strategy, when thinking what the corporate centre can do to add value to the business units. How can the centre help in building a core competence and ensuring its widespread application across all business units?

When to be wary

Michael Porter is one of many who believe that a firm's value resides at business level ('corporations don't compete, business units do') and the role of corporate should be no more than resource allocator. Hamel and Prahalad might respond by saying that successful companies leverage their core competences across all business units and anyway their model works just as well at the business unit level.

Other critiques of the core competence model focus on the difficulty of deciding on what is or is not a core competence. Unlike a tangible asset, it is difficult to measure and managers may over-inflate the firm's worthiness for their own agenda. This is a criticism applied likewise to the Attractiveness/Advantage Matrix (Tool 36) and suggests that a degree of objective oversight, along with a rigorous customer survey and benchmarking exercise, might be beneficial in the application of the model. It does not invalidate it.

64 Strategically valuable resources (Collis and Montgomery)

The tool

Porter + Hamel and Prahalad = Collis and Montgomery?

David Collis and Cynthia Montgomery set out to blend the best of two largely competing views of corporate strategy – the externally focused industry/market positioning view, as espoused by Porter, GE/McKinsey, BCG *et al.*, and the resource-based view, as championed by Hamel and Prahalad, Grant, Barney, Kay and others.

They did so by introducing the concept of strategically valuable resources and defining them in such a way that resources could only be valuable if they were recognised strategically *within an industry/market context*. Thus were the two views blended.

They focus on three types of resources:

- *Physical* – such as plant and equipment
- *Intangible* – such as brand
- *Organisational capability* – 'as embedded in a company's routines, processes and culture'.

They give the example of Marks & Spencer, whose strategically valuable resources can be seen as:

- *Physical* – freehold locations
- *Intangible* – brand reputation, employee loyalty
- *Organisational capability* – supplier chain, managerial judgement.

It is the 'dynamic interplay between three fundamental market forces that determines the value of a resource or capability' – scarcity, appropriability and demand.

They stress that a resource cannot be valued in isolation, since its value emerges from the interplay of market forces. 'A resource that is valuable in a particular industry or at a particular time might fail to have the same value in a different industry or chronological context' – thereby tacking head-on the main critique of the resource-based view.

For a resource to be strategically valuable, it must pass five external market tests of its value (see Figure 64.1):

- *The test of inimitability*: is it hard to copy? They identify four main barriers to imitation (physical uniqueness, path dependency, causal ambiguity and economic deterrence) which are similar to those set out by Barney in his VRIN model, where the I is for inimitability (see Tool 65).

- *The test of durability*: how long will it last? They give the example of the evergreen Disney brand, which has outlasted the death of Walt by decades.

- *The test of appropriability*: who captures the value that the resource creates? They give the example of leveraged buy-out firms, where the key resource of contact lists often walks out of the door as executives quit to start up their own funds.

- *The test of substitutability*: can a unique resource be trumped by a different resource? Again, one of Barney's VRIN attributes.

- *The test of competitive superiority*: whose resource is really better? 'Competence should not be an internal assessment of which activity the company performs best, it should be a harsh external assessment of what it does better than competitors, for which the term *distinctive competence* is more appropriate.'

Figure 64.1 Strategically valuable resources

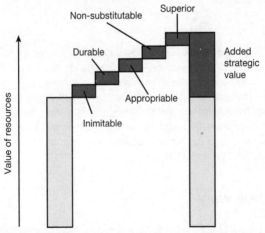

Source: Adapted from David J. Collis and Cynthia A. Montgomery, 'Competing on Resources: Strategy in the 1990s', *Harvard Business Review*, 1995, reprinted as *Competing on Resources*, July 2008

Collis and Montgomery have effectively done a Porter-style industry analysis on the resource-based school of strategy!

How to use it

Use Collis and Montgomery's guidelines to identify which of your resources are strategically valuable. Which are the most inimitable, durable, appropriable, non-substitutable and superior to the competition?

Then apply the Grant approach of Tool 30:

1 Identify strategically valuable resources.
2 Appraise them:
   - Assess their relative importance
   - Assess your relative strengths
   - Bring the appraisal together.
3 Develop strategy implications.

Collis and Montgomery suggest that you should invest in strategically valuable resources for sustainable competitive advantage, perhaps in three ways:

- *Invest in those you have* – for example, Disney reinvesting in animation.
- *Leverage those you have* – for example, Disney leveraging its brand name into retailing and publishing.
- *Upgrade those you should have* – for example, Intel moving into consumer branding with 'Intel Inside'.

When to use it

The authors' conclusion says it all (my italics):

> Whether a company is building a strategy based on core competencies, is developing a learning organization, or is in the middle of a transformation process, those concepts can all be interpreted as a mandate to build a unique set of resources and capabilities. However, this must be done with a *sharp eye on the dynamic industry context and competitive situation*, rigorously applying market tests to those resources. Strategy that blends two powerful sets of insights about capabilities and competition represents an enduring logic that transcends management fads.

When to be wary

The main critique that applies to all resource-based views of strategy development applies less evidently for this tool, but strategists would still be wise to conduct externally focused, Porter-esque industry/market analysis on the one hand and internally/externally focused Collis and Montgomery resource analysis on the other.

Virgin's brand as resource-based strategy

Richard Branson wrestled with a tricky decision. His launch of Virgin Atlantic had survived, much to the surprise of many pundits and despite fierce competition from British Airways. But bankers sought a large injection of cash to see it through the grim global economic downturn of the early 1990s. He could have brought in a strategic partner (as he was to do with Singapore Airlines later in the decade), but the terms would have been unfavourable.

Branson took a brave, ruthless decision. He sold off his beloved Virgin Music business to Thorn EMI for $1 billion and thereby secured his airline's future.

This is a classic example of portfolio planning in Virgin's corporate strategy – and not the only one. In the late 2000s Virgin Megastores was also sold off, becoming Zavvi and severing Branson's final link with the very High Street where he started.

But Virgin Group remains a highly diversified company, or rather a holding group of various equity participations in scores of businesses – in lifestyle, media & mobile, money, music and travel. Yet it is chosen here as an example of corporate strategy not so much due to its portfolio planning as to its core resources and capabilities.

To understand what these are, think back to 1984 and the launch of Virgin Atlantic. Branson had been an entrepreneur from the off, growing and selling budgerigars and Christmas trees as a schoolboy (without success) before launching a student magazine (with some success). Following school he opened a small record shop, moved into the recording business and, with a bit of luck, grew both businesses fast.

Astonishingly he then announced his intention to move into the airline business. 'The newspapers said calling an airline Virgin was mad', he reflects. They had a point. Airlines are highly risky enterprises and many investors won't go near them. History is littered with airlines that have gone under. Remember Pan Am? Eastern? Laker, the original, no-frills, cut-price, trans-Atlantic carrier? All these airlines went under despite being run and backed by people who knew the industry. But Branson? And the name Virgin?

Virgin Atlantic survived and thrived for a number of reasons, but one stands out: an extraordinary brand name – a name associated not just with quality, value-for-money service, but also of a man-of-the-people David fighting against a global Goliath. All brushed with more than a hint of glamour and excitement. And Branson raised this image to new heights following the airline launch, embarking personally on a series of world speed record attempts to keep the brand affixed to the headlines.

In 1986 his boat, *Virgin Atlantic Challenger II*, broke the record for crossing the Atlantic Ocean. A year later he did the same in the hot-air balloon, *Virgin Atlantic Flyer*. He later achieved the same feat flying across the Pacific Ocean, before making several attempts to circumnavigate the globe in a hot-air

▶

balloon. Foiled by weather, these attempts proved unsuccessful, though by no means so in terms of publicity.

Buoyed by this unique and unprecedented corporate branding, Branson's airline has succeeded. It has held its own both with British Airways and with American trans-Atlantic carriers. It has survived two severe downturns in the air industry without government subsidisation or recourse to Chapter 11.

The brand and the customer benefits it conveys are the secret to Virgin Group's success. It applies across the group, from Virgin Active to Virgin Books, Virgin Media to Virgin Money – even to Virgin Trains, which at one stage threatened to tarnish the brand but has persevered, investing in sleek, fast, tilting trains.

The brand is now being extended to the space-tourism business, with Virgin Galactic planning to offer its maiden commercial sub-orbital voyage in 2013. No prizes for guessing who will be one of the six passengers.

Strategically distinctive resources (Barney)

65

The tool

How strategic are your firm's resources? Are they valuable? Rare? Are they inimitable and non-substitutable?

The resource-based view of strategy, initially conceived by Edith Penrose in 1954 but rediscovered four decades later, bestrode the 1990s. Jay Barney was one of its earliest, leading proponents.

The resource-based view focuses on the internal competitiveness of a firm, rather than its external positioning, in determining sustainable competitive advantage. It is an inside-out more than an outside-in perspective, more supply-driven than demand-driven.

Barney argues that to build sustainable competitive advantage a firm must have resources characterised by four attributes: they must be valuable, rare, inimitable and non-substitutable – see Figure 65.1:

1 *Valuable* – they need to be of demonstrable value, enabling the strengthening of competitive position and/or the exploitation of market opportunities (or mitigation of market risks).

2 *Rare* – they must not be possessed by most competitors; they are possessed by few or by your firm alone; if too many players possess this resource, competitive advantage cannot be sustainable.

3 *Inimitable* – they cannot be readily imitated by competitors, or the advantage is not sustainable. Barriers to imitation include:

- *Distinctive location* – for example, the unique atmospheric conditions of San Daniele del Friuli in northern Italy for making its distinctive dark, sweet *prosciutto crudo*

- *Path dependency* – where a firm has acquired its resource as a result of its distinctive history and experience, not easily or at all replicable

- *Causal ambiguity* – the link between the resource and sustainable competitive advantage is not evident to the competition and they are unsure which resource to attempt to imitate – competitors in many of Virgin's businesses face this difficulty.

- *Social complexity* – where a firm's resource has been created through complex social interactions, either within the firm, its managers and staff, or between the firm and its customers, suppliers and other stakeholders.

4 *Non-substitutable* – they must not be readily substitutable; even if the resource is rare or inimitable, if it can be substituted by means of a resource which achieves more or less the same purpose, sustainable competitive position will be eroded and pricing driven down.

Figure 65.1 VRIN resources

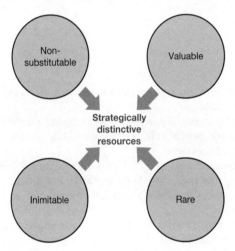

Source: Adapted from Jay Barney, 'Firm Resources and Competitive Advantage', *Journal of Management* 17, 1991

Barney argues that a firm must possess resources with all four of these attributes to build competitive advantage that is sustainable. The absence of any one attribute renders that resource unsustainable.

How to use it

Blend Barney's VRIN model with Grant's resource-based strategy development approach as set out in Tool 30 and summarised below:

1 Identify your strategically distinctive resources.
2 Appraise them for adherence to the VRIN model:
   - Assess their relative importance
   - Assess your relative strengths
   - Bring the appraisal together.
3 Develop strategy implications.

In principle, you should invest in your VRIN resources to obtain and defend sustainable competitive advantage.

When to use it

Use it in corporate or business strategy as an aid to assessing which of your resources is truly strategic and worth focusing investment on.

When to be wary

Critics have challenged the somewhat tautological nature of the V component of the VRIN categorisation. 'Resources can create shareholder value if they are valuable' is indeed a tautology, but substitution of the phrase 'if they are valuable' by 'if they strengthen competitive position' less so.

Others claim that it is difficult to conceive of and find resources that are each of V, R, I and N. And the model says little about how resources and capabilities change over time.

The main critique applies to all resource-based views of strategy development. They suggest that a firm with the right resources can succeed in any given industry, irrespective of competitive intensity. Market demand may be falling, competitors may be engaging in a price war, unable to exit due to high barriers, with prospective entrants from Asia knocking on the door, yet the firm with VRIN resources can be profitable? Unlikely.

The internally focused, resource-based view should best be blended with the externally focused, Porter-esque industry/market view before jumping to strategic conclusions.

66 Distinctive capabilities (Kay)

The tool

Does your firm's reputation confer a sustainable and non-appropriable competitive advantage? And what of its network of relationships? And innovation?

John Kay is very much of the resource-based school. He believes that 'the success of corporations is based on those of their capabilities that are distinctive. Companies with distinctive capabilities have attributes which others cannot replicate, and which others cannot replicate even after they realise the benefit they offer to the company which originally possesses them'.

'Business strategy involves identifying a firm's capabilities, putting together a collection of complementary assets and capabilities, and maximising and defending the [returns] which result.'

A distinctive capability he sees as a necessary but not sufficient characteristic for success. It must also be:

- *Sustainable* – defensible and long lasting
- *Appropriable* – benefiting mainly the firm, not its employees, who can walk out of the door, nor its customers, who can shop elsewhere.

Distinctive capabilities derive from three areas (see Figure 66.1):

- *Innovation* – whether in products, production or processes, a firm's innovation should be geared towards the creation of distinctive capabilities that are sustainable and appropriable.
- *Architecture* – the network of relationships both within the firm, between and among employees and managers, and outside the firm, with customers, suppliers, alliance partners and government, even competitors; 'architecture does not create extraordinary organizations by collecting extraordinary people – it does so by enabling very ordinary people to perform in extraordinary ways'.
- *Reputation* – the standing of the firm in the marketplace as a result of the

exploitation of its distinctive capabilities over time, perhaps as a result of architecture or innovation, engendering a sense of trust and enabling the firm to secure regular repeat business and perhaps charge premium pricing.

Figure 66.1 Distinctive capabilities

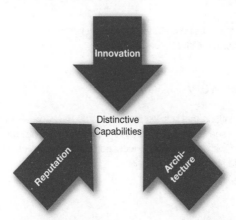

Source: Adapted from John Kay, *Foundations of Corporate Success: How Business Strategies Add Value*, Oxford, 1995

Distinctive capabilities may include skills or processes embedded in the firm, developed and honed over the years, knowledge management, patents or copyrights, customer and supplier relationships, image, brand.

You need to marshall your distinctive capabilities to develop sustainable competitive advantage. But what if you don't possess the distinctive capabilities needed for success in your marketplace? If they are truly distinctive, they may be irreproducible, as a result perhaps of industry structure, history or again what Barney calls 'causal ambiguity' (see Tool 65).

If the required capabilities are indeed irreproducible, you may be better off competing in those markets which play to your distinctive capabilities rather than aim for markets and distinctive capabilities to which you aspire.

How to use it

Categorise your distinctive capabilities using Kay's definitions and then apply Grant's resource-based strategy development approach as set out in Tool 30 and summarised below:

1 Identify distinctive capabilities.
2 Appraise them:
   - Assess their relative importance
   - Assess your relative strengths
   - Bring the appraisal together.
3 Develop strategy implications.

In principle, you should invest in your distinctive capabilities to gain sustainable competitive advantage.

When to use it

Use it in corporate or business strategy to identify which of your capabilities are truly distinctive and worthy of investment focus.

When to be wary

Again the main critique that applies to all resource-based views of strategy development applies – see Tool 65. The internally focused, resource-based view should best be blended with the externally focused, Porter-esque industry/market view before jumping to strategic conclusions.

Distinctive competences (Snow and Hrebiniak)

67

The tool

Are you a prospector, a defender, an analyser or a reactor? And do you have what it takes to succeed as one?

A decade before Hamel and Prahalad's work on core competences, Charles Snow and Lawrence Hrebiniak were researching the distinctive competences of firms and their relationships with strategy and organisational performance.

Figure 67.1 Aggressive and proactive strategies

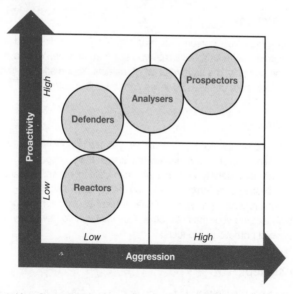

Source: Adapted from Charles C. Snow and Lawrence G. Hrebiniak, 'Strategy, Distinctive Competence, and Organizational Performance', *Administrative Science Quarterly*, June 1980

Indeed the term 'distinctive competence' was first coined in 1957 by Philip Selznick, a sociologist, as 'those things an organization does especially well in comparison to its competitors'. That definition has held.

Snow and Hrebiniak focused on the perceptions of top managers in four industries – plastics, semiconductors, automotive and air transportation. They found that these managers perceived four strategy types, categorised by degrees of aggression and proactivity, which they termed prospectors, defenders, analysers and reactors (see Figure 67.1).

They argued that several strategies are potentially feasible within a particular industry, but to achieve high performance the strategy must be backed up by the relevant distinctive competences.

How to use it

Which of these strategies most resonates with your firm's?

Prospector strategy

This is the most aggressive of the four strategies. You are constantly seeking to develop new products, enter new markets, exploit opportunities, often with little research or analysis. You like to play at the embryonic or development stage of the product life cycle. You aim for first mover advantage. Your marketing is typically offensive, advertising is a high proportion of sales. Business units have autonomy.

Defender strategy

You do not aggressively pursue new markets. You look to find and hold share in stable, mature markets. You insulate yourself from change. You have a limited product range and play in a narrow range of markets. Your marketing is defensive, advertising a low share of sales. Business units have little autonomy.

Analyser strategy

You are neither a prospector nor a defender, you are in between, like most businesses. You take less risk and make fewer mistakes than prospectors, but you are less concerned with stability and maturity than defenders. You expand in areas close to your existing core competences. You make improvements to your products rather than total redesign – in your R&D department you focus more on D than R. You gradually expand your markets rather than venture into new ones. You like to have a balanced portfolio of products.

Reactor strategy

You have no proactive strategy, rather you react as events occur – whether macro- or micro-economic. Your strategy is without direction, whether through poor articulation from the top, poor alignment of organisation with strategy or inadequate response to change. It is the least effective of the four.

To perform successfully when following these strategies you need these distinctive competences:

- *Prospectors* – general management, product R&D, marketing and basic engineering
- *Defenders* – general management, financial management, production and applied engineering
- *Analysers* – general management, production, applied engineering, marketing/selling
- *Reactors* – no distinct pattern (though reactor managers typically perceive themselves to have the same distinctive competences as defenders).

Do these distinctive competences match yours?

When to use it

Use it to gain a different perspective on your strategy and resources.

When to be wary

This was very much an academic study, deploying sophisticated statistical correlations. The distinctive competences analysed across the four industries were rather broad, like general or financial management and R&D, and to be really useful might have been further disaggregated, like product speed to market.

But strategy is often best-viewed from a helicopter perspective and the categorisation of prospectors, analysers *et al.* and their related distinctive competences may be illuminating.

68

Dynamic capabilities (Teece, Pisano and Shuen)

The tool

How dynamic are your firm's capabilities? How well do they respond in times of rapid change?

In 1997 the Berkeley team of David Teece, Gary Pisano and Amy Shuen addressed one of the seeming weaknesses of Barney's resource-based VRIN model (Tool 65) – that it was an essentially static analysis.

They set out to show how firms can achieve and sustain competitive advantage by developing, sustaining and renewing the dynamic capabilities a firm needs to compete in environments of rapid technological change.

They argue that a firm's competitive advantage rests on these dynamic capabilities (see Figure 68.1):

- *Distinctive processes* – ways of coordinating and combining
- *Basket of assets* – especially the firm's difficult-to-trade knowledge and complementary assets
- *Path dependencies* – whether adopted or inherited.

A firm's organisational and managerial processes need to fulfil three functions:

- Coordination and integration of internal and external resources, erecting barriers to imitation
- Organisational learning, benefiting from experimentation, experience and internal dissemination
- Reconfiguration and transformation of the firm, organisationally, culturally and technologically, as appropriate.

Second, they maintain that a firm's basket of assets defines its competitive advantage at any point, including technological, financial, reputational, structural, institutional and market (structure) assets, as well as knowledge and reputational assets.

Figure 68.1 Dynamic capabilities

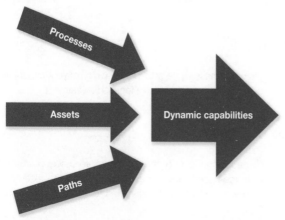

Source: : Adapted from David J. Teece, Gary Pisano and Amy Shuen, 'Dynamic Capabilities and Strategic Management', *Strategic Management Journal* (18) 7, 1997

Third, path dependencies define largely where a firm can actually move in its industry landscape. 'History matters', since such things as firm knowledge, experience, fixed assets, etc. cannot be changed in the short run and narrow the firm's scope of options. In particular, the firm's experience, expertise and processes in innovation and technology greatly affect strategic options.

The extent to which a firm's competitive advantage can be eroded depends on the stability of market demand and the sustainability of these dynamic capabilities, which in turn depends on the ease of replicability (expanding internally) and imitability (replication by competitors).

They suggest sustained value creation in regimes of rapid technological change depends in large measure on honing internal technological, organisational and managerial processes within the firm. Identifying new opportunities and organising effectively and efficiently to embrace them should add greater value than 'strategising', as defined by engaging in business conduct that keeps competitors off balance, raises rivals' costs and excludes new entrants.

How to use it

Consider to what extent the distinctive capabilities of your firm are or can be made to be dynamic. Then apply again the Grant approach of Tool 30:

1 Identify dynamic capabilities.
2 Appraise them:
   - Assess their relative importance
   - Assess your relative strengths
   - Bring the appraisal together.
3 Develop strategy implications.

In principle, you should invest in your distinctive, dynamic capabilities to gain sustainable competitive advantage.

When to use it

Use it in corporate or business strategy to identify which of your capabilities are truly distinctive and dynamic and should receive focused investment.

When to be wary

These are unabashed proponents of the resource-based school. Again this internally focused, resource-based view is best blended with the externally focused, Porter-esque industry/market view before jumping to strategic conclusions.

Deliberate and emergent strategy (Mintzberg)

69

The tool

'And now for something completely different', Monty Python might say here. Having set out in the last half a dozen tools the main proponents of the resource-based school of strategy, we turn to an iconoclast – Henry Mintzberg of McGill University.

Is all this strategising a waste of time? Worse, could it lead to the wrong actions?

Is strategic planning too restrictive, too structured, too analytical, too centralised, done by too many people, clever, yes, but unblooded, unexposed to the frontline?

Would strategy not be better conducted by line managers, responding to events as they unfold, as they see them, taking risks, testing the market, probing for opportunities?

Strategy should be as much emergent as deliberate, says Mintzberg (see Figure 69.1). Strategic planning remains useful, but it needs to be:

- More decentralised
- More intuitive.

Figure 69.1 Deliberate and emergent strategies

It is better done by managers than strategists. Five-year plans can be out of date within a year in mature industries or before the ink has dried in technology industries.

Industry boundaries have become more fluid. The value chain is more dispersed and more shared. 'Black swan' events (see Tool 87) throw plans off course more frequently. Industry analysis can be redundant, even misleading.

Firms need to be fleet of foot, strategically flexible. Organisations need to be structured as an 'adhocracy', the diametric opposite of a bureaucracy, with flat lines of responsibility, decentralised decision-making and small-team project work, with appropriate liaison mechanisms.

Strategy should emerge over time as intentions collide with and respond to a changing reality.

This is emergent strategy. It is what works in practice.

How to use it

Proceed regardless with the essential tools in this book, from the HOOF approach to demand forecasting (Section 3) to the Suns & Clouds (Section 9), via Porter's Five Forces (Section 4), competitive matrices (Section 5–7) and resource-based views (Section 8).

But be cognisant throughout of the need for strategic flexibility. Listen to your line managers. Build them into your strategy process. Encourage them to think on how unfolding events are impacting on strategy. Be aware of emergent strategy.

Adapt and amend strategy, as required, as you go along, but only if a sound case can be made to do so.

When to use it

The more change you witness in your market, the more strategy should evolve. But whether that should result in a succession of deliberate strategies or a shift towards emergent strategy is your call for your organisational culture.

When to be wary

Emergent strategy is no substitute for deliberate strategy. Taken to its extreme, emergent strategy equals no strategy, just flying by the seat of the pants.

Yes, industry boundaries can become fluid, yes, value chains are less rigid. But this is not new and these changes mostly take time. The future market environment can be envisioned. Your strategy can be deliberate.

Yes, there are black swan events – in recent years we have had EU sovereign debt, the banking collapse, Fukushima, Deepwater Horizon, Katrina, 9/11 – and these have indeed blown away the strategic plans of many companies.

But this has ever been the case. For the sovereign debt crisis, read the Latin American debt crisis, the shipping debt crisis, the LBO debt crisis, the southeast

Asian financial crisis, the dot-com bust of earlier years. Or go back further to the South Sea Bubble.

Strategy is not set in stone. It responds and evolves.

Read Mintzberg, he is a breath of fresh air. Here is his spiel on the back cover of *Strategy Bites Back*: 'OK, strategy is crucial. We all know that. But why must it be so deadly serious? So plodding, uncreative, *boring*? Dull strategy books create dull strategists that produce dull strategies that fail. Now here's an antidote.'

If so inspired, let your strategy be emergent!

P.S. Mark Maletz and Nitin Nohria followed similar lines to Mintzberg in their 2001 research on 'whitespace', the 'large but mostly unoccupied territory in every company where rules are vague, authority is fuzzy, budgets are nonexistent, and strategy is unclear – and where entrepreneurial activity that helps reinvent and renew an organization most often takes place'. They describe how senior executives should nurture whitespace projects by putting aside the traditional planning, organising and controlling techniques deployed in the 'blackspace'. In effect, they let the strategy emerge.

70

Stick to the knitting (Peters and Waterman)

The tool

'I believe the true road to pre-eminent success in any line is to make yourself master in that line. I have no faith in the scattering of one's resources, and in my experience I have rarely if ever met a man who achieved pre-eminence in money making ... who was interested in many concerns.'

Thus spake a nineteenth-century Scottish-American who specialised in steel, and only steel. From modest beginnings, Andrew Carnegie's company did well. So did the many beneficiaries of his philanthropy.

Tom Peters and Robert Waterman published *In Search of Excellence* in 1982, just before I started at business school. It was an instant sensation, a must-read and the topic of many a heated group debate.

Its impact has faded over the years, due mainly to the dip in performance by a number of their supposedly 'excellent' case studies, such as Delta Airlines, Digital Equipment, Eastman Kodak and K Mart, but its influence is felt to this day – not only because it sold more copies than virtually any business book in history, but because one or two of the elements specified as necessary for success had longevity.

They were two consultants at McKinsey and were tasked to travel the world talking to senior executives of top-performing companies to find out what they could about organisation – structure and people. They did, their bosses were impressed and the book followed.

They identified eight principles of a successful organisation (see Figure 70.1):

- *A bias for action* – active decision-making, 'getting on with it'
- *Close to the customer* – learning from the people served by the business, with customer satisfaction paramount
- *Autonomy and entrepreneurship* – fostering risk-taking and innovation and nurturing 'champions'
- *Productivity through people* – treating employees with respect and motivation

- *Hands-on, value-driven* – company values permeate the firm, with management as role models
- *Stick to the knitting* – focusing on what the company knows and does best
- *Simple form, lean staff* – minimal staff at HQ, authority dispersed to the business units
- *Simultaneous loose–tight properties* – autonomy at shop-floor along with centralised guidance.

Figure 70.1 Eight principles of corporate excellence

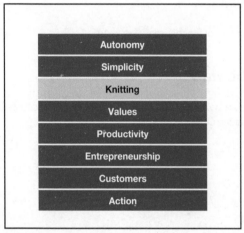

Source: Adapted from Tom Peters and Robert H. Waterman, Jr, *In Search of Excellence: Lessons from America's Best Run Companies*, Profile, 1982

Of these it is the sixth, stick to the knitting, that has arguably proved most closely associated with the book.

It was nothing new (nor indeed the last word – see Zook's Tool 71), just freshly espoused. And it offered a counter to the prevailing strategic orthodoxy of the age, where diversified conglomerates were run, successfully in the short term, generally unsuccessfully in the long term, by financial engineers and bean counters.

It echoes the logic of Igor Ansoff's product/market matrix (Tool 32). Venturing into new products and new markets is the riskiest strategic option.

Companies who may wish in retrospect that they had stuck to the knitting include AOL, rulers of the new media world before their ill-fated merger with old-media house, Time Warner.

Examples of successful companies who have stuck to the knitting abound, from Intel to LVMH, BMW to IKEA.

How to use it

If your strategy is to venture with a new product to a new market, whether organically or through acquisition, think very carefully.

What are your transferable strengths in resources and/or capabilities?

What is the balance of risk and opportunity (see the Suns & Clouds chart of Tool 83)?

Might you not get a better return for lower risk by sticking to the knitting?

When to use it

Always be cognisant of the maxim.

When to be wary

Be vigilant when a colleague proposes a venture requiring capabilities other than knitting or resources other than needles.

Profit from the core (Zook)

71

The tool

Has your firm, like an overly curious cat, strayed too far from home?

Most growth strategies fail to deliver value because they venture too far, concluded Chris Zook. The timeless strategic precept, that of building power in a well-defined core, remains the key source of competitive advantage and the most viable platform for successful expansion.

Successful companies operate in an F-E-R cycle:

- Focus on, understand and reach full potential in the core business.
- Expand into logical adjacent businesses surrounding that core.
- Redefine pre-emptively the core business in response to market turbulence.

These were the findings of a study of over 2000 companies and interviews with over 100 CEOs by management consultants Bain & Co and summarised in Zook's 2001 book, *Profit from the Core*.

In other words, as suggested in the previous tool, stick to the knitting.

How to use it

First you need to identify your core. Consider the key assets in your firm – your most potentially profitable customers, your most strategic capabilities, your most critical product offerings, your most important channels and any other critical strategic assets such as patents or brand name.

Now consider these three strategic growth alternatives (see Figure 71.1).

Strengthen and defend the core

Define business boundaries, confirm sources of differentiation and assess whether the core is functioning at or near full potential.

Grow through adjacencies

Consider expansion into adjacent markets that utilise and preferably reinforce your strengths in the profitable core.

Redefine your core business

Consider whether you need to redefine your core business – is this the right time, what methods work best, what lessons can be learnt from past successes or failures?

Figure 71.1 Profit from the core: the F-E-R cycle

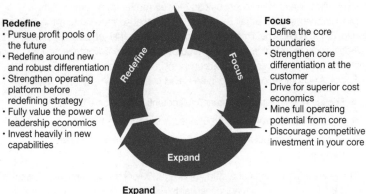

Redefine
• Pursue profit pools of the future
• Redefine around new and robust differentiation
• Strengthen operating platform before redefining strategy
• Fully value the power of leadership economics
• Invest heavily in new capabilities

Focus
• Define the core boundaries
• Strengthen core differentiation at the customer
• Drive for superior cost economics
• Mine full operating potential from core
• Discourage competitive investment in your core

Expand
• Project and extend strengths
• Expand into related adjacencies
• Push core boundaries out
• Pursue repeatable growth formula

Source: Chris Zook, *Profit from the Core*, Harvard Business School Press, 2001

Be careful in defining adjacencies. Zook stresses that adjacency expansion differs from other growth strategies in its use of existing customer relationships, technologies or core business skills to build competitive advantage in a new area.

Here is one process example in mapping adjacency opportunities:

● Rank your cores from strongest to weakest based on economics and relative competitive strength, as well as richness of adjacent growth opportunity.

● Develop the adjacencies in greater detail, considering new products, new markets, new businesses, new capabilities or vertical integration – see Figure 71.2.

- Rank adjacency opportunities by size, strength of transferable advantage, competition, importance to core (offensive or defensive), coherence with long-term strategy and ability to implement.
- Develop a cluster of moves or develop scenarios.
- Draw up implementation plans.

Figure 71.2 Profit from the core: exploring adjacencies

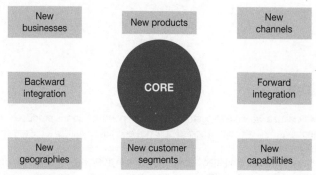

Source: Chris Zook, *Profit from the Core*, Harvard Business Press, 2001

When to use it

Any time you find your strategy veering too far from your core business, think on Zook's F-E-R cycle and consider whether you would be better off in the Focus or Redefine stage or, if the Expand stage is where you are at, whether more adjacent opportunities can be exploited.

When to be wary

This is a research-based, definitive affirmation of the dangers of wayward diversification and straying too far from your core business or core capabilities.

72

The market-driven organisation (Day)

The tool

Ted Levitt claimed we were all customer satisfiers now, not goods producers. Fellow marketing sage Philip Kotler exhorted 'it is not enough to satisfy a customer – you must delight them'.

But it was strategic marketer George Day who in 1994 put together a framework for creating the capabilities demanded by a market-driven organisation. Like Collis and Montgomery (Tool 64), also writing at the same time, he blended the resource-based view of strategy with Porter's strategic positioning view, specifically with regard to creating a market-driven organisation.

Indeed he saw that the choice of which of a firm's core competences or distinctive capabilities should be nurtured must be 'guided by a shared understanding of industry structure, the needs of the target customer segments, the positional advantages being sought and the trends in the environment'.

Two capabilities are especially important in bringing these external realities to the attention of the firm (see Figure 72.1):

- *Market-sensing capability* – how the firm is equipped to monitor and pick up discernible shifts in industry or market trends and customer behaviour and preferences and to anticipate customer response to specific marketing actions, in their broadest 4P sense (product, place, price promotion – see Tool 53).

- *Customer-linking capability* – the skills, abilities and processes needed to achieve collaborative customer relationships, so individual customer needs become apparent rapidly across the organisation, and with clear processes in hand on how to deal with them.

He then borrowed from total quality management ('TQM') manuals to set out a process on how to create a market-driven organisation, summarised below:

- Diagnosis of current capabilities

- Anticipation of future needs for market-oriented capabilities
- Bottom-up redesign of relevant processes
- Top-down direction from senior managers, ensuring that the redesign is geared towards putting customer needs first
- Use of IT, in particular customer relationship management ('CRM') tools as appropriate
- Monitoring of progress towards performance-improvement targets.

Figure 72.1 Market-driven organisation

Source: Adapted from George S. Day, *The Market Driven Organization: Understanding, Attracting, and Keeping Valuable Customers*, Simon and Schuster, 2007

Market-sensing and customer-linking capabilities alone, however, are not sufficient to create a market-driven organisation. The latter is characterised by:

- market-driven capabilities
- market-driven culture, so the capabilities may be nurtured within an environment of values, beliefs and staff behaviour wholly aligned to market and customer orientation
- market-driven configuration (or organisational structure and systems) with processes of control, motivation, incentives and decision-making geared towards supporting market and customer orientation.

The latter two themes are explored further in Day's 2007 book, in which he quotes examples such as Wal-Mart, Virgin Airlines, Disney and Gillette to illustrate how intimate knowledge of customers and markets has given them sustainable competitive advantage. He also uses the familiar examples of IBM's loss of leadership of the computer market or Motorola's stumble in shifting from analogue to digital cellular phone systems to show the results of failure to align the firm with the market.

How to use it

If you feel that yours is not as market-driven an organisation as it should be, Day's book comes with a roadmap, questionnaire and toolkit.

When to use it

Use it to become a market-driven organisation.

When to be wary

Becoming a market-driven organisation will not happen overnight. It may require a full change-management process.

Much of the research is ex-post – Virgin Group has been successful because it is a market-driven organisation. Little is ex-ante – along the lines, for example, of XYZ formerly being a product-driven organisation but, following a three-year change programme, is now more market-driven and this has shown through in improved performance.

Day is aware of this and uses case studies such as Eurotunnel and Sears as a guide.

Value disciplines (Treacy and Wiersema)

73

The tool

Is your firm product leading? If not, is it customer intimate? If neither, is it operationally excellent?

Michael Treacy and Fred Wiersema asked how come Dell emerged from nowhere to outmanoeuvre Compaq, how come customers deserted other DIY chains and flocked to Home Depot and how come the upstart Nike managed to sprint past Adidas.

The answers were the same in all three cases. And in 37 other cases where the authors examined the secrets to extraordinary success. The winning companies:

* Redefined value in their markets
* Built powerful delivery systems
* Raised customer expectations beyond the reach of competitors.

No revolutionary insights there, perhaps. What was new, they found, was in how customers defined value. In the past it was some combination of product and price. Now customers have an expanded concept of value, which includes convenience, after-sale service and reliability.

To succeed, then, do companies need to provide each of these elements of value? Treacy and Wieresma believe not. Companies succeed by providing one of three 'value disciplines':

* *Operational excellence* – providing customers with reliable product (or service), delivered cost-effectively and with minimal inconvenience – the Dell model, so too on a smaller scale with gocompare.com or Laithwaites.
* *Customer intimacy* – segmenting and targeting markets precisely and tailoring product to meet specific customer needs, which are understood well and promptly, thanks perhaps to Day's market-sensing and customer-linking capabilities (see Tool 72) – the Home Depot model, so too with IKEA or Pets at Home.

- *Product leadership* – offering the customer leading-edge product that enhances its use, enabling premium pricing and rendering competitive products obsolete – the Nike model, so too with Apple or Google.

Companies pursuing operational excellence aim to lead on price and delivery. They seek to drive down cost at every opportunity, at every link in the value chain. Theirs is Porter's generic low-cost strategy (Tool 45), but with a focus as much on convenience of delivery as price.

Those pursuing the customer intimacy discipline continually reshape product to meet the evolving needs of the customer, increasingly finely defined. This may be expensive, but they see it as a long-term investment in loyalty. It is one aspect of Porter's generic differentiation strategy.

And those pursuing the product leadership discipline are the consummate innovators, turning out a never-ending stream of enhanced product. They must constantly create product, commercialise it and, as appropriate, cannibalise it – before the competition does. This is another aspect of Porter's differentiation strategy.

Companies need to meet basic industry standards in each of the three value disciplines. But those that excel in one, or rarely two, can gain sustainable competitive advantage because they will have aligned all aspects of their operational model – their systems, processes, culture, incentives – to deliver that particular value discipline.

Other less disciplined competitors will find it hard to keep up. The disciplined company can just tweak its model continuously to stay ahead, while its challenger may have to undergo a complete business transformation to get on the same page. The advent of low-cost carriers caused havoc amongst the traditional national carrier airlines. Some went out of business, others merged, but all survivors had to reinvent their model, not just in demand pricing but in all supporting operational systems. Having done so, they still could not become as lean, flexible and low cost as their upstart rivals.

Treacy and Wiersema observed that companies that follow the same value discipline have similar characteristics to others following that discipline, even in totally different sectors. Thus the business systems at Wal-Mart and Federal Express are similar, since they both pursue the discipline of operational excellence. An employee leaving one for the other would feel quite at home. Not so, however, if he or she left to join Facebook, who pursue the discipline of product leadership.

How to use it

What are the key success factors ('KSFs') required to attain operational excellence in your industry (see Tool 24)? How should they be weighted?

On a scale of 1–5, how would you rate your firm against each of these KSFs?

Given the weighting, how does your firm rate against the value discipline of operational excellence?

Do the same with the value discipline of customer intimacy. Then product leadership.

Figure 73.1 Value disciplines

Source: Adapted from Michael Treacy and Fred Wiersema, 'Customer Intimacy and Value Discipline', *Harvard Business Review*, January 1993

Draw up a chart as in Figure 73.1. Plot the triangle which emerges from your ratings. In the example, the company performs most strongly against operational excellence (a rating of 4 out of 5), less so against customer intimacy (around 3) and least against product leadership (1).

From your chart, is it clear which value discipline you should be investing in? It should be the most pointed corner of the triangle.

How do your competitors rate? How do their triangles look?

If your chart looks like an equilateral triangle, you could be in trouble. You may be vulnerable to a lower-cost competitor, a more customer-responsive competitor, a product-leading competitor, or to all three.

If one of your competitors has an equilateral triangle, they may be vulnerable to your assault.

If a competitor has a highly pointed triangle, they could be formidable – especially if their prime value discipline is the same as yours. Should you invest to strengthen your position in that discipline or should you redirect your energies to another discipline?

These ratings cannot be trotted off without due care and discussion. You may choose to address them in a series of two or three workshops with your top managers.

When to use it

It offers a different perspective from the standard Porter generic strategies. Use it when you feel the need for fresh insight.

When to be wary

Don't focus on one value discipline to the extent of neglect of the others. Your firm needs to achieve a floor level in each. And ceiling level in one.

Or possibly two. Facebook was mentioned above – by any definition, they have attained product leadership, disposing of the likes of MySpace on the way. But they would also claim a very high level of customer intimacy. Given their direct access to the eyes, minds and, perhaps, souls of millions of users, particularly the young, they would have a point, scarily so to some observers.

Disruptive technologies (Christensen)

74

The tool

Great firms can fail by doing everything right.

All is going fine, then along comes a new technology, usually of inferior, seemingly retrogressive quality and hence resisted, often disparaged, by the firm and its customers, and all is disrupted – says Clayton Christensen.

Christensen's 1997 book, *The Innovator's Dilemma: When New Technologies Cause Great Firms to Fail*, exploded into the business world. Everyone knew of large firms being tumbled by new technologies, but this was research which showed that many of them had done nothing wrong to merit such a fall, strategically or managerially. They were doing what they should have done, not realising that their very successes and capabilities were obstacles to changing markets and technologies.

He sets out two types of technology: sustaining and disruptive. Established companies are adept at keeping abreast of the former, less so the latter. A sustaining technology is one which enhances an existing product, typically improving its performance and benefits to the customer. Successful established companies have processes which enable them to stay on top of these technologies, resulting in continuous product improvement and sustained customer satisfaction.

A disruptive technology is one which radically alters the benefit/price algorithm. Typically it produces a product of distinctly inferior quality or performance (though often smaller, simpler and/or more convenient), at least in the short term, but at such a lower price point that customers either rethink their rationale for purchasing the product or new customers are attracted into the market.

Examples abound – rail carriage producers lost out to saloon car manufacturers, Facit to Canon, Olivetti to Amstrad, Concorde to Learjet, mainframe producers to mini-computers to personal computers to laptops to tablets/smart phone producers, offset to digital printers, Encyclopaedia Britannica to Wikipedia, music companies and CD producers to Apple's iTunes.

Christensen studied the hard disk industry in depth and found that established companies tended to lag two years or so behind newcomers coming in with a new, typically smaller product generation. Seagate, leaders in the 5.25-inch disk, invented the 3.5-inch disk, but found little interest from their customers, who were happy with the status quo. Some Seagate employees left to form their own start-ups, producing the smaller disk, while Seagate continued to invest heavily in the larger disk, improving performance and sales. Over time the performance of the new smaller disks improved and started to displace the larger disks in the laptop and PC markets. Seagate belatedly fought back, but never reached the market share it had enjoyed in the larger disk market.

Two things from this research proved illuminating and not confined to hard disks:

- Barriers to technological change come as much from major customers as from within the major producers themselves – often what the customer says is what the producer wants to hear, so they can carry on with what they are doing.

- Disruptive technologies are very often promoted by new players to the market, not constrained by old technologies, old processes, old positioning, old sales pitches and, importantly, as above, the old thinking of old customers.

Disruptive technologies succeed because they sneak in surreptitiously. They do not appeal to the top end of the market at first, due to their inferior product performance. Other attributes, such as size, simplicity or convenience, enable them to gain a beachhead in the market, from where they start to gain share either by improving performance or by driving cost down through the experience curve (Tool 46). Soon enough they dominate the market – see Figure 74.1.

This is what Christensen calls the 'innovator's dilemma'. At what stage does the innovator have to overcome cultural bias against the inferior product, both within

Figure 74.1 Disruptive technologies

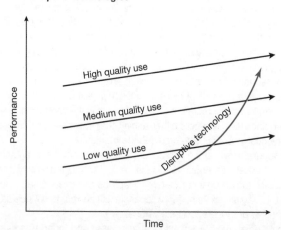

Source: : Adapted from Clayton M. Christensen, *The Innovator's Dilemma: When New Technologies Cause Great Firms to Fail*, Harvard Business School Press, 1997

and outside the firm, especially with customers, and embark on an investment pro-gramme with guaranteed cannibalisation of the firm's existing products to protect against the possibility of an upstart doing the same thing?

Think of the example of the humble razor blade. Global market leader Gillette's introduction of the Trac II was bound to cannibalise its double-edged safety razor, in production for decades. Later the Mach 3 did the same to the Trac II, but if Gillette hadn't done so, a competitor or new entrant might have done it for them with a disruptive technology.

A ubiquitous example of the innovator's dilemma is the world of ecommerce. Despite the huge advantages enjoyed by incumbent retailers, throughout the value chain, it is the upstarts who have dominated the market – the likes of Amazon, GoCompare, Trainline. It is only in food retailing, inevitably, due to the vastly different distribution challenges of the fresh, chilled and frozen food supply chain, banking, with its stability (formerly!) and security issues, and information – for example, the BBC, where the 'bricks and clicks' model has worked.

How to use it

Solving the innovator's dilemma is easier said than done. Your challenge is to iden-tify those emerging technologies which could threaten to steal share from or even supersede your current, sustaining technologies.

The trouble is, according to Christensen, that 'markets that don't exist can't be analysed'. Yes, to an extent, but that applies to any new venture – and one answer is to conduct pilot test marketing. Christensen suggests an alternative, discovery-driven planning, where you learn by doing and making real-time adjustments in strategy and planning. You should establish small, creative teams, bold and unafraid of failure, prepared to engage with freer-thinking customers on a range of what-if scenarios.

You should also consider setting up a wholly independent firm charged with exploiting the new technology, in effect competing with your sustained technologies.

It will be a firm created to disrupt.

When to use it

Use it when you suspect new technologies may prove disruptive.

When to be wary

Stay within the bounds of probability – otherwise you will fritter away resources pur-suing alternative technologies which are highly unlikely ever to become disruptive.

75

Co-opetition (Brandenburger and Nalebuff)

The tool

'Most businesses succeed only if others also succeed. It's mutual success rather than mutual destruction. It's win-win. It's simultaneously war and peace.'

So say Adam Brandenburger and Barry Nalebuff. Suppose that, instead of competing ferociously with your industry rivals, you could also cooperate with them, legitimately, to change industry competitive forces in your favour, would that be worth pursuing?

OK on paper, you may think, little chance in practice? Brandenburger and Nalebuff, whom we met in Tool 27 for their work on complements as the sixth addition to Porter's five forces, beg to differ. They used game theory to develop a strategic framework to do just that in their book, *Co-opetition*, of 1996.

Game theory has been around since the 1950s. It is a mathematical approach to resolving psychological, sociological and economic interaction and response by rational participants in the decision-making process.

Its most famous game is the prisoners' dilemma. Two prisoners are arrested, but the police have no evidence and must rely on confession. Because of the likely prison sentences for each course of action, it is in the interests of each prisoner acting individually and rationally to confess. Yet it is manifestly in their joint interest to stay silent. Their likely individual and combined prison sentences would be shorter. In this paradox the irrational is paramount.

This dilemma can apply to a whole range of situations. It would have been infinitely more beneficial, economically, socially and politically, for neither the US nor the USSR to have spent a cent on the arms race, let alone trillions of dollars. It would be better for no Americans to carry guns. The Great Depression might have been a regular recession if major nations had maintained free trade policies rather than erecting protectionist barriers.

In the world of business the dilemma is most evident in marketing – whether in price discounting or advertising. No matter to what extent Coke or Pepsi flood the airwaves, their market shares, other things being equal, tend to remain steady. One will respond emphatically to the other's campaign. As in the prisoners' dilemma, they would jointly be better off staying silent.

How to use it

The authors' apply co-opetition theory to everyday business via their PARTS system (see Figure 75.1):

- *Players* – what opportunities exist for cooperation and competition for each of the main players in your value net – your network of customers, suppliers, competitors and complementors? Can you bring in new parties, could your competitors? How would that impact on you?

- *Added value* – what is your added value and how can you enhance it, for example through building loyalty? What value do other players in your value net add? Who has the power?

- *Rules* – which rules help you, hinder you? What new rules would help you? What contracts would you like with customers and suppliers? Do you have sufficient power to get such rules introduced? Could another party overturn your rules?

- *Tactics* – how do other players perceive the game? How can you influence those perceptions in your favour? Should you make your value net transparent or opaque?

- *Scope* – should you try to link (or delink) your value net to (from) another one? How would that create value?

Approach these PARTS questions methodically and regularly and you may find the chance to change your value net to your advantage.

Figure 75.1 Value net, co-opetition and PARTS

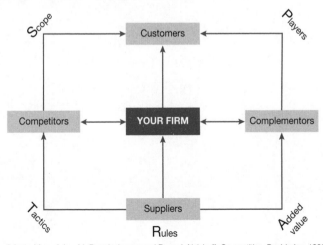

Source: Adapted from Adam M. Brandenburger and Barry J. Nalebuff, *Co-opetition*, Doubleday, 1996

When to use it

Use it when you would benefit from a structured framework to think how co-opetition might help in changing the rules of the game in your favour.

When to be wary

The authors claim that co-opetition is a 'revolutionary mindset'. This is somewhat of an exaggeration, given that elements of cooperation between industry players have existed for decades in every industry association. Likewise strategic alliances, from basic exclusive supplier arrangements right through to joint ventures, long predated the 1990s. But the authors provide a stimulating perspective, with a useful framework and set of checklists.

Growth and crisis (Greiner)

76

The tool

Is your firm facing a growth crisis? Will it?

All organisations go through different phases of growth and in so doing face tricky transition points along the way.

Larry Greiner's categorisation of common growth phases and transition points, which he highlights as potential crises, first appeared in 1972 – see Figure 76.1.

An organisation typically goes through six phases of growth:

1 *Creativity* – driven by the creative energy and inspiration of the founder, intent on creating distinctive value propositions to the customer, fostering innovation and orchestrating staff morale to the cause of survival and prosperity; this leads to a LEADERSHIP CRISIS, where the founder finds that the hands-on skills needed to start up a company are not the same as the organisational and delegating skills needed to manage it.

2 *Direction* – professional managers are drafted in, strategy, planning and financial controls brought in and a longer-term horizon set; this leads to an AUTONOMY CRISIS, where managers seek a greater share of decision-making and rewards, due in large part, they believe, to their endeavours.

3 *Delegation* – organisational structure is broadened, dividing and ruling top management; new departments are added, such as sales and marketing, and possibly new business units, and middle managers appear; this leads to the CONTROL CRISIS, where in the more complex organisation direction from above is not always implemented below and where managers in the functional or business units take autonomous decisions, leading to a loss of control.

4 *Coordination* – greater emphasis on reporting and communication, often through sophisticated management information systems; independent business teams are integrated; this leads to a RED TAPE CRISIS, where

the organisation develops extra layers to handle the information flow and becomes more bureaucratic.

5 *Collaboration* – the crisis is resolved through a process of debureaucratisation and rehumanisation of reporting lines, leading to a flatter structure, more collaboration, more trust and greater buy-in of middle management, with remuneration systems geared towards the attainment of common organisational goals; this leads to a GROWTH CRISIS, since it is now difficult to achieve growth targets with this more collaborative structure without overloading it.

6 *Alliances* – the solution to constrained organic growth is sought through mergers, acquisitions and alliances, informal and formal; this sixth phase was added by Greiner in his 1988 revision, reflecting perhaps the booming M&A market of the mid to late 1980s, driven in part by leveraged buyouts, and it will no doubt lead to another crisis – perhaps the Debt Crisis?!

Figure 76.1 Growth and crisis model

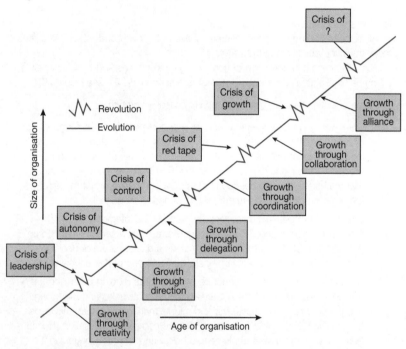

Source: Adapted from Larry E. Greiner, 'Evolution and Revolution as Organizations Grow', *Harvard Business Review*, Jul–Aug 1972 and May–Jun 1988

How to use it

At what growth phase is your business? Is it facing or due to face one of Greiner's crises? Might you be able to resolve that by proceeding to the next phase?

Are there any early warning signals? Are procedures getting in the way of front-line staff doing their job? Are staff forever clogging up meeting rooms with each other rather than with the customer? Do staff feel they are getting adequately remunerated for their contribution to firm growth? Are too many leaving the firm?

Think through the implications of what needs to be done in terms of responsibility-sharing, delegation, specialisation, communication, motivation, incentivisation. Think carefully about administrative procedures, which should be there to help not hinder growth.

When to use it

Use it when your firm is approaching a natural transition point in its growth. Could that transition point become a crisis?

When to be wary

Greiner's model is a generalisation and inevitably a simplification of a firm's growth path. Look only for elements that might be applicable to your situation. Be aware too that the duration of each phase and the intensity of the crises experienced will vary from firm to firm, depending largely on leadership and organisational flexibility, and that some growth phases may be repeated.

77 Good strategy, bad strategy (Rumelt)

The tool

'For many people in business, education and government the word "strategy" has become a verbal tic. A word that can mean anything has lost its bite.'

This was Richard Rumelt in his 2011 best-seller, *Good Strategy, Bad Strategy*.

He sees bad strategy as that often expressed in an interminable PowerPoint presentation, replete with vision, mission, goals and objectives, forcefully expressed and communicated with gusto and apparent conviction. But it is built on sand. It is a propaganda tool, for both staff and investors. Its goals have no bearing on achievable reality.

Bad strategy tends to display one of four hallmarks:

- *Fluff* – esoteric jargon serving to befuddle the reader or listener and convey a sense of 'I know best' to the presenter
- *Waywardness* – insufficient definition of the challenge, and therefore no means of properly evaluating the strategy
- *Desire* – goals which are exhortations rather than plans for overcoming challenges
- *Woolliness* – objectives which fail to address critical issues ('dog's dinner') or are impractical ('blue sky').

Good strategy is rooted in diagnosis – a thorough analysis of the business challenge ahead, warts and all, the designing of a guiding policy ('an approach to dealing with the obstacles called out in the diagnosis') which will create and sustain a competitive advantage and the translation of that policy into specific and coherent actions.

Those three aspects (see Figure 77.1) represent the 'kernel' of a good strategy.

Figure 77.1 Good strategy

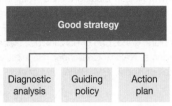

Source: Adapted from Richard P. Rumelt, *Good Strategy, Bad Strategy: The Difference and Why It Matters*, Profile, 2011

Beyond that, a good strategy works by 'harnessing power' and applying it to where it will have the greatest effect. Rumelt elaborates on nine such power sources, admittedly non-exhaustive but fundamental:

- *Using leverage* – a channelling of activity and energy on a pivotal objective to achieve a tipping point and a 'cascade of favourable outcomes'

- *Proximate objectives* – challenging but attainable objectives (for example, the SMART objectives of Tool 8)

- *Chain-link systems* – if there is one link in your chain that is so weak that its breaking will bring down the whole venture, there is no point in strengthening other links until that link is fixed – for example, the faulty O-ring in the booster engine of the spacecraft *Challenger* in 1986

- *Using design* – framing the user experience so intimately that it drives product development, engineering, manufacturing and sales

- *Focus* – identify your competitive advantage, don't be swayed into deviation into superficially attractive areas where your advantage counts for little (see Tool 70)

- *Growth* – this should be the reward for competitive advantage, innovation or efficiency, not for financial engineering through grandiose and value-destroying mergers and acquisitions (see Tool 60)

- *Using advantage* – deepen it, broaden it, reinforce it (see Tool 71)

- *Using dynamics* – ride the crest of any exogenous new wave, whether technological, environmental or socio-cultural

- *Inertia and entropy* – exploit any such organisational shortcomings in your rivals, to which market leaders are particularly prone, and renew your own organisation if and when necessary to repel any such encroachment.

How to use it

By following this book you will avoid many of the pitfalls of bad strategy. Your strategy will have been grounded in Rumelt's diagnosis – micro-economic analysis (Sections 3 and 4), competitive analysis (Sections 5 and 6) and rounded off by risk analysis (Section 9).

This is an immensely readable book, choc-a-bloc with lively, often quirky examples. It opens with Admiral Nelson plotting the destruction of the Spanish fleet at Trafalgar by aiming his more flexible (and heavily outnumbered) ships directly at his foe.

Other strategy exemplars, good, bad or ugly, include General Schwarzopf, David and Goliath, Iraqi insurgents, NASA's *Challenger*, Hannibal and Galileo, as well as the more customary likes of Apple, IBM, BMW, GM *et al*.

When to use it

To help you think strategically, read it at leisure and enjoy.

When to be wary

There is an element of self-back-slapping, with some examples chosen where the good professor himself has advised wisely. There are also so many examples that it can be difficult at times to see what the point being made is and where it fits into the overall scheme of things.

But such shortcomings are par for the genre. Read on and discover the next, surprising and revelatory strategic vignette.

Innovation hot spots (Gratton)

78

The tool

Does your organisation have a creative buzz? Should it?

Do your competitors have the buzz? Shouldn't you?

As Linda Gratton asks in her 2007 book, *Innovation Hot Spots: Why Some Companies Buzz with Energy and Innovation… and Others Don't*, why do some companies buzz with energy, innovation and creativity? Why do these flares of activity occur in some companies and teams within them and not in others? How can you avoid the Big Freeze and instead encourage the creation of these centres of creativity, action and energy?

Gratton says that you always know when you are in a hot spot. You feel energised and vibrantly alive. The atmosphere is charged with a buzz of ideas and dynamic creativity. Hot spots are the 'times and places in some companies and teams where unexpected cooperation and collaboration flourish, creating great energy, productivity and excitement'.

Gratton asked these questions of 57 different companies, from Adidas to Unliever, BP to Goldman Sachs, exploring the conditions and environments that are conducive to the creation of hot spots. She found four essential elements for their nourishing:

- *A cooperative mindset* – fostered through a culture of mutuality and collegiality

- *An ability to span boundaries* – working with people with new ideas from outside your group

- *The collective igniting of purpose* – through a vision, challenge or task, to focus energy and not let it dissipate

- *The achieving of productive capacity* – requiring skills of discourse, conflict-resolution and teamwork.

She expressed this as the formula in Figure 78.1 to show that each of the first three elements has a multiplicative effect on the others and that the absence of one

Figure 78.1 Innovation hot spots

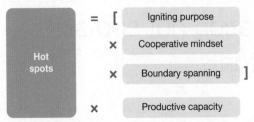

Source: Adapted from Linda Gratton, *Innovation Hot Spots: Why Some Companies Buzz with Energy and Innovation ... and Others Don't*, FT Prentice Hall, 2007

will have a major impact on the potential energy of a hot spot. The capacity of this potential energy to be translated into productive energy – hence innovation and value creation – depends on the productive capacity of the people in the emerging hot spot.

Gratton sees the role of the leader in nurturing hot spots as less one of direction and control but as orchestrator, process-builder and network creator.

How to use it

Is your firm as innovative as the competition? Should it be? How can you create more buzz, become more innovative? Follow Gratton's approach.

When to use it

Use it when you need to make your firm more innovative.

When to be wary

It won't happen overnight. Gratton's approach may represent a cultural shift for your firm. Tread lightly but steadily.

Strategy as orientation or animation (Cummings and Wilson)

79

The tool

Are you an orienteer or an animator?

Stephen Cummings and David Wilson make a stimulating distinction between strategy as orientation and strategy as animation.

In the former camp they place the likes of Michael Porter and his generic strategies (see Tool 45) for seeking sustainable competitive advantage. In the latter they point to the likes of Henry Mintzberg and his bottom-up emergent strategy (Tool 69), which is more concerned with the energising effect of strategy on the organisation, resulting in a common sense of purpose, vision and drive.

Chris Bilton has developed this distinction further to examine the creative implications of these two approaches to strategy (see Figure 79.1). With strategy as orientation, the leader is seen as a visionary. With strategy as animation, the leader is an orchestrator of visionary staff.

Figure 79.1 Strategy as orientation or animation

Strategy as orientation	Strategy as animation
Differentiation	Emergence
Strategy by specialists	Strategy by line managers
Leader as visionary	Leader as orchestrator
Divergent thinking	Divergent then convergent thinking
Revolutionary change	Evolutionary change
Fixed and communicated down	Continual adaption from below

Sources: Adapted from Stephen Cummings and David Wilson, *Images of Strategy*, Blackwell, 2003 and Chris Bilton, *Management and Creativity: From Creative Industries to Creative Management*, Wiley-Blackwell, 2007

Strategy as orientation requires divergent thinking. So too does strategy as animation, but the orchestrator will need to converge all the divergent thinking from below into a coherent strategy.

How to use it

Think on how you wish to develop strategy creation in your firm. Would you like your staff to be oriented, animated or a bit of both? Could strategy be used for morale-building, for raising creativity, for upping productivity, for obtaining buy-in?

When to use it

When you feel the firm would benefit from greater staff involvement in the strategy creation process. This may be particularly pertinent in the media and other creative industries, as well as in my own field of management consulting and other professional services.

When to be wary

Be aware of the old maxim: a little learning is a dangerous thing. And too many cooks spoil the broth. But then again: many hands make light work!

The knowledge spiral (Nonaka and Takeuchi)

80

The tool

'True knowledge exists in knowing that you know nothing', said Socrates, in a useful maxim for the business world. There is always more to know.

Knowledge is a resource, possessed to a greater or lesser degree, and to a greater or lesser degree of importance, by every firm. Knowledge management is a capability which is seen by some strategists and in some sectors as a key ingredient of success.

Ikujiro Nonaka and Hirotaka Takeuchi saw the process of knowledge conversion as key to building a firm's knowledge base. They differentiated between two types of knowledge: tacit and explicit. The former is subjective and experience-based, difficult to express in words or numbers, often because it is context specific, and is internalised in the form of know-how. The latter is objective and rational, able to be expressed externally and generally in words, numbers, even formulae.

Companies need to convert tacit into explicit knowledge to enable replication of successful activities throughout the organisation. Nonaka and Takeuchi developed a model of a continuous cycle of four integrated processes in knowledge conversion: socialisation, externalisation, combination and internalisation (see Figure 80.1). But the conversion process should become more than a cycle, more of a spiral, since the knowledge base of the firm should deepen as it travels round the four processes.

Tacit knowledge transfer from one person to another is termed *socialisation*. It is experiential, active and involves direct interaction with fellow employees, customers and suppliers. People share their experience and acquire skills and common mental models. Socialisation is primarily a process between individuals.

The process for making tacit knowledge explicit is *externalisation*. This is the articulation of one's own tacit knowledge or that of others – customers or experts, for example – into a readily understandable form, typically through dialogue. People share beliefs and learn how better to articulate their thinking through instant feedback and the exchange of ideas. This is a process among individuals within a group.

Figure 80.1 The knowledge spiral

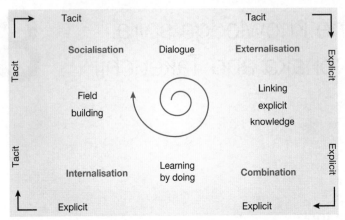

Source: Adapted from Ikujiro Nonaka and Hirotaka Takeuchi, *The Knowledge-Creating Company*, Oxford University Press, 1995

Once knowledge is explicit, it can be transferred as explicit knowledge through *combination*. This can be conveyed in documents, email, databases, as well as through meetings and briefings. Key steps involve the collecting of relevant knowledge and its editing/processing to make it more usable. Combination allows knowledge transfer among groups across organisations.

Internalisation is the process of understanding and absorbing explicit knowledge, thereby transferring it to tacit knowledge held by the individual. Internalisation is largely experiential, with concepts and methods put into practice, either through actual doing or through simulation.

How to use it

You can stimulate the workings of the knowledge spiral through workshops, which are good for externalisation, and a culture of sharing experiences, ideas, beliefs, whether in the canteen or via email or teleconferencing.

When to use it

Use it when you feel that there are pockets of wisdom hidden in the cellars of your firm which would be to the benefit of others once exposed to daylight.

When to be wary

Not all time spent in the canteen can be classified as productive!

The eight phases of change (Kotter)

81

The tool

'Change, before you have to', advised Jack Welch.

But Peter Drucker was more circumspect: 'Company cultures are like country cultures. Never try to change one. Try, instead, to work with what you've got.'

This is not a book on strategy implementation, let alone on the complexities of change management, but it is an inescapable fact that strategy formulation is only as value-enhancing as its eventual implementation.

So strategy needs to be implementable. Implementation may require change. And one recognised change-management guru has long been John Kotter.

He introduced his *8 Step Process for Leading Change* in 1996. The steps, as displayed in Figure 81.1, are:

- *Establishing a sense of urgency* – examine market and competitive realities and identify and discuss crises, potential crises or major opportunities

- *Creating the guiding coalition* – assemble a group with enough power to lead the change effort, and encourage the group to work as a team

- *Developing a change vision* – create a vision to help direct the change effort, and develop strategies for achieving that vision

- *Communicating the vision for buy-in* – use every vehicle possible to communicate the new vision and strategies, and teach new behaviours by the example of the guiding coalition

- *Empowering broad-based action* – remove obstacles to change, change systems or structures that seriously undermine the vision, and encourage risk-taking and non-traditional ideas, activities and actions

- *Generating short-term wins* – plan for visible performance improvements, create those improvements, recognise and reward employees involved in the improvements

- *Never letting up* – use increased credibility to change systems, structures and policies that don't fit the vision, also hire, promote and develop employees who can implement the vision, and finally reinvigorate the process with new projects, themes and change agents

● *Incorporating changes into the culture* – articulate the connections between the new behaviours and organisational success, and develop the means to ensure leadership development and succession.

Figure 81.1 An eight-step process for leading change

Source: Adapted from John P. Kotter, *Leading Change*, Harvard Business School Press, 1996

How to use it

Follow the above steps. Read up too on other important thinkers on the change-management process, like Kurt Lewin's organisational change model (Unfreeze-Change-Refreeze) or Elisabeth Kubler-Ross's Change Curve. Adapt them appropriately for your own situation and apply them methodically.

When to use it

When formulating your strategy think on what you may have to do to implement it through a change-management programme.

When to be wary

Each change-management situation is different from the next. Adapt this and other models as appropriate to your context.

[SECTION 9]

Addressing risk and opportunity

Overview

Essential tools

82 Strategic due diligence and the market contextual plan review
    (Evans)

83 The suns & clouds chart (Evans)

Useful tools

84 The composite risk index and the 5×5 risk matrix

85 The risk management matrix

86 Expected value and sensitivity analysis

87 Black swans (Taleb)

88 Strategic bets (Burgelman and Grove)

Overview

'In these matters, the only certainty is that nothing is certain', professed Pliny the Elder.

No change there then since Roman times.

Many managers see the concept of uncertainty as a black box. They are aware of so many tomes on the theory and measurement of risk as to make the eyes glaze over.

Managers may feel that only rocket scientists can understand risk – the latter have to, for the consequences of getting things wrong can be grim – so they don't need to bother. They can proceed with the strategies they feel to be correct and the risks will take care of themselves.

There is a middle way. Between gut feel and complex algebra lie some simple tools which can really help the manager reach an informed, balanced decision.

The first is strategic due diligence, a risk-management process normally undertaken to screen a prospective acquisition, but one which lends itself readily to screening the output of the strategy development process. The main outputs of strategic due diligence are the Market Contextual Plan Review and the Suns &

Clouds chart and these essential tools can be applied to your emergent strategy as a form of quality control.

Other useful tools include the Composite Risk Index (or the 5×5 Matrix), a simple quantitative but less visual alternative to the Suns & Clouds; the Risk Management Matrix, a useful construct on the manageability of risk, and the old staples of expected value and sensitivity analysis. Also included are stimulating contributions from Nasim Taleb on black swans and Burgelman and Grove on strategy bets.

82

Strategic due diligence and the market contextual plan review (Evans)

The tool

Strategy development and strategic due diligence are as two peas in the same pod. They feed off the same nutrients – market demand, industry supply, competitive advantage.

They are mirror images of one another. In strategy development you assemble the micro-economic and competitive information and conjure up a means of creating sustainable competitive advantage. In strategic due diligence you review that strategy in the context of the same micro-economic and competitive information.

Strategic due diligence ('SDD') is used primarily in mergers and acquisitions – see Tool 60. Without a thorough assessment of the market, industry and competitive risks and opportunities facing the target, the acquirer runs the risk of paying too much to gain control. The penalties of inadequate due diligence can be catastrophic – ask then-shareholders of RBS (or Lloyds TSB) how good an idea it was to have bought ABN AMRO (or HBoS).

But it can also be used constructively as a check on the strategy development process. Think of the latter as the manufacturing shop-floor of a one-off, made-to-order, very large item of capital equipment. SDD then is the quality control unit, tasked with verifying that the output has emerged as it should.

This equipment, this strategy, should be fit for purpose – it should be what the market is prepared to pay for and stand out from the competition. If not, it should be resubmitted to the shop-floor for final adjustments.

Let SDD fine-tune your strategy.

How to use it

SDD seeks the answer to one basic and one supplementary question.

The basic question is: Is this firm likely to achieve its plan over the next few years? And the supplementary: do the opportunities to beat the plan outweigh the risks of not achieving it?

You will deal with the supplementary question in Tool 83. To address the basic question, you need to review your strategy using the Market Contextual Plan Review tool.

Throughout this strategy development process you have been urged to frame your strategy in the context of the micro-economy in which you operate. Now is the time to see how well you have done.

Start with your revenue forecasts. You need to check that these are compatible with your assumptions on market demand growth and future competitive position.

For each of your business units draw up a table as in Figure 82.1 with at least eight columns and possibly (preferably, unless you find too many columns confusing) 14 (the extra 6 are shown in italics), as follows:

1 Main product/market segments

Sales

2 Sales in latest year, and possibly also:

   a. *Budgeted sales for next year*

   b. *Sales in previous year*

   c. *Sales in year before that*

   d. *Sales growth (per cent/year) over last three years*

   e. *Market demand growth in nominal terms over last three years*

Market demand

3 Market demand growth forecasts in nominal terms over next three years (note that there is no entry in the bottom row, since you are forecasting by specific segment – also for column 4)

4 Your firm's average competitive position rating (0–5) in that segment over the next three years, or current rating in this column and in the next:

   a. *Likely rating in three years' time, showing impact of strategy*

Sales forecasts

5 Your firm's planned sales in three years' time

6 Your firm's planned sales growth rate over the next three years

A backer's perspective

7 How achievable? Look at planned sales in the context of market dynamics from the perspective of a backer (and finally how achievable is the overall sales number for the business in the bottom row)

8 Your firm's more likely sales – what a backer would be more prepared to finance.

You have looked at your emergent strategy and plan from a top-down perspective, that of a backer doing SDD.

Figure 82.1 Market Contextual Revenue Review

Product/Market segments	Revenues (£000)	Market demand growth (%/year)	Competitive position (0-5)	Plan revenues (£000)	Plan revenue growth (%/year)	How achievable?	Likely revenues (£000)
	This year	Next three years	Next three years	In three years	Next three years		In three years
1	2	3	4	5	6	7	8
A							
B							
C							
Others							
Total							

Your backer will be looking for inconsistencies. In general, your sales forecasts in each segment should be consistent with:

- Your track record of sales growth
- Market demand prospects
- Your competitive position, now and over the next few years.

Any inconsistencies need justification.

If your track record in a segment is good and your competitive position strong, poised to get stronger, your backer would expect your sales forecasts, *ceteris paribus*, to exceed those of market demand, to gain market share.

If, however, your track record is not good and/or your competitive position is currently only tenable and your sales forecasts still exceed those of market demand, your backer would be concerned at the apparent inconsistency and would need to know why.

Can your strategy, designed to strengthen that competitive position, support such a forecast? Is it robust?

The second element of the Market Contextual Plan Review concerns margins. Draw up another table with 11 columns (see Figure 82.2), as follows:

1 The same product/market segments

Profits

2 Sales in latest year again

3 Profit margin in latest year (preferably contribution margin, but, if unavailable at that level of disaggregation, gross margin will do)

4 Profit in latest year – contribution (or gross profit) = column 2 × column 3

Industry competition

5 Competitive intensity in this segment currently (low/medium/high) – from Porter's Five Forces analysis (see Tool 22)

6 Competitive intensity over the next three years – is it likely to augment, subside or stay flat?

Profit forecasts

7 Planned profit margin in three years' time

A backer's perspective

8 How achievable? Look at planned margin in the context of industry competition dynamics from the perspective of a backer (and finally how achievable is the overall margin for the business in the bottom row)

9 Your firm's more likely profit margin – what a backer would be more prepared to finance

10 Your likely sales – from Figure 82.1

11 Your likely profit – column 9 × column 10.

Figure 82.2 Market Contextual Margin Review

Segments	Revs (£000)	Profit margin (%)	Profit (£000)	Competitve intensity (L/M/H)		Plan profit margin (%)	How achiev-able?	Likely profit margin (%)	Likely revs (£000)	Likely profit (£000)
	This year	This year	This year	Now	Next three years	In three years		In three years	In three years	In three years
1	2	3	4	5	6	7	8	9	10	11
A										
B										
C										
Others										
Total										

Again, you, through the eyes of a prospective backer, should be looking for consistency. If your forecasts show flat margins within a context of little anticipated change in competitive intensity, they are consistent. Likewise if they show rising margins in an industry where competition is easing.

But if your forecasts show rising margins in an industry where competition is getting tougher, they are inconsistent. They are not necessarily wrong, but they do need justification. Reasons for such performance improvement are manifold, but may include:

● Improved purchasing

- Higher utilisation
- Greater productivity
- Product line rationalisation
- Economies of scale (Tool 25)
- Experience curve effects (Tool 46)
- Business process redesign (Tool 57)
- Outsourcing (Tool 58)
- Belt tightening.

But they need to be coherent, consistent and convincing.

When to use it

Use strategic due diligence and the Market Contextual Plan Review when you need to fine-tune your strategy. The aim should be that the strategy emerges sufficiently robust to withstand the forensic cross-examination of a specialist strategic due diligence house engaged by a highly diligent private equity client.

When to be wary

Don't be one of these guys whose rather absurd but commonly found character traits are set out in more detail in the *FT Essential Guide to Writing a Business Plan*:

- *The dreamer* – whose sales forecasts bear no relation to those of market demand
- *The loner* – who recognises no significant competition
- *The magician* – whose sales forecasts are convincing but who claims they can be achieved from a steady cost base, resulting in ridiculous margins
- *The macho* – who struts his 'hockeystick' forecasts
- *The deluded* – whose sales volume and cost forecasts are convincing, but whose pricing assumptions are wishful thinking.

Make yours a robust strategy, a backable business plan.

The suns & clouds chart (Evans)

83

The tool

'When written in Chinese the word crisis is composed of two characters. One represents danger, and the other opportunity', said John F. Kennedy.

Risk and opportunity may indeed be two sides of the same coin. They are juxtaposed illuminatingly in the Suns & Clouds chart.

Strategic due diligence ('SDD') seeks to address the balance of risk and opportunity in meeting your plan. It looks for risks and opportunities in four main areas:

- *Demand risk* – how risky is future market demand?
- *Competition risk* – how risky is future competitive intensity?
- *Competitive position risk* – how risky is your firm's future competitive position?
- *Business plan risk* – how risky is your firm's plan?

Figure 83.1 The risk jigsaw of strategic due diligence

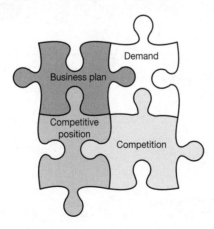

Each of these areas of risk and opportunity goes towards making up a risk jigsaw, as shown in Figure 83.1. SDD seeks to put together the four pieces of the jigsaw and assess the overall balance of risks and opportunities.

You can readily assemble the raw material for the risk analysis on your firm:

- Previously you drew up forecasts of market demand (Section 3); what are the main risks of those forecasts not being met? What are the opportunities that could enable those forecasts to be exceeded? How likely are these risks and opportunities to occur? How big an impact would they have if they were to occur?

- Do the same for the main industry competition risks and opportunities you found earlier (Section 4)

- And for the main risks and opportunities concerning your competitive position (Section 5) …

- … and your emerging strategy (Sections 6–8).

You are now ready for these key risks and opportunities to be assessed in a Suns & Clouds chart.

How to use it

I first created the Suns & Clouds chart in the early 1990s. Since then I've seen it reproduced in various forms in reports by my consulting competitors. They say imitation is the sincerest form of flattery, but I still kick myself that I didn't copyright it back then!

Figure 83.2 The Suns & Clouds chart

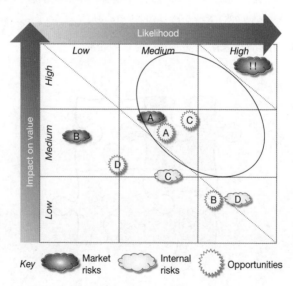

The reason it keeps getting pinched is that it works. It manages to encapsulate in one chart conclusions on the relative importance of all the main strategic issues. It shows, diagrammatically and visually, whether the opportunities surpass the risks. Or vice versa. In short, in one chart it tells you whether your strategy is backable. Or not.

The chart (Figure 83.2) forces you to view each risk (and opportunity) from two perspectives: how likely it is to happen, and how big an impact it would have if it did. You don't need to quantify the impact, but instead have some idea of the notional, relative impact of each issue on the value of the firm.

In the chart risks are represented as clouds, opportunities as suns. For each risk (and opportunity) you need to place it in the appropriate position on the chart taking into account both its likelihood and impact.

The Suns & Clouds chart tells you two main things about how backable your strategy is: whether there are any *extraordinary* risks (or opportunities), and whether the overall *balance* of risk and opportunity is favourable.

Extraordinary risk

Take a look at the top right-hand corner of the chart. There's a heavy thundercloud in there, with two exclamation marks. That's a risk that is both very likely *and* very big. It's a show-stopper risk. If you find one of them, your strategy is unbackable.

The closer a cloud gets to that thundercloud, the worse news it is. Risks that hover around the diagonal (from the top-left to the bottom-right corners) can be handled, as long as they are balanced by opportunities. But as soon as a cloud starts creeping towards that thundercloud (for example, to around where opportunity C is placed), that's when you should start to worry.

But imagine a bright shining sun in that spot where the thundercloud is. That's terrific news, and you'll have suitors clambering over each other to back you.

The balance

In general there's no show-stopper risk. The main purpose of the Suns & Clouds chart will then be to present the *balance* of risk and opportunity. Do the opportunities surpass the risks? Given the overall picture, are the suns more favourably placed than the clouds? Or do the clouds overshadow the suns?

The way to assess a Suns & Clouds chart is to look first at the general area above the diagonal and in the direction of the thundercloud. This is the area covered in Figure 83.2 by the parabola. Any risk (or opportunity) there is worthy of note: it's at least reasonably likely to occur *and* would have at least a reasonable impact.

Those risks and opportunities below the diagonal are less important. They are either of low to medium likelihood *and* of low to medium impact. Or they're not big enough, or not likely enough, to be of major concern.

Take a look at the pattern of suns and clouds in your chart around the area of the parabola. The closer each sun and cloud to the thundercloud, the more important it is. If the pattern of suns seems better placed than the pattern of clouds, your strategy may be backable.

In the chart above there are two clouds and two suns above the diagonal. But risk D lies outside the parabola. The best placed is opportunity B. Risk A and opportunity A more or less balance each other out, likewise other risks and opportunities. Opportunity B seems distinctly clear of the pack. The opportunities seem to surpass the risks. The business looks backable.

One of the best features of the Suns & Clouds chart is that it can be made dynamic. If the balance of risk and opportunity shown on the chart is unfavourable, you may be able to do something about it – and the chart will show this clearly.

For every risk there are mitigating factors. Many, including those relating to market demand and competition (the darker clouds in Figure 83.2), will be beyond your control. Those relating to your firm's competitive position, however, are within your power to influence. They may indeed be an integral part of your emergent strategy.

Likewise, your strategy may improve the likelihood of achieving a key opportunity on the chart, thereby shifting the sun to the right.

Risk mitigation or opportunity enhancement in the Suns & Clouds chart can be illuminated with arrows and target signs. They'll show where your firm should aim for and remind you that it's a target. Your strategy should improve the overall balance of risk and opportunity in your firm.

When to use it

You can the Suns & Clouds chart in so many situations. It was designed for SDD purposes in transactions such as acquisitions, alliances and investments, but it is just as useful in project appraisal, strategy review (as here) or even in career development and change. It would even have been useful in deciding whether or not to back the Beatles (see text box).

When to be wary

Don't worry if your Suns & Clouds chart doesn't make that much sense initially. This chart changes with further thought and discussion. *Always*. Arguably its greatest virtue is its stimulus to discussion. It provokes amendment.

Remember, you cannot be exact in this chart. Nor do you need to be. It is a pictorial representation of risk and opportunity, designed to give you a *feel* for the balance of risk and opportunity in your strategy.

What about highly improbable but potentially catastrophic risks, you might ask? The chart deals with them too. In the autumn of 2001 my colleagues and I were advising a client on whether to back a company involved in airport operations. After the first week of work, we produced an interim report and a first-cut Suns & Clouds chart. In the top left-hand corner box, we placed a risk entitled 'major air incident'. We were thinking of a serious air crash that might lead to the prolonged grounding of a common class of aircraft. It seemed unlikely, but would have a very large impact if it happened.

9/11 came just a few days later. We never envisaged anything so devastating, so inconceivably evil, but at least we had alerted our client to the extreme risks involved in the air industry. The deal was renegotiated and completed successfully.

Were the Beatles worth the risk?

If you were a music producer at Parlophone in the first few months of 1962, would you have backed the Beatles?

Remember that this was a distinguished record company that had never previously backed any rock 'n' roll groups. At the time, there were dozens of such groups with persistent promoters doing the rounds of the studios. One such group, the Beatles, had done a couple of tours in Hamburg and had developed a following at a night club in their home town of Liverpool.

You knew that one other record company, Decca, had shown some interest but had turned them down in favour of a similar group, Brian Poole and the Tremeloes. Some Decca executives also believed – in a now classic quote – that 'guitar groups are on the way out'. For your studio's first venture into rock 'n' roll, would you have chosen these four mop-topped lads from Liverpool?

Let's look at their Suns & Clouds (see figure).

Early 1962: would you have backed the Beatles?

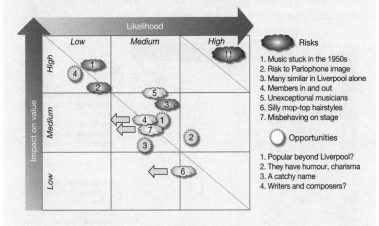

It couldn't have been an easy decision. On the one hand, there were so many wannabe groups around (risk 3) and the Beatles seemed unexceptional musically (risk 5). On the other hand, they had charisma and humour (opportunity 2). And, on the back of their Hamburg experience, they had built a loyal following among club-goers in Liverpool (opportunity 1). These may have been the four issues that stood out, two risks and two opportunities, above the diagonal, within the parabola.

No one would blame you, you would have thought, if you turned these guys down. Yet you had a hunch. They seemed to have something. Maybe they could improve their musical abilities. Maybe they could be marketed. Maybe some of the risks could be mitigated – perhaps they could develop their singing and songwriting capabilities, bin (contractually) their drinking and swearing on stage. You backed them.

Good call.

As a postscript, let's envisage how the backing decision would have changed one year later, in spring 1963. The Beatles' first single, 'Love Me Do', had reached the UK Top 20. Their second single, 'Please Please Me', and their first album, of the same name, were riding high as number one in both the single and album charts. Was this a flash in the pan? Were these guys to come and go with little trace like many before them?

You weren't to know then that their album would stay at number one for 30 weeks, before being replaced by, yes, their second album! That their fourth single, 'She Loves You', would become the biggest seller of all time, topping hits by their role model, Elvis Presley, and would remain so for more than a decade.

What you did know was that you'd sure made the right decision the year before. You'd also greatly underestimated them as musicians. They could write and compose catchy songs. The Suns & Clouds chart was transformed.

Spring 1963: now would you back the Beatles?

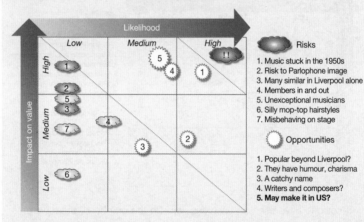

All the risks in the earlier Suns & Clouds chart had retreated leftward into insignificance. Even the risk of the four members splitting up was greatly reduced. Meanwhile, the opportunities were dazzling. Their popularity as performers had soared. Their potential as songwriters was formidable. And to cap it all, a new, huge opportunity had arisen (number five). Could they conceivably become the first British group to wow a US audience?

Would you have backed the Beatles in the spring of 1963? The Suns & Clouds says it all. Would you play the lottery if you knew what number was coming up?

The composite risk index and the 5×5 risk matrix

84

The tool

What preceded the Suns & Clouds, you may ask.

There are a host of other tools for assessing risk, all useful in their own right, but arguably of lesser effectiveness:

- Most focus on risk, not on opportunity, so can present an unbalanced picture.
- Most are less visually emphatic, thereby less appealing to a busy manager, let alone to his or her boss, banker or investor.

The composite risk index and the 5×5 risk matrix are simple, effective and widely used tools.

How to use them

As you did for the Sun & Clouds, pull together all the main risks you have identified through the strategy development process, whether market, competition, competitive position, strategic or operational risks.

Against each risk, again as before, assess them for likelihood of occurrence and impact on value should they occur. This time, however, assign each risk numerical grades, as shown below.

Likelihood of occurrence

1 Most unlikely, a rare occurrence

2 Unlikely, but conceivable

3 Quite likely, possible

4 Likely, probable

5 Most likely, not quite certain, but not far off

Impact on value (or, often found, Consequences)

1 Low – of negligible impact

2 Low-medium – of minor impact

3 Medium – of moderate impact

4 Medium-high – of major impact

5 High – of severe impact

Now multiply the grades together to obtain a *composite risk index*.

You can now categorise your risks according to their composite scores, for example as follows:

1 to 8:   Small risks

9 to 16:   Medium risks

20 or 25:   Big risks

Big risks, defined as at least likely (4) and high impact (5), or most likely (5) and medium-high impact (4), are show-stoppers if they are market risks which your firm can do little about. You should walk away from that market.

If these big risks are internal, over which your firm has control, your strategy should include robust ways of mitigating these risks for it to have any credibility.

But your best bet may again be to avoid such big risks and exit that business, as portrayed graphically in the *5×5 Risk Matrix*. In the example of Figure 84.1, 'big risks' are taken to include not just composite scores of 20 and 25, but also of 15 and 16 and even 10, where the risk is unlikely but the consequences severe. This would be a matrix typical of the aviation or space industries.

Figure 84.1 The 5×5 risk matrix: an example

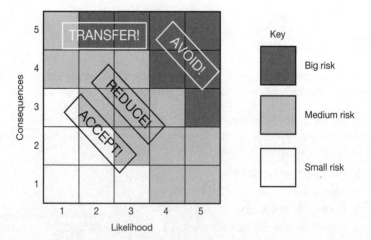

The four basic strategies for managing risk, as shown in the figure, are:

- Where possible, avoid the big risks, or, where not possible …
- … transfer them to your insurers.
- Reduce the medium risks through mitigation.
- Accept the small risks, live with them, though also consider how they could be further mitigated cost-effectively.

When to use them

The composite risk index is ubiquitous – not just in business, but in diverse areas of risk assessment, from project to prison management, from space stations to healthcare. I am a governor of a secondary school and we use the index across all aspects of school governance – in obvious areas of health and safety concern, like classics trips to Pompeii or rugby trips to Cornwall, but also in areas such as funding risk, information security risk and reputational risk. Against each risk we assess which of the 4Ts we should apply – terminate (avoid), transfer (to government or insurers), treat (reduce, mitigate) or tolerate (accept).

When to be wary

Be careful that your risk assessment doesn't degenerate into a box-ticking exercise.

And don't let the exercise grind you down. The trouble with many risk assessment and management exercises is that they can be unbalanced. The beauty of the Suns & Clouds chart is that it acknowledges risk, lives with it and balances it with opportunity. The composite risk index has no such balance, no opportunities. It would be all cloud on a Suns & Clouds chart. It can be unremitting gloom, a thorough downer on getting any strategy agreed or funded, let alone implemented.

85 The risk management matrix

The tool

'Risk comes from not knowing what you're doing', declared Warren Buffett.

The risk management matrix is another alternative to the Suns & Clouds, though, as with the composite risk index of Tool 84, it looks only at risk, not at opportunity.

This tool places emphasis on the management of risk, the 'knowing what you are doing' about it. It asks you to consider each risk not just by likelihood of occurrence and impact on value, but on manageability.

How to use it

Pull together all the main risks identified in your strategy development process to date. Rate them as you did in the Sun & Clouds, by likelihood of occurrence and by impact on value.

Now rate them also on manageability, as follows:

- *Zero* – this risk is unmanageable, wholly beyond your control to influence – it includes all market demand and industry supply risks, as well as others specific to your company but which you can do little about; you cannot influence the likelihood of occurrence, but you may be able to mitigate the impact (thus the loss of key personnel or of property due to fire or extremes of weather can be minimised through insurance).

- *Low* – this risk is difficult to manage: for example, competitive retaliation.

- *Medium* – this risk can be managed: for example, customer response to a new product launch (which can be redeveloped if required).

- *High* – this risk is easily managed: for example, customer response to a marketing initiative (which can be redirected as required).

Plot the risks on a chart of manageability versus impact on value, using circles proportionate in scale to likelihood of occurrence – see Figure 85.1.

Figure 85.1 The risk management matrix: an example

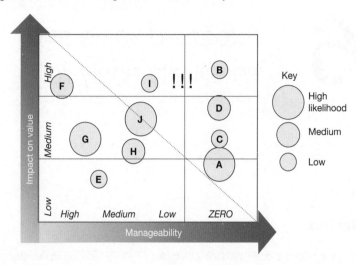

With luck your circles will be predominantly below the diagonal. And you won't have any large circles towards the upper-right corner.

Now see what you can do to improve overall positioning on your risk management matrix. What steps can you take to transfer risk on unmanageable risks? Or to enhance the manageability of certain risks?

When to use it

Use it as a call to action. Force yourself to think harder on managing risk, on transferring and mitigating risk, and how such steps can make your strategy more robust.

When to be wary

Again, as with the composite risk index (Tool 84), this is all about risk management and, unlike with the more balanced Suns & Clouds chart, with its compensating opportunities, the process can get bogged down in negativity.

Expected value and sensitivity analysis

The tool

'It is great to be a blonde. With low expectations it's very easy to surprise people', said Pamela Anderson.

So too in business – set expectations low, then super-please your board or backer.

Expected value is a concept that has been around since the days of Pascal, Fermat and Huygens in the mid-seventeenth century. It is no less useful today.

The principle behind it is that future gain should be directly proportional to the chance of getting it. Thus, the real value of a piece of business to you today should be the nominal value of the order multiplied by the probability of winning it.

This concept is most useful in forecasting, especially if yours is a lumpy business with few, sporadic, large orders – such as in automotive components (where the supplier either wins a place on a programme which can last for years or doesn't), capital equipment, outsourcing or management consulting.

Each prospective order can be probability weighted and the resultant expected values totted up to yield an overall expected value total.

This total then becomes the base case order forecast, against which you can apply sensitivity testing.

An example may help.

How to use it

Suppose your firm has existing orders totalling 1000 units and 10 prospective new orders, ranging from 30 to 300 units, over the next three years – see Figure 86.1.

One commonly found way of forecasting future orders would be to take different scenarios – a downside case, where only the more likely orders come in, and an upside case, where they all come in. The base case would then split the difference.

Thus, in this example a downside case (taking only new orders where probability is greater than 50 per cent, say) would give total orders in Year 3 of 1490 units. The upside case gives 2000 units, so the base case could be 1745 (halfway).

Figure 86.1 Expected value: an example

Orders	Y1	Y2	Y3	Prob-ability	Downside case Y3	Expected value Y3
Existing	1000	1050	1100	100%	1100	1100
New:						
A	40	40	40	90%	40	36
B	50	50	50	80%	50	40
C	30	30	30	45%		13.5
D	80	80	80	20%		16
E		180	180	60%	180	108
F		30	30	55%	30	16.5
G		40	40	40%		16
H			60	30%		18
I			90	70%	90	63
J			300	10%		30
Total	1200	1500	2000		1490	1457

But this greatly over-estimates likely future orders. The largest one, for 300 units, has just a 10 per cent probability. It is excluded from the downside case, but included in the upside case, therefore part included in the base case – with an *implied* probability of 50 per cent, when in reality it should be just 10 per cent. The second largest order, for 180 units, is included in both the downside and upside cases, and accordingly has an implied probability in the base case of 100 per cent, when it should be just 60 per cent.

Far more realistic for future planning purposes is to apply *individual* probabilities to each *individual* new order to obtain expected values, the total of which should be a more usable base case – in this case, 1457 units in Year 3.

That should be the base around which sensitivity testing can proceed. Sensitivity analysis is another time-tested tool for testing for uncertainty of inputs and analysing the impact on outputs. Values of selected inputs can be varied, typically by 5 to 10 per cent, to assess impact on output.

In this case, having established a base case, appropriate sensitivity tests could be:

- With Order E – giving total expected value orders in Year 3 of 1529 units (note that base case rises by only 72, the difference between 60 per cent and 100 per cent of 180)
- Without Order E – 1349 units
- With Order J – 1727 units
- Without Order J – 1427 units
- With Orders E and J – 1799 units
- Without Orders E and J – 1319 units.

The impact of these sensitivity tests on sales, the P&L and cash flow can then be measured and appropriate flexibility built into the firm's operations to be able to handle each outcome competently.

The most common type of sensitivity tests come from varying key parameters such as:

- Sales volume forecasts up/down 5–10 per cent
- Unit pricing forecasts up/down 2–3 per cent
- Labour costs up 5 per cent
- Capex up 10 per cent.

Again, the impact of these varied inputs can be evaluated on the key financial and operational outputs and appropriate action taken.

When to use it

Expected value is most appropriately used where there are yes/no moments which can have a major impact on your business. It is less useful in businesses where there are large numbers of customers, such as in consumer goods or services, but even there it can be used on the revenue side to allow for the success of individual segment initiatives or on the cost side for major lumpy items, such as lease renewal.

Sensitivity analysis should be used in all investment appraisals, whether expected values are used or not.

When to be wary

Take care with the individual probabilities. It is human nature to over-inflate expectations. Over-optimism may help in team motivation, but is unhelpful in business planning.

Black swans (Taleb)   87

The tool

'As rare as a black swan' was a commonplace phrase in medieval times.

It meant that the event under discussion was impossible, since all knew that swans were white and white only. Then, in the late seventeenth century, mutant black swans were discovered in Australia and the phrase came to mean something entirely different – a perceived impossibility, subsequently proved to be possible.

Nassim Nicholas Taleb uses the term 'black swan' to denote a very rare event, one of such magnitude and improbability that people choose to ignore it. They brush it under the carpet.

Yet when such an event happens it seems quite evident with hindsight.

Taleb specifies three characteristics of black swan events. They are

- Rare, at the time seemingly highly improbable, even impossible, they are extreme outliers in the normal bell curve of probability distribution
- Extreme in their impact
- Explicable and justifiable retrospectively.

Thus, the financial meltdown of 2008 was a black swan event (see Figure 87.1) – banks suddenly illiquid, worldwide, due to exposure to an esoteric financial instrument called securitised sub-prime mortgages. Yet, with hindsight, a meltdown was inevitable. So too was the dot-com bubble a black swan. Even 9/11.

According to Taleb we live in the world of 'Mediocristan', where rare events don't occur, whereas we should be living in 'Extremistan', where unpredictable events can and do take place, now and again, with devastating consequences.

We are like turkeys. We get fed by seemingly kind farmers, evidently concerned for our welfare, day after day, until just before Christmas a rare and unpredictable event occurs which has a devastating, and in this case terminal, effect on our lives.

Like turkeys, we don't include such black swan events in our plans. They aren't programmed into the forecasting models of businessmen, financiers, economists or politicians.

But they could and should be allowed for and managed.

Figure 87.1 Black swans: an example

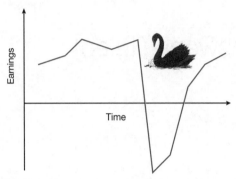

Source: Adapted from Nassim Nicholas Taleb, *Fooled by Randomness: The Hidden Role of Chance in Life and in the Markets*, Allen Lane, 2002

How to use it

Pull out your Suns & Clouds chart of Tool 83. What risks have you placed in the top left-hand corner? Are any of these black swan events – most unlikely but potentially devastating and rationally explicable in retrospect?

If you have one, what steps can you take to manage that black swan risk? Using the terms of the risk management matrix of Tool 85, what scope do you have to:

- Avoid the risk altogether, perhaps by segment withdrawal?
- Transfer the risk in part or in whole to insurers?
- Mitigate the risk through contingency planning?

If you choose to retain the black swan risk by sweeping it under the carpet, you are trusting to luck.

When to use it

There was little new in the black swan discussion that had not been covered previously in tomes on risk management. What was new was the catchy terminology and the condemnation heaped on those in Wall Street in particular who blithely ignored the existence of highly improbable, hugely impactful risks, understandable in hindsight, but by then catastrophically late.

When to be wary

Don't categorise all low-probability, high-impact risks as black swans or you'll never get out of bed in the morning.

Strategic bets (Burgelman and Grove)

88

The tool

'You should never bet against anything in science at odds of more than about 1012 to 1', teased nuclear scientist Ernest Rutherford.

You may find such odds unattractive. But that depends on whether yours is a strategic bet ...

Stanford professor Robert Burgelman and former Intel CEO Andrew Grove conducted lengthy research on the dynamics of strategy, based in large part on the evolution of Intel. They differentiated between *autonomous strategy*, where the CEO has the luxury of time, flexibility and autonomy, and *induced strategy*, where the CEO needs to respond, often rapidly, to market change.

They concluded that 'corporate longevity, especially in high tech sectors, depends on matching cycles of autonomous and induced strategy processes to different forms of strategic dynamics, and that the role of alert strategic leadership is to appropriately balance the induced and autonomous processes throughout these cycles'.

Furthermore, in autonomous strategy development, a critical top management strategic role is to understand the fundamental *strategic bet* the firm is making.

This depends on two factors:

- The extent to which the opportunity has been validated (through the process of determining the strategic context)
- The extent to which available cash reserves are sufficient to protect the firm from disaster in case the project, once fully scaled up, fails.

They identify four types of strategic bet situation (see Figure 88.1):

- *The 'safe bet'* – where the opportunity has been validated and cash is sufficient
- *The 'wait-to-bet'* – where the opportunity is yet to be validated and cash is sufficient

- *The 'bet-the-company'* – where the opportunity has been validated but cash reserves are insufficient and will need topping up, whether from equity or debt

- *The 'desperate bet'* – where the opportunity is not yet validated and where cash reserves are insufficient.

Figure 88.1 Strategic bets

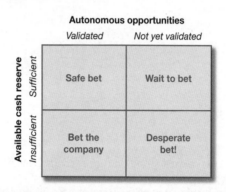

Source: Adapted from Robert A. Burgelman and Andrew S. Grove, 'Let Chaos Reign, then Rein in Chaos Repeatedly: Managing Strategic Dynamics for Corporate Longevity', *Strategic Management Journal* 28, 2007

How to use it

The y-axis in the Suns & Clouds chart (Tool 83) examines the impact on value, or impact on discounted cash flow. But that implies a net figure – discounted cash inflows less discounted cash outflow's of strategic risks and opportunities.

What if the cash inflows have been overestimated? And what if the net cash outflows exceed the available cash reserves? Then, assuming you have done your utmost to validate the opportunity and are not venturing into the murky depths of 'desperate betting', you are 'betting the company'.

You need to take great care with your sensitivity analysis.

When to use it

It is always wise to think not just on the potential net benefits of an investment opportunity, but also on the total costs. Costs will be inevitable, benefits not so.

When to be wary

If the costs are so high as to endanger the firm if the benefits do not work out as planned, take great care with your validation process.

Conclusion

A final cautionary word from Michael Porter: 'The company without a strategy is willing to try anything.'

Yours won't be one such company. By following this book, yours will have direction. You will try only those things that are in concert with your strategy.

In the introduction to this book it was asked whether you as a manager or entrepreneur find the idea of drawing up a strategy daunting.

You have now read this book. Strategy isn't that grim, is it?

As long as you follow the process, the Strategy Pyramid, and deploy at least the essential tools in each of the pyramid's building blocks, you will have a strategy.

What is more, that strategy should be robust, able to pass the scrutiny of your board, even to withstand the forensic cross-examination of an external backer.

And, just in case the chairman takes you to one side after the meeting and asks how you did it, how you managed to come up with such an impressive strategy, let him or her in on the secret.

The key to a winning strategy, a backable strategy, as opposed to a run-of-the-mill strategy, is threefold:

- Appreciating the micro-economic context
- Creating a sustainable competitive advantage
- Fine-tuning the balance of risk and opportunity.

Enjoy and good luck!

References and further reading

Section 1

Andrews, Kenneth R. (1994) *The Concept of Corporate Strategy*, Irwin Professional.

Bridges, William (1998) *Creating You & Co: Learn to Think Like the CEO of Your Own Career*, Da Capo Press.

Evans, Vaughan (2011) *The FT Essential Guide to Writing a Business Plan: How to Win Backing to Start Up or Grow Your Business,* FT Publishing.

Juran, Joseph M. (1951) *Quality Control Handbook*, McGraw-Hill.

Koch, Richard (2007) *The 80/20 Principle: The Secret of Achieving More with Less*, 2nd edn, Nicholas Brealey Publishing.

Koch, Richard (2011) *The FT Guide to Strategy: How to Create, Pursue and Deliver a Winning Strategy*, 4th edn, FT Prentice Hall.

Minto, Barbara (2002) *The Pyramid Principle: Present Your Ideas so Clearly that the Ideas Jump Off the Page and into the Reader's Mind*, Pearson Education.

Mullins, John (2010) *The New Business Road Test: What Entrepreneurs and Executives Should Do Before Writing a Business Pla*n, 3rd edn, FT Prentice Hall.

Pareto, Vilfredo (1906) *Manuale di Economia Politica*.

Section 2

Collins, James C. and Porras, Jerry I., 'Building Your Company's Vision', *Harvard Business Review*, September–October, 1996.

Collins, James C. and Porras, Jerry I. (1997) *Built to Last: Successful Habits of Visionary Companies*, Random House.

Doran, G. T., 'There's a S.M.A.R.T. Way to Write Management's Goals and Objectives', *Management Review*, November 1981.

Drucker, Peter F. (1954) *The Practice of Management*, HarperCollins.

Friedman, Milton, 'The Social Responsibility of Business Is to Increase Profits', *New York Times Magazine*, 13 September 1970.

Geus, Arie de, 'The Living Company', *Harvard Business Review*, March–April 1997.

Handy, Charles (1993) *Understanding Organisations*, 4th edn, Penguin.

Handy, Charles (1995) *Gods of Management: The Changing World of Organisations*, 3rd edn, Penguin.

Handy, Charles, 'What's a Business For?', *Harvard Business Review*, December 2002.

Handy, Charles, Porter, Michael E., Kramer, Mark R., Prahalad, C. K. and others (2003) *Harvard Business Review on Corporate Responsibility*, Harvard Business Press.

Henderson, David (2001) *Misguided Virtue: False Notions of Corporate Social Responsibility*, Institute of Economic Affairs, December 2001.

Kaplan, Robert S. and Norton, David P. (1996) *The Balanced Scorecard: Translating Strategy into Action*, Harvard Business Press.

Kaplan, Robert S. and Norton, David P. (2000) *The Strategy-Focused Organization: How Balanced Scorecard Companies Thrive in the New Business Environment*, Harvard Business Press.

Kaplan, Robert S. and Norton, David P. (2004) *Strategy Maps: Converting Intangible Assets into Tangible Outcomes*, Harvard Business Press.

Kotler, Philip and Lee, Nancy (2004) *Corporate Social Responsibility: Doing the Most Good for Your Company and Your Cause*, Wiley.

Latham, Gary P. and Locke, Edwin A., 'Building a Practically Useful Theory of Goal Setting and Task Motivation', *American Psychologist*, September 2002.

Orlitzky, Marc, Schmidt, Frank L. and Rynes, Sara L., 'Corporate Social and Financial Performance: A Meta-Analysis', *Organization Studies*, 24, 2003.

Porter, Michael E. and Kramer, Mark R., 'Strategy & Society: The Link between Competitive Advantage and Corporate Social Responsibility', *Harvard Business Review*, December 2006.

Porter, Michael E. and Kramer, Mark R., 'Creating Shared Value', *Harvard Business Review*, January–February 2011.

Rappaport, Alfred (1986) *Creating Shareholder Value: The New Standard for Business Performance*, Free Press.

Rumelt, Richard P. (2001) *Good Strategy, Bad Strategy: The Difference and Why It Matters*, Profile.

Stern Stewart & Co. (www.sternstewart.com) on *EVA®*.

Werther, William B. and Chandler, David B. (2010) *Strategic Corporate Social Responsibility: Stakeholders in a Global Environment*, 2nd edn, Sage Publications.

Section 3

Chase, Charles (2009) *Demand-Driven Forecasting: A Structured Approach to Forecasting*, Wiley.

Evans, Vaughan (2011) *The FT Essential Guide to Writing a Business Plan: How to Win Backing to Start Up or Grow Your Business*, FT Publishing.

Section 4

Brandenburger, Adam M. and Nalebuff, Barry J., 'The Right Game: Use Game Theory to Shape Strategy', *Harvard Business Review*, July–August 1995.

Brandenburger, Adam M. and Nalebuff, Barry J. (1995) *Co-opetition*, HarperCollins.

Coyne, Kevin P. and Subramaniam, Soma, 'Bringing Discipline to Strategy', *McKinsey Quarterly*, No 3, 2000.

Gillespie, Andrew (2007) *Foundations of Economics (additional chapter on Business Strategy, including PESTEL Analysis)*, Oxford University Press.

Hamel, Gary and Prahalad, C. K. (1994) *Competing for the Future*, Harvard Business School Press.

Porter, Michael E., 'How Competitive Forces Shape Strategy', *Harvard Business Review*, March–April 1979.

Porter, Michael E. (1980) *Competitive Strategy: Techniques for Analyzing Industries and Competitors*, Free Press.

Rumelt, Richard P., 'Does Industry Matter Much?', *Strategic Management Journal*, 12, 1991.

Section 5

Ansoff, Igor M. (1965) *Corporate Strategy*, McGraw-Hill.

Ansoff, Igor M. (1984) *Implanting Strategic Management*, Prentice Hall.

Ansoff, Igor M. (1988) *The New Corporate Strategy*, John Wiley.

Camp, Robert C. (1989) *Benchmarking: The Search for Industry Best Practices that Lead to Superior Performance*, ASQ Quality Press.

Grant, Robert M. (2011) *Contemporary Strategy Analysis*, 7th edn, Wiley-Blackwell.

Kaplan, Robert S., 'Limits to Benchmarking', *Harvard Business Publishing Newsletters*, November 2005.

Porter, Michael E. (1984) *Competitive Advantage*, Free Press.

Section 6

Bain & Company (www.bain.com) on *The Opportunity/Vulnerability Matrix*.

The Boston Consulting Group (www.bcg.com) on *The Growth/Share Matrix*.

Grant, Robert M. (2011) *Contemporary Strategy Analysis*, 7th edn, Wiley-Blackwell.

Hamel, Gary and Prahalad, C. K. (1994) *Competing for the Future*, Harvard Business School Press.

Koch, Richard (2007) *The FT Guide to Strategy: How to Create, Pursue and Deliver a Winning Strategy*, 4th edn, FT Prentice Hall.

L.E.K. Consulting (www.lek.com) on *The Opportunity/Vulnerability Matrix*.

Arthur D. Little Inc (www.adl.com) on *The Strategic Condition Matrix*.

McKinsey & Company (www.mckinsey.com) on *The Advantage/Attractiveness Matrix* and *The 7S Framework*.

Section 7

Brealey, Richard, Myers, Stuart and Allen, Franklin (2007) *Principles of Corporate Finance*, McGraw-Hill.

The Chartered Institute of Marketing, *Marketing and the 7Ps*, 2009.

Collins, Jim, 'Best Beats First', *Forbes*, August 2000.

Collins, Jim (2001) *Good to Great: Why Some Companies Make the Leap ... and Others Don't*, Random House Business.

Gladwell, Malcolm (2000) *The Tipping Point: How Little Things Can Make a Big Difference*, Little Brown.

Hammer, Michael, 'Reengineering Work: Don't Automate, Obliterate', *Harvard Business Review*, July–August 1990.

Hammer, Michael and Champy, James (2001) *Reengineering the Corporation: A Manifesto for Business Revolution*, 3rd edn, Nicholas Brealey.

Hartung, Adam (2008) *Create Marketplace Disruption: How to Stay Ahead of the Competition*, FT Press.

Hartung, Adam, 'How Facebook Beat MySpace', *Forbes.com*, 14 January 2011.

Henderson, Bruce (1973) *The Experience Curve Reviewed*, The Boston Consulting Group, (reprint No 135).

Kano, N., Seraku, N., Takahashi, N. and Tsuji, S., 'Attractive Quality and Must-be Quality', *Hinshitsu: The Journal of the Japanese Society for Quality Control*, April 1984.

Karamchandani, Ashish, Kubzansky, Mike and Lalwani, Nishant, 'The Globe: Is the Bottom of the Pyramid Really for You?', *Harvard Business Review*, March–April 2011.

Kim, W. Chan and Mauborgne, Renee (2005) *Blue Ocean Strategy: How to Create Uncontested Market Space and Make the Competition Irrelevant,* Harvard Business School Press.

Koller, Tim, Goedhart, Marc and Wessels, David (all McKinsey & Co) (2010) *Valuation: Measuring and Managing the Value of Companies*, 5th edn, Wiley.

Lauterborn, Robert F., Schullz, Don E. and Tannenbaum, Stanley I. (1993) *Integrated Marketing Communications*, NTC Business Books.

Marshall, Alfred (1890) *Principles of Economics*, Macmillan.

Maslow, Abraham H., 'A Theory of Human Motivation', *Psychological Review* 50, 1943.

McCarthy, E. Jerome (1960) *Basic Marketing. A Managerial Approach*, R. D. Irwin.

Porter, Michael E. (1980) *Competitive Strategy: Techniques for Analyzing Industries and Competitors*, Free Press.

Prahalad, C. K. (2004) *The Fortune at the Bottom of the Pyramid: Eradicating Poverty Through Profits,* Wharton.

Prahalad, C. K. and Lieberthal, Kenneth, 'The End of Corporate Imperialism', *Harvard Business Review*, July–August 1998.

The Strategic Planning Institute (www.pimsonline.com) on *PIMS*.

Tracy, Brian (2004) *Million Dollar Habits: Proven Power Practices to Double and Triple Your Income*, Entrepreneur Press.

Section 8

Barney, Jay, 'Firm Resources and Competitive Advantage', *Journal of Management* 17, 1991.

Bilton, Chris (2007) *Management and Creativity: From Creative Industries to Creative Management,* Wiley-Blackwell.

Bower, Joseph L. and Christensen, Clayton M., 'Disruptive Technologies: Catching the Wave', *Harvard Business Review*, January–February 1995.

Brandenburger, Adam M. and Nalebuff, Barry J. (1996) *Co-opetition*, Doubleday.

Christensen, Clayton M. (1997) *The Innovator's Dilemma: When New Technologies Cause Great Firms to Fail*, Harvard Business School Press.

Collis, David J. and Montgomery, Cynthia A., 'Competing on Resources: Strategy in the 1990s', *Harvard Business Review*, July–August 1995, reprinted as 'Competing on Resources', July 2008.

Cummings, Stephen and Wilson, David (2003) *Images of Strategy*, Blackwell.

Day, George S. (1990) *Market Driven Strategy: Processes for Creating Value*, Free Press.

Day, George S. (2007) *The Market Driven Organization: Understanding, Attracting, and Keeping Valuable Customers*, Simon and Schuster.

Goold, Michael, Campbell, Andrew and Alexander, Marcus (1994) *Corporate-Level Strategy: Creating Value in Multi-Business Companies,* Wiley.

Gratton, Linda (2007) *Innovation Hot Spots: Why Some Companies Buzz with Energy and Innovation… and Others Don't*, FT Prentice Hall.

Greiner, Larry E., 'Evolution and Revolution as Organizations Grow', *Harvard Business Review*, July–August 1972 and May–June 1988.

Hamel, Gary and Prahalad, C. K. (1994) *Competing for the Future*, op. cit.

Kay, John (1995) *Foundations of Corporate Success: How Business Strategies Add Value*, Oxford.

Koller, Tim, Goedhart, Marc and Wessels, David (all McKinsey & Co) (2010) *Valuation: Measuring and Managing the Value of Companies*, 5th edn, Wiley.

Kotter, John P. (1996) *Leading Change*, Harvard Business School Press.

Maletz, Mark C. and Nohria, Nitin, 'Managing in the Whitespace', *Harvard Business Review*, February 2001.

Mintzberg, Henry (1994) *The Rise and Fall of Strategic Planning*, Free Press.

Mintzberg, Henry, Ahlstrand, Bruce W. and Lampel, Joseph (1998) *Strategy Safari: A Guided Tour through the Wilds of Strategic Management*, Financial Times Prentice Hall.

Mintzberg, Henry, Ahlstrand, Bruce W. and Lampel, Joseph (2005) *Strategy Bites Back: It Is A Lot More, And Less, Than You Ever Imagined…*, Financial Times Management.

Nonaka, Ikujiro and Takeuchi, Hirotaka (1995) *The Knowledge-Creating Company*, Oxford University Press.

Penrose, Edith T. (1959) *The Theory of the Growth of the Firm*, John Wiley.

Peters, Tom and Waterman Jr, Robert H. (1982) *In Search of Excellence: Lessons from America's Best Run Companies*, Profile.

Porter, Michael (1984) *Competitive Advantage*, Free Press.

Rumelt, Richard P. (2011) *Good Strategy, Bad Strategy: The Difference and Why It Matters*, Profile.

Snow, Charles C. and Hrebiniak, Lawrence G., 'Strategy, Distinctive Competence, and Organizational Performance', *Administrative Science Quarterly*, June 1980.

Teece, David J., Pisano, Gary and Shuen, Amy, 'Dynamic Capabilities and Strategic Management', *Strategic Management Journal* (18) 7, 1997.

Treacy, Michael and Wiersema, Fred, 'Customer Intimacy and Other Value Disciplines', *Harvard Business Review*, January–February 1993.

Treacy, Michael and Wiersema, Fred (1996) *The Discipline of Market Leaders: Choose Your Customers, Narrow Your Focus, Dominate Your Market,* Perseus.

Zook, Chris (2001) *Profit from the Core*, Harvard Business School Press.

Section 9

Burgelman, Robert A. and Grove, Andrew S., 'Let Chaos Reign, then Reign in Chaos – Repeatedly: Managing Strategic Dynamics for Corporate Longevity', *Strategic Management Journal* 28, 2007.

Evans, Vaughan (2009) *Backing U!: A Business-Oriented Guide to Backing Your Passion and Achieving Career Success*, Business and Careers Press.

Evans, Vaughan (2011) *FT Essential Guide to Writing a Business Plan: How to Win Backing to Start Up or Grow Your Business*, FT Publishing.

Taleb, Nassim Nicholas (2002) *Fooled by Randomness: The Hidden Role of Chance in Life and in the Markets*, Allen Lane.

Taleb, Nassim Nicholas (2007) *The Black Swan: The Impact of the Highly Improbable*, Allen Lane.

Glossary

Advantage See **competitive advantage**.

Attractiveness See **market attractiveness**.

Balanced scorecard A means of translating corporate goals and strategy into a series of defined, measurable objectives, spanning key departmental functions (Tool 13).

Benchmarking A systematic approach to measuring key metrics in a firm's operations, systems and processes against best practice, whether found in the same industry or others (Tool 34).

Black swan event A very rare event, one of such magnitude and improbability that people choose to ignore it, yet explicable and justifiable with hindsight (Tool 87).

Blue oceans Uncontested market space, as distinct from the 'red oceans' of existing market space (Tool 49).

Brainstorming A structured process for the generation of ideas, done individually or in a group setting (Tool 43).

Business Strategic business unit.

Business process redesign (or re-engineering) Radical, comprehensive rethinking of key business processes to attain step-up levels of cost, production, quality, speed or service performance (Tool 57).

Business strategy Gaining a sustainable competitive advantage in a single strategic business unit.

Capabilities How a firm deploys its resources.

Capability gap The gap in performance between where your firm is currently positioned against key success factors and where it aims to be.

Competitive advantage The strategic advantage possessed by one firm over others in a product/market segment or industry which enables it to make superior returns.

Competitive intensity The degree of competition in a given industry and a main determinant of industry profitability.

Competitive position A rating of a firm's relative competitiveness in a given product/market segment or industry.

Complement The opposite of a substitute – where an increase in demand for one good (or service) results in an increase in demand for another.

Composite risk index A numerical assessment of key risks, where grades of likelihood of occurrence are multiplied by those of value impact to attain a composite grade (Tool 84).

Co-opetition Cooperating with your competitors legitimately to change industry competitive forces in your favour (Tool 75).

Core competence An integrated bundle of skills and technologies, the sum of learning across individual skill sets and individual organisational units (Tool 63).

Corporate social responsibility How firms address the social, environmental and economic impacts of their operations and so help meet sustainable development goals (Tool 10).

Corporate strategy Optimising value from a portfolio of businesses and adding value to each through exploiting the firm's core resources and capabilities.

Customer purchasing criteria (CPCs) What customers need from their suppliers (Tool 23).

Discounted cash flow analysis Projected annual cash inflows less outflows, including the upfront capital outflow, discounted at the opportunity cost of capital and summed to yield a net present value.

Disruptive technology One which radically alters the benefit/price algorithm (Tool 74).

Distinctive capability One which is a necessary but not sufficient characteristic for success and is sustainable and appropriable (Tool 66).

Distinctive competence Something an organisation does especially well relative to its competitors (Tool 67).

Dynamic capability One that is sufficiently dynamic to cope in times of rapid change, namely distinctive processes, knowledge assets and path dependencies (Tool 68).

Economic Value Added® A measure of a higher than expected return on capital employed (Tool 12).

Economies of scale The reduction in unit costs in a firm arising from an increase in the scale of its operations (Tool 25).

Economies of scope The reduction in unit costs in a firm arising from the production of similar or related goods or services.

Emergent strategy That which emerges over time as intentions collide with and respond to a changing reality (Tool 69).

Expected value The parameter value multiplied by the probability of that value being realised (Tool 86).

Experience curve An effect whereby the unit cost of a standard product declines by a constant percentage each time cumulative output doubles (Tool 46).

Generic strategies Those which relate to an entire genus or class: namely, differentiation, low-cost or focus strategies (Tool 45).

Ideal player The theoretical competitor who achieves the highest possible rating against each key success factor.

Income elasticity of demand The percentage change in demand for a good (or service) divided by the percentage change in income (Tool 19).

Industry maturity The stage of evolution of an industry, from embryonic through to growing, mature and ageing (Tool 40).

Industry supply The aggregate supply by producers of a product (or product group) over a specified period of time, typically one year.

Innovation hot spots The times and places in some companies and teams where unexpected cooperation and collaboration flourish, creating great energy, productivity and excitement (Tool 78).

Internal rate of return That discount rate in discounted cash flow analysis which delivers a net present value of zero.

Issue A matter under discussion or in dispute, often due to future uncertainty – a risk or an opportunity.

Key success factors (KSFs) What firms need to do to meet customer purchasing criteria and run a sound business (Tool 24).

Macro-economics The study of the aggregate economy, whether regional, national or international.

Market attractiveness A composite measure of the relative attractiveness of a product/market segment, taking into account factors such as market size, market growth, competitive intensity, industry profitability and market risk.

Market contextual plan review An assessment of the achievability of the revenues and margins forecast in a business plan by key product/market segment (Tool 82).

Marketcrafting Creating estimates of market size (and growth) and market share (and growth) from the bottom up, by using index numbers to gauge the relative scale of key producers, present and past (Tool 16).

Market demand The aggregate demands of customers for a product (or product group) over a specified period of time, typically one year.

Market-driven organisation Focus on capabilities guided by a shared understanding of industry structure, the needs of target customer segments, positional advantages being sought and trends in the environment (Tool 72).

Market-positioning school Proponents of the view that strategy should be focused at the level of the business, where all meaningful competition resides, and corporate strategy limited to portfolio planning.

Micro-economics The study of small economic units, such as the consumer, the household, the non-profit organisation or, most commonly, the firm.

Moving average A method of smoothing a time series (typically annual) by averaging a fixed number of consecutive terms (typically three years) (Tool 18).

Net present value The end-result of discounted cash flow analysis.

Offshoring Outsourcing carried out by foreign, usually lower-cost suppliers.

Outsourcing The process of buying in business processes from independent providers as opposed to performing them in-house (Tool 58).

Parenting advantage The creation of synergies not just between strategic business units but between them and the centre (Tool 62).

Payback The number of years it takes for net cash inflows to recoup initial investment costs.

PESTEL analysis A framework for identifying external issues affecting industry competition, namely political, economic, social, technological, environmental and legal issues (Tool 28).

PIMS An independent database which measures the profit impact of market strategy (Tool 52).

Portfolio The collection of key product/market segments in a business or of businesses in a multi-business company.

Price elasticity of demand The percentage change in demand for a good (or service) divided by the percentage change in price (Tool 51).

Profit from the core Build power in a well-defined core (Tool 71).

Resource-based school Proponents of the view that strategy should be focused on leveraging the resources and capabilities of the corporation as a whole (Tools 63–68).

Resources A firm's productive assets, whether human, physical, financial or intangible, as distinct from capabilities, which are how a firm deploys its resources.

Scenario A coherent and consistent portrayal of a series of future events based on specific parameter assumptions made by the strategist (Tool 44).

Segment A slice of business where the firm sells one product (or product group) to one customer group (strictly a 'product/market segment').

Sensitivity analysis The tweaking of parameter value assumptions to test overall impact on key financials (Tool 86).

Shareholder value The value a shareholder gains from investing in a firm through dividend and other payouts and capital appreciation/gain upon exit.

SMART objectives Those which are specific, measurable, attainable, relevant and time-limited (Tool 8).

SME Small or medium-sized enterprise.

Stakeholder Persons and organisations with a non-shareholding stake in the success of the firm: for example, employees, customers, suppliers, national and local government, the local community.

Stick to the knitting Focus on what the company knows and does best (Tool 70).

Strategically valuable resources Those which are valuable only if recognised strategically within an industry/market context (Tool 64).

Strategic bet One which takes into account validation and available cash reserves in case of failure (Tool 88).

Strategic business unit (SBU) A profit centre entity with a closely interrelated product (or service) offering and a cost structure largely independent of other business units.

Strategic due diligence (aka **market or commercial due diligence**) An assessment of the key risks and opportunities in market demand, industry competition, competitive position, strategy and the business plan facing a target company (Tool 82).

Strategic investment decision Go/no go decision on an investment of strategic importance (Tool 48).

Strategic repositioning Adjusting strategic position through investing, holding, exiting or entering segments (for business strategy) or businesses (for corporate strategy).

Strategic resources Those that are valuable, rare, inimitable and non-substitutable (Tool 65).

Strategy How a firm achieves its goals by deploying its scarce resources to gain a sustainable competitive advantage.

Strategy map The translation of a balanced scorecard into a two-dimensional chart, showing how a firm can create value by connecting strategic objectives in cause-and-effect relationships (Tool 13).

Structured interviewing Systematised interviewing of customers, suppliers and other industry observers to gain strategic information (Tool 35).

Substitute The opposite of a complement – where an increase in demand for one good or service results in a decrease in demand for another.

SWOT analysis A matrix of the strengths, weaknesses, opportunities and threats of a firm (Tool 6).

Synergy Where the whole is greater than the sum of the parts and specifically where the value of a merged entity is greater than the pre-bid, standalone values of acquirer plus target (or partner).

The 4Ps The product, place, price and promotion components of the marketing mix (Tool 53).

The 7S framework Seven elements of corporate success: namely, strategy, structure, systems, skills, staff, style and shared values (Tool 41).

The five forces Key forces driving industry competition: namely, internal rivalry, the threat of new entrants or substitutes and supplier and customer bargaining power (Tool 22).

The HOOF approach Forecasting market demand by assessing the historic (H) rate of growth, identifying key drivers (D), assessing how these and potentially new drivers may change (D) and thereby deriving demand forecasts (F) – Tool 17.

The innovator's dilemma Do you or do you not invest heavily, with inevitable cannibalisation of existing sales, to protect against the possibility of an upstart doing likewise (Tool 74)?

The knowledge spiral A continuous cycle of four integrated processes in knowledge conversion: socialisation, externalisation, combination and internalisation (Tool 80).

The Suns & Clouds chart An assessment of key risks and opportunities, portrayed visually as suns and clouds, by likelihood of occurrence and value impact should they occur (Tool 83).

The value chain The key primary and support activities of a firm (Tool 31).

Tipping point A point beyond which ideas, products or social norms, which may have been around for a while, suddenly catch alight and spread like wildfire (Tool 50).

Value disciplines The three disciplines which create value are operational excellence, customer intimacy and product leadership (Tool 73).

Whitespace The large but mostly unoccupied territory in a company where rules are vague, strategy is unclear and where entrepreneurial activity most often takes place (Tool 69).

Index

4Cs approach 217
4Ps marketing mix 214–17, 286
5C situation analysis 29–30
5×5 risk matrix 327, 328–9
7Ps 217
7S framework 167–9
80/20 Principle (Pareto) 24–6

addressed and addressable markets 66–7
adjacency opportunities 284–5
advertising 25, 216
aggressive strategies 271–2
aims 6, 37, 160
    see also goals; objectives
airlines 76–7, 95, 113, 137, 182, 263, 290
Airwalk shoes 205
Aldi 224
Alexander, Marcus 252
alien territory business 254
alliances 113, 188, 240, 242–4, 248, 298, 300
analyser strategy 271–3
Andrews, Kenneth R. 31
Anglo-Saxon business model 43, 45, 60–1, 240
animation, strategy as 307–8
Ansoff, Igor 131–2, 200, 224, 281
AOL 281
Apple 181, 197, 200, 290
appropriability 261, 268
architecture 268–9
Ashridge Strategic Management Centre 252
assets 61, 124, 274–5, 283
    see also resources
Attractiveness/Advantage Matrix 9, 91, 145,
        146–50, 153–4, 238, 239, 259

bad strategy 302–4
Bain & Co. 170–1, 283
balanced scorecard 55–7
ballast business 253–4
Barney, Jay 256, 261, 265–6, 269, 274
barometric method 87
barriers to entry 28, 30, 94, 96
barriers to exit 93
BCG Growth/Share Matrix 9, 151–4, 170–1, 223,
        238, 239
The Beatles 325–6
benchmarking 123, 125, 136–8, 259
big, hairy, audacious goals (BHAGs) 58, 59
Bilton, Chris 307
black swan events 157, 278, 335–6
blue ocean strategy 197–200
BMW 281

The Body Shop 47
Boeing 58, 201
Boston Consulting Group (BCG) 146
    experience curve 183–5
    Growth/Share Matrix 9, 151–4, 170–1, 223,
        238, 239
Bottom of the Pyramid 223–5
boundary spanning 305–6
BP 47
brainstorming 21, 30, 173–4, 220
    PESTEL analysis 116
    profiling the ideal player 156, 157
    SWOT analysis 31, 32
Brandenburger, Adam 112, 296
Branson, Richard 263–4
Bridges, William 17
British Aerospace (BAe) 23
British Airways 182, 263, 264
Burgelman, Robert 337
business process redesign (BPR) 189, 226–8,
        249, 320
business segments see product/market segments
business strategy 6–7, 9, 145, 150, 166, 179
business-to-business (B2B) companies 14, 84,
        98, 99

Camp, Robert 136–7
Campbell, Andrew 252
capabilities
    capability gap 144, 158–62, 179, 187–8
    distinctive 256, 268–70, 286
    dynamic 256, 274–6
    market-driven organisation 286–7
    parenting 253
    profiling the ideal player 156, 157
    resource and capability strengths/importance
        matrix 124–6
    strategically valuable resources 262
capital asset pricing model 53, 193
Carnegie, Andrew 280
'cash cows' 152–3
cash flow
    discounted 191, 192–3, 194, 195, 245–6,
        338
    forecasting 65
    shareholder value 43, 44
Caterpillar 163
Cereal Partners Worldwide (CPW) 248
chain-link systems 303
Champy, James 226
change, eight phases of 311–12
Christensen, Clayton 293–5

Cirque du Soleil 197
co-opetition 296–8
Cobra Beer 108, 127
collaborators 29
Collins, Jim 58, 201
Collis, David 256, 260–2, 286
comb charts 133–5
combination of knowledge 309, 310
communication
    4Cs approach 217
    change management 311
    with shareholders 249, 251
    strategy map 56
community, business as a 60–2
competences
    core 190, 228, 231, 256–9, 286
    distinctive 256, 261, 271–3
competition 39, 65, 90–1, 105
    5C situation analysis 29, 30
    Attractiveness/Advantage Matrix 147
    blue ocean strategy 197
    core competences 257
    experience curve 184–5
    Five Forces analysis 92–6, 106
    Growth/Share Matrix 154
    key segments 15, 16
    Market Contextual Plan Review 319
    market sizing 67–9
    PESTEL analysis 115
    risk 321, 322
    Segmentation Mincer 28
    supplier interviews 142
competitive advantage 2, 118, 127, 316, 339
    competitive position rating 119–23
    distinctive capabilities 268, 269
    dynamic capabilities 274, 275, 276
    generic strategies 180–1
    good strategy 303
    incumbents 103
    resources and capabilities 125
    scenario planning 176
    shareholder value 44
    strategically valuable resources 262
    value chain analysis 128
    value disciplines 290
    VRIN model 265–6, 267
competitive intensity 68, 92–6, 106, 147, 175,
        192, 319, 321
competitive position 30, 97, 118, 119–23, 139
    Attractiveness/Advantage Matrix 148, 149
    capability gap 158, 160, 161, 162
    key success factors 104
    Market Contextual Plan Review 318
    PIMS database 212
    risk 321, 322, 324
    Strategic Condition Matrix 164–6
    VRIN model 267
competitiveness 4–6, 65, 91, 265
complements 95, 112–13
composite risk index 315, 327–9

computer reservation systems (CRSs) 76–7
context 29, 30
Continental European business model 45–6
convenience 217
cooperation 297, 298, 305–6
core competences 190, 228, 231, 256–9, 286
core ideology 58–9
core, profit from the 283–5
corporate environment 95, 110–11
corporate governance 45, 61
corporate restructuring hexagon 249–51
corporate social responsibility (CSR) 43, 46–8,
        49, 50
corporate strategy 6–7, 9, 145, 166, 179, 235–6,
        237, 256, 258
costs
    4Cs approach 217
    blue ocean strategy 197–8
    competitive position 120, 121
    cost leadership 39, 180–2, 290
    economies of scale 102, 107–9, 153, 188
    employees treated as 61
    experience curve 183–4
    key success factors 102, 103, 104
    mergers and acquisitions 246–7
    new products 189
    Opportunity/Vulnerability Matrix 171
    outsourcing 229, 231
    profit growth options 187, 188
    Segmentation Mincer 28
    short-term profit 44
    strategic bets 338
    sunken 191
    switching 94, 103
    WACC 53, 54
Coyne, Kevin 96
creativity 299, 305
cross charts 133–5
Cummings, Stephen 307
customer purchasing criteria (CPCs) 28,
        90–1, 97–100, 101–2, 133, 135, 141,
        149
customers 39, 217, 280, 286
    5C situation analysis 29, 30
    balanced scorecard 55, 56, 57
    customer intimacy 289–92
    customer-linking capability 286, 287, 289
    emerging markets 223–5
    Five Forces analysis 92–4, 106
    generic strategies 182
    hierarchy of needs 221–2
    key success factors 104
    market sizing 67
    mergers and acquisitions 246
    Pareto Principle 25
    product quality and satisfaction 218–20
    segmentation 14, 17, 28
    structured interviewing 139–42
    surveys 82–3, 123
    value disciplines 289–90

Day, George 286–8, 289
de Geus, Arie 62
debt 53
decision making 191–6, 280
defender strategy 271–3
deliberate strategy 277–8
Dell 154, 289
Delphi method 83–4
demand *see* market demand
differentiation 102, 108, 109, 180–2, 189, 290
    blue ocean strategy 197
    competitive position 120, 121
    experience curve 185
    key success factors 104
    marketing 214
    Opportunity/Vulnerability Matrix 171
    strategy as orientation 307
discounted cash flow (DCF) 191, 192–3, 194,
    195, 246, 338
disintermediation 77
Disney 139, 261, 262, 287
disruptive technologies 224, 293–5
distinctive capabilities 256, 268–70, 286
distinctive competences 256, 261, 271–3
diversification 131–2, 239, 281
divestment 153, 165–6, 239, 249, 250
'dogs' 151, 152–3, 172
downsizing 228
Drucker, Peter 41, 45, 55, 237, 311
due diligence 244–5, 315, 316–20, 321–2,
    324
durability 261
dynamic capabilities 256, 274–6

easyJet 181, 182
ecomagination 51
ecommerce 295
economic cycle 74
economic factors 114–15
economic value added (EVA) 53–4
economies of scale 102, 107–9, 153, 187, 246,
    320
edge of heartland business 253–4
effectiveness of product 98, 99
efficiency 98, 99, 108, 184, 228
Einstein, Albert 29, 183
elasticity of demand 74, 80–1, 187, 188–9, 200,
    207–10
emergent strategy 277–9, 307
emerging markets 224–5
Emerson, Ralph Waldo 201
employees 38, 45, 61, 217, 280, 308
    7S Framework 167–8
    balanced scorecard 57
    change management 311–12
    outsourcing impact on 230
entertainment retailing 105–6
environmental issues 47, 49, 50–1, 61, 114–16
equity, cost of 53, 193
ethical issues 40, 47, 50–1

European business model 45–6
executive compensation 48
exit 93, 149, 164–6, 186, 188, 189
expected value 175, 332–4
experience curve 183–5, 223, 320
explicit knowledge 309–10
externalisation 309, 310

F-E-R cycle 283–5
Facebook 201–3, 290, 292
FAIRTRADE 47
Federal Express 290
finance
    balanced scorecard 55, 56, 57
    corporate restructuring hexagon 249
    financial goals 38, 39–40
financial crisis 62, 336
first mover advantage 201, 272
Five Forces analysis 90, 92–6, 105, 106, 223
    complements as sixth force 95, 112–13
    corporate environment as sixth force 95,
        110–11
    criticisms of 95–6, 197
    PESTEL analysis 115–16
focus strategy 180–2, 183
Ford Motor Company 182
forecasting 65, 122, 320, 322
    discounted cash flow 192–3, 245–6
    expected value 332–4
    Growth/Share Matrix 152
    HOOF approach 70–5, 86, 87, 115, 116
    income elasticity of demand 80–1
    Market Contextual Plan Review 317–20
    statistical methods 85–7
    survey methods 82–4
Friedman, Milton 43

game theory 296
gap analysis 158–62, 167
    see also strategic gap
General Electric (GE) 51, 211, 237
    Attractiveness/Advantage Matrix 9, 91, 145,
        146–50, 153–4, 238, 239, 259
General Mills 248
generic strategies 180–2, 197–8, 290, 307
Gillette 287
Gladwell, Malcolm 204–6
Go 182
goals 6, 36–7, 41, 158
    big, hairy, audacious 58, 59
    long-term 38–40
    non-financial 194–5, 196
    see also objectives
Google 39, 201, 203, 290
Goold, Michael 252
government 93, 110, 114
Grant, Rob 124, 162, 262, 266, 269, 275
Gratton, Linda 305–6
Greiner, Larry 299–301
Grove, Andrew 337

growth
    Attractiveness/Advantage Matrix 147
    competitive position 122
    corporate restructuring hexagon 249
    crises 299–301
    F-E-R cycle 284
    good strategy 303
    Growth/Share Matrix 151–4
    HOOF approach to forecasting 70–5
    industry maturity 164
    product/market matrix 131, 132
    smoothing with moving averages 78–9
    trend projection 85–6
Growth/Share Matrix 66, 145, 151–4, 170–1, 223,
    238, 239
Guinness 108

Hamel, Gary 200, 256–9
Hammer, Michael 226, 228
Handy, Charles 60–2
Hartung, Adam 202
Harvard Business School 146, 211
harvesting 148, 149, 153, 165–6
heartland business 253–4
Henderson, Bruce 185
Henderson, David 47
Hewlett, Bill 61
hexagon, corporate restructuring 249–51
hierarchy of needs 221–2
historic growth 71–2, 74, 86
Home Depot 289
Honda 181
HOOF approach 65, 70–5, 86, 87–8, 115, 116
horizontal integration 239
hot spots 305–6
Hrebiniak, Lawrence 256, 271–2
human resource management 129, 130

IBM 154, 287–8
Icahn, Carl 151
ideal player 155–7, 158–9, 174
ideology, core 58–9
IKEA 181, 281, 289
imitation 261, 265–6, 274, 275
income elasticity of demand 80–1
incumbents 103
indivisibility economies of scale 108
industry maturity 164–6
industry supply 4, 65, 90, 330
    see also competition
infrastructure 129
innovation 50, 58, 280
    blue ocean strategy 197–8, 199
    distinctive capabilities 268–9
    hot spots 305–6
    'innovator's dilemma' 294–5
Intel 113, 262, 281
internal business processes 55, 56
internal rivalry 92–3, 106, 111, 115–16
internalisation 309, 310

interviewing 119, 139–42
investment
    Attractiveness/Advantage Matrix 148, 149
    capability gap 162
    forecasting 65
    making the decision 191–6
    optimising the portfolio 237–9
    outsourcing 230
    profit growth options 186, 187–8, 190
    sensitivity analysis 334
    strategic bets 338
    Strategic Condition Matrix 164–6
iPhone/iPod 222
issue analysis 19–22
iTunes 94, 197, 200, 293

Juran, Joseph M. 25

Kano, Noriaki 218–20
Kaplan, Robert 55, 56, 138
Kay, John 256, 268
Kennedy, John F. 42, 58, 321
key segments see product/market segments
key success factors (KSFs) 90–1, 97, 101–4, 135,
    180
    Attractiveness/Advantage Matrix 149
    blue ocean strategy 199
    capability gap 159–60
    competitive position 119–23
    must-have 104, 122
    new products 189
    parenting-fit matrix 253–4
    profiling the ideal player 156, 157
    resources and capabilities 125
    structured interviewing 142
    value chain analysis 130
    value disciplines 290–1
Kim, Chan 197, 199, 200
knowledge spiral 309–10
Koch, Richard 25, 27
Komatsu 163
Kotler, Philip 286
Kotter, John 311
Kraft 242
Kramer, Mark 50
Kravis, Henry 64
Kubler-Ross, Elisabeth 312

labour efficiency 184
leadership 168, 307
learning 55, 56, 274
legal factors 114–16
L.E.K. 170
leverage 126, 162, 179, 303
Levi jeans 222
Levitt, Steve 205
Levitt, Ted 286
Lewin, Kurt 312
Lieberthal, Kenneth 224
Little, Arthur D. 146, 164

logistics 128–9
Lotus 150
luxury brands 208, 222
LVMH 281

Magnet 239
Maletz, Mark 279
management 55, 102, 103, 104
managers 1, 240, 277, 278, 299, 314
market capitalisation 43, 61
Market Contextual Plan Review 315, 317–20
market demand 4, 65, 111, 122
    Attractiveness/Advantage Matrix 147
    computer reservation systems 76–7
    Five Forces analysis 93
    Growth/Share Matrix 151–4
    HOOF approach to forecasting 70–5, 115, 116
    income elasticity of demand 80–1
    key segments 15, 16
    long-term 39
    Market Contextual Plan Review 317–18
    price elasticity of demand 187, 188–9, 200,
        207–10
    Risk Management Matrix 330
    smoothing with moving averages 78–9
    statistical methods of forecasting 85–7
    Strategic Condition Matrix 165
    survey methods of forecasting 82–4
market-driven organisation 286–8
market positioning school 235, 260
market research 67, 71, 72
market-sensing capability 286, 287, 289
market share 39, 41, 42, 44
    competitive position 120, 121, 122
    core competences 257
    experience curve 184
    Growth/Share Matrix 151–4
    key success factors 102–3, 104
    market sizing 66, 68–9
    Opportunity/Vulnerability Matrix 171–2
    PIMS database 212
    profit growth options 187
    Segmentation Mincer 28
market size 30, 65, 66–9, 84, 146, 147
market value 249–51
marketcrafting 65, 67–9, 71
marketing 128–9, 190
    5C situation analysis 29, 30
    4Ps marketing mix 214–17
    pilot tests 84, 295
    PIMS database 212
Marks & Spencer 51, 260
Marshall, Alfred 200, 207
Maslow, Abraham 221–2
Mauborgne, Renee 197, 199, 200
McCarthy, E. Jerome 214, 217
McDonald's 224
McKinsey 280
    7S framework 167–9
    Attractiveness/Advantage Matrix 9, 91, 145,

      146–50, 153–4, 238, 239, 259
    corporate restructuring hexagon 249–51
mergers and acquisitions (M&A) 182, 238–9,
    240–8, 281, 300, 303
    corporate restructuring hexagon 249, 250
    Opportunity/Vulnerability Matrix 171
    strategic due diligence 316
micro-economic context 3–4, 64–5, 90, 316,
    339
Microsoft 201
Microtel Communications 23
military strategy 150
Minto, Barbara 19
Mintzberg, Henry 202, 213, 277, 279, 307
mission 37
Montgomery, Cynthia 256, 260–2, 286
motivation 38, 39
Motorola 288
moving averages 78–9
Mullins, John 17
multi-dimensional scaling (cross charts) 133–5
MySpace 201, 202

Nalebuff, Barry 112, 296
needs 17, 99, 100, 182, 289
    hierarchy of 221–2
Nestlé 51, 242, 248
net present value (NPV) 192, 193, 195, 247
new entrants 92, 93, 94, 106
Nike 289, 290
Nohria, Nitin 279
Nokia 58
Nonaka, Ikujiro 309–10
Norton, David 55, 56

objectives 6, 36–7, 38–9, 303
    balanced scorecard 55, 56, 57
    mergers and acquisitions 241–2, 243
    SMART 37, 41–2
    see also goals
offshoring 129, 161, 190, 230
Ohmae, Kenichi 2
operational excellence 289–91
opportunities 7, 19, 339
    adjacency 284–5
    core competences 258
    mergers and acquisitions 245, 247
    strategic bets 337–8
    strategic due diligence 316
    Suns & Clouds chart 321, 322–4, 325–6, 329,
      331
    SWOT analysis 31–2
Opportunity/Vulnerability Matrix 170–2
organisational culture 58, 260, 287, 311, 312
organisational structure 167–8, 287, 299
orientation, strategy as 307–8
Osborn, Alex F. 173
outsourcing 129, 161, 190, 229–31, 239, 249,
    320
overheads 16, 102, 189

packaging 217
Packard, Dave 61
paralysis by analysis 18, 132
parenting value 252–5
Pareto (80/20) Principle 24–6
PARTS system 297
path dependencies 265, 274, 275
payback method 191, 194–5
Penrose, Edith 265
PESTEL analysis 114–16
Peters, Tom 97, 280
Pets at Home 188, 289
pilot test marketing 84, 295
PIMS database 146, 211–13
Pioneer-Migrator-Settler chart 198–9
Pisano, Gary 256, 274
place 214, 215–16
planning 136–7
political factors 114–15
Porras, Jerry I. 58
Porter, Michael 200, 228, 258, 286, 339
    Five Forces analysis 90, 92–6, 105, 110, 111,
        113, 197, 256
    generic strategies 180–2, 290, 307
    shared value 50
    value chain analysis 128–9
portfolio gap 144
portfolio planning 9, 179, 237–9, 263
positioning 217, 235, 245, 257, 260
Prahalad, C. K. 200, 223, 256–9
premises 98, 99
pressure groups 110, 111
Pret A Manger 181
price
    customer purchasing criteria 98, 100
    key success factors 102, 103, 104
    marketing mix 214, 216
    Opportunity/Vulnerability Matrix 171
    premium 153
    profit growth options 187, 188–9
    Segmentation Mincer 28
    short-term profit 44
price elasticity of demand 187, 188–9, 200,
        207–10
Primark 47
primary activities 128–9
prisoners' dilemma 296–7
proactive strategies 271–2
process efficiency 184
Procter & Gamble 225
procurement 129, 130
product/market matrix 131–2
product/market segments 2–3, 9, 13–18, 23
    Attractiveness/Advantage Matrix 146–50
    blue ocean strategy 198–9
    capability gap 160–1, 162
    competitive position 120, 122, 123
    customer purchasing criteria 97
    Five Forces analysis 95
    generic strategies 180–2

Growth/Share Matrix 151–4
income elasticity of demand 81
industry maturity 164, 166
Market Contextual Plan Review 317–18
mergers and acquisitions 245, 246
Pareto Principle 25–6
pilot test marketing 84
profit growth options 186–90
Segmentation Mincer 27–8
strategic gap 144, 145
productive capacity 305–6
productivity 50, 56, 280, 320
products
    attributes 133–5, 218–19
    competitive position 120, 121
    core competences 257
    customer purchasing criteria 98–100
    marketing mix 214, 215
    product leadership 290–1
    quality and satisfaction 218–20
profiling the ideal player 155–7, 158–9, 174
profit 2–3, 12, 44, 45
    Attractiveness/Advantage Matrix 147, 148
    from the core 283–5
    firm effects 96
    key segments 13, 16, 18, 23, 25–6
    Market Contextual Plan Review 318–19
    Pareto Principle 25–6
    profit growth options 186–90, 215, 218
    relative market share 153
    Segmentation Mincer 28
    value distinction 43
promotion 214, 216
prospector strategy 271–3
purchasing economies of scale 107
purpose 37, 58, 59, 305–6
pyramid of questions 20, 21, 22

'question marks' 152–3, 172
questionnaires 140–1
questions, pyramid of 20, 21, 22

radar (spider) charts 133–5
raiders 250–1
range of products 98, 99
reactor strategy 271–3
regression analysis 86
regulation 61, 93, 110
relationship with producer 98, 99
relative market share (RMS) 151–4, 171–2, 184
reputation 268–9
resources 2, 9, 65, 257, 274
    capability gap 162
    leveraging 126, 162, 179
    resource and capability strengths/importance
        matrix 124–6
    resource-based school 235, 256, 260–1,
        265–7, 268, 276
    strategically valuable 256, 260–2
    SWOT analysis 31

VRIN model 265–7
return on capital employed (ROCE) 54, 172
return on investment (ROI) 211, 212
risk 7, 19, 192, 314–15, 339
    Attractiveness/Advantage Matrix 147
    composite risk index 315, 327–9
    diversification 131–2
    economic value added 53
    investment 193, 195–6
    mergers and acquisitions 245, 247–8
    new products 200
    Risk Management Matrix 315
    strategic due diligence 316, 321–2
    Suns & Clouds chart 321, 322–4, 325–6, 329, 336
Risk Management Matrix 315, 330–1, 336
Rover Group 23
Royal Bank of Scotland (RBS) 49, 316
Royal Dutch Shell 175, 248
Rumelt, Richard 42, 96, 302–4
Ryanair 181

S-C-Q framework 19–21
sales
    business segments 14–15
    forecasting 317–18, 319, 320
    marketcrafting 67–8
    Pareto Principle 25
    product/market matrix 131
    value chain analysis 128–9
salesforce estimation 83
Samsung 163
scenario planning 155–7, 175–6
Seagate 294
segmentation
    British Aerospace 23
    competitive position 120, 122, 123
    Five Forces analysis 95
    identifying key segments 13–18
    income elasticity of demand 81
    Pareto Principle 25–6
    Segmentation Mincer 27–8
    see also product/market segments
sensitivity analysis 175, 332, 333–4, 338
service-related key success factors 104
shared value, creating 50–2
shared values 168
shareholders 60, 249, 251
    shareholder-stakeholder trade-off 38, 40, 45
    shareholder value 37, 43–4, 50–2, 191, 240, 245
Shell 51, 175, 176, 248
Shuen, Amy 256, 274
situation analysis 29–30
skills 167–8
small and medium-sized enterprises (SMEs) 66
SMART objectives 37, 41–2
Smith, Adam 45
smoothing with moving averages 78–9
Snow, Charles 256, 271–2

social factors 114–15
social responsibility 43, 46–8, 49
socialisation 309, 310
spider charts 133–5
stakeholders 37, 38, 40, 43, 45–8, 50–2
'stars' 152–3
start-up ventures 16–17
statistical methods of forecasting 85–8
Stern Stewart & Co. 53
stick to the knitting 280–2
strategic alliances 113, 188, 298
strategic bets 337–8
strategic business units (SBUs) 9, 145, 146, 182
Strategic Condition Matrix 164–6, 238, 239
strategic due diligence (SDD) 244–5, 315, 316–20, 321–2, 324
strategic gap 91, 122, 144–5, 163
    7S framework 169
    Attractiveness/Advantage Matrix 146, 150
    capability gap 144, 158–62, 179, 187–8
    profit growth options 190
Strategic Planning Institute (SPI) 211
strategic repositioning 186–90
strategically valuable resources 256, 260–2
strategy
    autonomous and induced 337
    definitions of 2
    emergent 277–9, 307
    good and bad 302–4
    implementation 311
    as orientation or animation 307–8
    7S framework 167–8
    strategy canvas (comb chart) 133–5
    strategy map 56, 57
    Strategy Pyramid 2–9, 339
    see also business strategy; corporate strategy
strengths 31–2, 91, 124–6
    benchmarking 136
    capability gap 162
    competitive position 119, 122
    transferable 242
structured interviewing 119, 139–42
Subramaniam, Somu 96
substitution, ease of 105, 106, 116, 261
    Five Forces analysis 92–4
    price elasticity of demand 207
    VRIN model 266
Sun Tzu 2
Suns & Clouds chart 115, 245, 315, 321–4, 325–6, 329, 331, 336, 338
suppliers 92–4, 99, 106, 113, 142
supply see industry supply
support activities 129
survey methods of forecasting 82–4
sustainability 268
switching costs 94, 103
SWOT analysis 31–3, 115
synergies 150, 153

mergers and acquisitions 241, 242, 245, 246–7
  parenting value 252–3
systems 167–8

tacit knowledge 309–10
Takeuchi, Hirotaka 309–10
Taleb, Nassim Nicholas 335–6
technical economies of scale 108
technology
  business process redesign 226
  disruptive technologies 224, 293–5
  experience curve 184
  outsourcing 230
  PESTEL analysis 114–16
  value chain analysis 129
Teece, David 256, 274
Tesco 163
threats 31–2
tipping point 203, 204–6, 303
Toshiba 113
Tracy, Brian 217
travel industry 76–7
Treacy, Michael 289, 290
trend projection 85–6

uncertainty 7, 96, 314, 333
Unilever 248

value
  drivers 175–6
  expected 175, 332–4
  market 249–51
  net present 192, 193, 195, 247
  parenting 252–5

value-based management 192
value chain analysis 125, 128–30
value disciplines 289–92
value innovation 197–8, 199
value-related goals 38, 40
value trap business 254
values 37, 46, 58, 59, 168, 281
vertical de-integration 229, 239
vertical integration 239
Virgin 253, 263–4, 266, 287, 288
vision 37, 59, 305, 311
VRIN model 256, 261, 265–7, 274

Wal-Mart 287, 290
Waterman, Robert 280
weaknesses 31–2, 91, 125
  benchmarking 136
  capability gap 162
  competitive position 119, 122
web (spider) charts 133–5
weighted average cost of capital (WACC) 53, 54
Welch, Jack 237, 311
whitespace 201, 202, 279
Wiersema, Fred 289, 290
Wilson, David 307
Woolworths 105–6

Xerox Corporation 137

Yohn, George 205

Zook, Chris 283–5
Zuckerberg, Mark 202